Wanderlost

FALLING FROM GRACE AND FINDING
MERCY IN ALL THE WRONG PLACES

NATALIE TOON PATTON

PARACLETE PRESS
Brewster, Massachusetts

2021 First Printing

Wanderlost: Falling from Grace and Finding Mercy in All the Wrong Places

Copyright © 2021 by Natalie Toon Patton

ISBN 978-1-64060-674-6

The Paraclete Press name and logo (dove on cross) are trademarks of Paraclete Press.

Scripture quotations are from New Revised Standard Version Bible, copyright © 1989 National Council of the Churches of Christ in the United States of America. Used by permission. All rights reserved worldwide.

Some names and identifying details have been changed to protect the privacy of individuals.

Library of Congress Cataloging-in-Publication Data
Names: Patton, Natalie Toon, 1982- author.
Title: Wanderlost : falling from grace and finding mercy in all the wrong places / Natalie Toon Patton.
Description: Brewster, Massachusetts : Paraclete Press, 2021. | Summary: "A coming-of-age travel memoir that probes thorny spiritual questions while taking the reader on a wild ride from the deep American South to the Middle East, Europe, and the Far East"-- Provided by publisher.
Identifiers: LCCN 2021025823 (print) | LCCN 2021025824 (ebook) | ISBN 9781640606746 (trade paperback) | ISBN 9781640606753 (epub) | ISBN 9781640606760 (pdf)
Subjects: LCSH: Patton, Natalie Toon, 1982---Travel. | Christian women--United States--Biography. | Christian biography--United States. | Women travelers--United States--Biography. | Divorced women--United States--Biography. | Women--Religious life--United States. | Spirituality--Christianity. | Christian life. | BISAC: RELIGION / Christian Living / Personal Memoirs | RELIGION / Christian Living / Spiritual Growth
Classification: LCC BR1725.P2734 A3 2021 (print) | LCC BR1725.P2734 (ebook) | DDC 248.8/43092 [B]--dc23
LC record available at https://lccn.loc.gov/2021025823
LC ebook record available at https://lccn.loc.gov/2021025824

10 9 8 7 6 5 4 3 2 1

Published by Paraclete Press
Brewster, Massachusetts
www.paracletepress.com
Digitally printed

FOR HENRY, MAGNOLIA, FRANCINA,

and all of those who dare to be "curiouser and curiouser"

CONTENTS

PART III

THE River

PART I

THE Woods

I wondered if the trees were God.
They were like God in many respects:
they stood silent, and most people
only noticed them when the need
arose. Maybe all the secrets of life
were written on the surface of leaves,
waiting to be translated. If I touched
them long enough, I might be given
some information no one else had.

—Silas House, *A Parchment of Leaves*[1]

CHAPTER 1

THE STORY

County Carlow, Ireland

The rain is colder in Ireland than just about anywhere. I'm running through the trees along a path, trying my best to ignore it. It runs down my neck and glides under my collar, making me do a weird shiver dance as if someone had just dropped a bunch of spiders on my head. Thank God nobody is around to see.

My Southern American blood is primed for gravy and humidity; it does not acquiesce to the cold. It's been years since I've lived in my home state of Arkansas, but right now I'm remembering the delicious, steamy summer rains of my childhood and how lovely they are compared to this frigid mess. The tunnel of trees ahead of me is a lousy shelter. The trees assault me like rude wedding guests pelting rice at my bare face. I wish I'd brought an umbrella. I'm sprinting now and trying not to slip on bits of grass and earth that litter the ancient, untrodden pathway. There's nobody around to ask how far to go; it's just me.

He said it wasn't too far away. But I don't see it. My husband's exaggerations make me irritable. *Who's going to take care of the kids when I get pneumonia?* My husband is waiting for me in the car with our sleeping brood as we take turns dashing in and out of various tourist sites in the rain. It feels ridiculous, but gone are the days of backpacking, crashing in hostels, and wandering wherever the wind blows. Tourism is different when you have small humans in tow.

I slow down so I can shield the rain from my eyes, looking frantically for the rock. Thailand, our current home, is a million miles away. I'd rather be on the sun-blessed shores of Railay Beach drinking a Tom Yum cocktail, building drip castles with my kids than getting dripped on by cold rain, but I've come too far to turn back. I hear thunder in the distance and speed up again. One foot in front of the other, I trudge forward in a rhythm that seems to sync with the rain.

The beat of my heart syncs with my feet, as if an unseen presence is propelling me. The presence is Mystery itself, and it is thrumming louder. I didn't always run in this lane. But today, I'm running for the girl who used to wear shame like a boxy boyfriend blazer, trying her best to accessorize her awkwardness. I'm running for the girl set free from a neat little box with straight, predictable edges. I'm running for the girl who turned into a woman and found a home in her own divine skin. I'm shivering, but my body hums with curiosity and lights a fire in my belly to keep running.

We are all running from something, right? I remember the days when I first ran away from home, when the wanderlust itch rooted in my soul, was nurtured by failure, and then transplanted me from the only place I'd ever called home. You could call it *running away*, but for me it wasn't. I was running toward the places where my heart could be reborn.

It was more than a pilgrimage; it was a *peregrination:* a one-way ticket to far-off lands. Like a peregrine falcon that migrates from the arctic tundra to the jungle to the desert and gets its name from the Latin word for wanderer, I would need to take flight to the most obscure corners of the world in order to resurrect the strangled, decaying parts of my soul and infuse it with new life. After ten years of wandering, I carry pieces of myself found strewn all over God's very good earth.

I can see it. *This has to be it.* I turn the corner and see the enormous gray rocks stacked up on the earth against a canvas of farmland, misty and still: the Brownshill Portal Tomb. The rain stops abruptly as if mother earth is calming and hushing the weather gods long enough for me to take it in. It's a dolmen burial chamber built by Ireland's first farmers between 4000 and 3000 BC. The plaque near the road told me it's the heaviest of its kind in Europe.

What in the devil? I can't imagine how anyone without a crane could have placed a 150-ton capstone on top of a group of rocks in the middle of a field. It used to sit like a table across a group of smaller rocks, but time has taken its toll; its rear is almost on the ground.

I want to touch it. I run my fingers across its bumpy, lichen-speckled surface. *Who were these people and the Druids that followed?* I wonder, as I stand on my ancestral grounds. I'm told these Neolithic dolmens are all over the world in places that don't seem to have much in common, like South Korea, Europe, and India. My toes are numb, but I'm paralyzed with curiosity imagining the love and care these ancient people must have had for each other to go through such great (heavy!) lengths to honor their dead. Or were they built for another purpose that has been lost to history? Archaeologists are unsure.

For a brief moment of marvel (or maybe it is much longer, as time seems to stand still), I'm transported from my ordinary life as a wife and mother and suspended in the flow of divine Mystery. The ancient Celts believed in "thin places," geographical locations where the veil between heaven and earth becomes papery thin. There's a particular energy that isn't seen, an ineffable realm that is felt with a sixth sense.

I've come to believe in the existence of this metaphysical phenomenon. For me, it's a feeling of nostalgia, as if I'm coming home to a place that I didn't know was home; it's pangs of deep belonging; it's echoes of sensations I felt only as a child—like having cousins come stay the night and waking up the next morning, ecstatic at the first remembrance of their presence.

Thin places can be found in nature—feeling a tropical waterfall at our face or watching the sunset over a coastal cliff. Or they can just as well be found in a Victorian library in Appalachia, a Zen garden in Japan, or in a dive bar in Budapest. This is what makes travel so exhilarating: finding the thin places . . . or letting them find us.

The rain picks up again, and I bid the dolmen farewell and turn back down the path. Drenched, I make it back to the edge of the road, where my husband is waiting for me in the car.

"Amazing, huh? Here, take this," he says, tossing me his sweater to wipe my face.

The rain drums steadily on the windshield of our rental van as we drive through winding roads in the Irish countryside. Shades of green and gray stretch for miles through dense forests and rocky clearings.

My husband behind the wheel is usually a man with a plan, but this day he is content to wander. Our plans to visit the Glendalough monastic site were spoiled by the weather, but the stars have aligned and all three kids are fast asleep in the back, so we take a long drive and relish the captive stillness and uninterrupted conversation, taking turns to see sites while the other sits with the kids.

The kids are jetlagged from the long trek from our home in Bangkok, Thailand, to America. We decided Ireland would be a good midway stopping point with fresh air and the chance for three city kids to collect chicken eggs from the coop and pet sheep, and for all of us to literally lie down in green pastures.

I glance back at their sleeping faces, buckled in car seats, snuggled in jackets they aren't used to wearing. How sweet they look when the batteries have slowed down.

I wipe the rain off my face, pop a few Advil, and dig around the diaper bag for a tube of mascara. I open the mirror on my sun visor and am alarmed to see the face of my mother staring back. I lift the edges of my cheeks and stretch out the deepening eleven between my eyes.

Singer-songwriter Brandi Carlile's song "The Story" plays faintly in the sleepy folds of my mind. It's a song about the stories our faces tell; the well-earned lines that come from our unique journeys and the need to share the lines with a lover like pages in a book.

It was the same song I once heard on a road trip from Amman, Jordan, to Damascus, Syria—when the lines were still baby fine and my wounds still gaping open, held together only with an artificial bandage—a flowery facade.

There's power in telling our stories honestly, and there's healing that comes when we can connect all our dots—the good, the bad, the proud, the embarrassing. The moments of our lives are strung together not like neat pearls on a strand—shiny and tidy and sequential. They're more like wild, pulsating stars in a constellation. Some stars are farther away, but might shine brighter. They say a star can be dead and dark now, but we wouldn't know it because we see the light from millions of years ago. Memories are like that too. They linger and glow in our consciousness, some blinking in the periphery and begging for our attention more than others, until one day we take the time to stop and put words to them, reframing our collection of stories to get a complete picture. I'm still learning to do that.

Carlile's bridge guitar riff plays in my head while my eye catches something up the road—"Wait! Let's stop here real quick!" I see an old church.

"We have tons of old churches to see tomorrow," my husband says, trying to dismiss this one.

There were other churches we'd passed. There were other churches up ahead. But something about this church was calling out to me like a dinner bell, clamoring: *come eat!*

As usual, the Hubs gives in to my impulsive request and pulls over. The rain picks up again. "You first!" he nudges.

I dash through the rain again, regretting my fresh mascara. It is a dark gray stone church, almost Gothic, with a small graveyard on one side and courtyard on the other. The wide, wooden doors are unlocked and the church is empty. I close the door behind me and absorb the silence that rings in my ears with the roaring rain outside. It smells like an old library. The lights are out, but the dark skies cast a soft light in the sanctuary.

It was my idea to stop here, but churches are hard for me. They can be both places of comfort—old swaying hymns that remind me of my grandparents in Arkansas or lullabies my mother sang—but they can also be painful triggers, as my background in the evangelical subculture conjures up feelings of shame and rejection. But this time I check all my spiritual baggage at the door. I breathe in a cool stream of air and exhale the dust of a meandering journey that has stretched the span of a decade. I am only passing through, but it feels so good to be *home*.

I belong in this space, I tell myself, as I walk slowly down the aisle. It's hard to make out the shadowy altar. It's so ill-lit that I wonder if perhaps I'm breaking and entering. Suddenly I'm stopped in my tracks by something crazy on the sidewall. It's an inscription that takes my breath away. Surely, it can't be there by accident . . .

CHAPTER 2

FIRE ON THE MOUNTAIN

Little Rock, Arkansas

ELEVEN YEARS PRIOR

I was so good at being good that I didn't know it wasn't necessary to wear pantyhose in Arkansas humidity on my first big-girl job selling TV commercials to mom-and-pop furniture stores. I was hired before graduating from college, and despite getting heck for working at the local Fox affiliate from my professor of organic gardening, I took my job selling air seriously.

I wore three Express skirt suits on rotation—a black, a brown, and a gray—accessorized with a handful of brightly colored old-lady costume jewelry found at estate sales. Like a little girl playing dress-up, I tried hard to look the part: businessy and professional, but also feminine and unique. Clutching my black Target workbag, I strutted around town with an effervescent gait, swinging blond ponytail, and a handful of rehearsed sales pitches. I was ready to take on the world, one mom-and-pop at a time.

It was never in my plan to work in TV sales. I had studied mass communications, film, and journalism and anchored my college TV news channel. I recorded every newscast on a VHS tape, and I'd carefully review it after the fact, analyzing my every move and working hard to smooth out my Southern drawl. Long *I*'s were the toughest for me; *ice* sounded more like *ass*.

I started at the Fox affiliate as an unpaid news intern, following reporters around town and peering over their shoulders as they typed their stories. It was part of my detailed plan of hustling as a reporter for several years before being hired as an anchor and then moving up the chain in larger markets. I had hoped that it was an inevitable ticket out of Little Rock.

I might have been naïve, but it didn't take long to figure out where the money in a television station came from. The sales department seduced me with the prospect of a steeply rising income and freedom and flexible work hours that a news career couldn't offer. What my well-intentioned gardening professor didn't understand was that I didn't have the luxury of living in the world of ideas. I had bills to pay and nobody to fall back on. So, I decided to keep my nonstandard American dialect and followed the well-worn path of shelving my dreams in order to be prudent and make ends meet. I would do my sales job with joy and gladness, or at least pretend to be happy if I wasn't truly feeling it because, I told myself, I needed to be grateful to even have a job.

Wearing a well-painted mask already came naturally. I was in church every time the doors were open. I did all the right things and checked all the boxes that my parents, teachers, and church leaders told me would put me on the straight-and-narrow path of success and blessings. I developed a stiff posture and practiced utmost care with every damn word that came out of my mouth, lest my foul language lead others astray and send them to hell. Nothing that had anything to do with making the world a better place, but that was beside the point. How others saw me was exponentially more important than enjoying my life. I couldn't trust my own thoughts and intuition because, I was taught, my true nature was dark and sinful. It never dawned on me that my own happiness and desires could factor into the equation. I sang "Amazing grace, how sweet the sound" and believed that good works couldn't save me, but I thought somehow God would love me more if I tried my hardest to serve him, worked extra hard at my job, and did all the right things.

Behind my glossy smile, smoothed-out hair, and polished facade was a deep secret and a hairline crack just waiting to be split right open.

* * *

After a day of earnest hustle at Fox 16 Arkansas, I shuffled through the door of my tiny apartment and kicked off my heels. I pulled my hair into a ponytail and sat down on my little couch to peel off my sticky pantyhose.

There was a knock at the door.

It startled me, as I hadn't been in that apartment long enough for anyone to know I was there. I hesitated to answer but decided it might be someone welcoming me to the neighborhood. *Not gonna miss out on free pie!* I stuffed the pantyhose in the crack of the couch cushions.

It was only the mailman. "Hello. I have a certified letter for you. Need your signature on this one," he mumbled.

Certified letter? My heart skipped a beat as I squiggled out my name, curious.

He turned to leave, and I immediately recognized my church letterhead. Two mountain peaks. *Why would my church need my signature for a letter?*

My eyes were drawn to the army of signatures at the bottom of the page. Black and blue jagged edges stood at attention in angry formation. Some of the names were recognizable—all men in my church—most of whom I had never spoken to face-to-face but recognized from the pulpit.

Dear Natalie,

The Elder Board has had a meeting to discuss your pending divorce. We have unanimously concluded that you have no grounds for divorce, and thus we have decided to withdraw our fellowship from you.

I thought I was invisible to these men. My Southern Baptist megachurch, which I'll call Mountaintop, described itself as a "campus," but it was so big it could have been a small theme park. I wondered how my personal life was suddenly important enough for the patriarchal Wizards of Oz to have a powwow behind the curtain on my behalf. Up to that point, my life had been secretly unraveling, and there were few, so I thought, who even knew I had filed for a divorce. I had been married less than a year to my high school sweetheart, and since then, everything except the beautiful facade I had created had fallen apart.

The bizarre combination of the words "withdraw our fellowship from you" sifted through my synapses. I read the line over and over until I was able to read between the lines.

They are kicking me out of church.

I instantly hated the word *fellowship*. Before, "fellowship" meant church potlucks with rows of steamy casseroles, home Bible studies, or being squeezed in tightly in the back of a stadium with church friends, tearing up as we listened to Mark Lowry and the Gaithers sing "Mary Did You Know?" at a Christmas Homecoming concert. It was a word attached to a vague sense of belonging, but the genuine pursuit of love and acceptance from the people you choose to worship with and call "church family."

Now every time I'd hear the word *fellowship* used in a warm and fuzzy way, it seemed disingenuous and deceptive. Had the letter said, "We are kicking you off the mountain, don't come back," or "You're being given the boot!" then maybe the crushing of my soul would have at least been less annoying. But that churchy, sanctimonious tone delivering such a damning blow only set my hair on fire.

What would happen if I tried to go back? Had everybody at Six Flags Over Jesus gotten the memo too? Were they all instructed to *withdraw their fellowship* from me? And did this extend outside the church walls? If I ran into folks at the grocery store, which would inevitably happen that same day, would they turn the other way because they were now *withdrawing their fellowship*?

Aside from the sinking questions, I was drowning in the quicksand of shame and rejection. The people pleaser in me was a naked girl on a whipping post. I had been a faithful member at Mountaintop, never failing to tithe ten percent of my poor college student earnings. I was active in women's Bible study. Served on the media team. I had friendships I thought were solid. *Was my sense of belonging all an illusion? Did everybody know my business?* I tossed the letter aside and fell to the floor.

I didn't know what was worse: getting an actual divorce or being shamed and condemned by those I once trusted for my spiritual formation. I thought about all the things I once was . . . The good daughter. The straight-A student. The faithful friend. The homecoming queen. The local pageant beauty queen. The campus crusader. The virgin bride. The girl who loved Jesus and fantasized about being a missionary.

And then, at the tender age of twenty-three, I was an excommunicated divorcée in a small town. In evangelical youth-pastor lingo, girls who have sex before marriage are like *chewed gum*. Or one particular illustration I recall—a piece of duct tape that's been reapplied so many times that it's lost its stickiness. A young woman who leaves her husband was somewhere below that. I didn't know what I was, but I knew I was no longer at the top of those two mountain peaks. I had taken a tumble off the edge and rolled all the way down to the valley below where I lay bruised and alone, sobbing into my wadded-up pantyhose. I was so good at being good that I didn't know how to nurse my own wounds, alone in the wilderness.

I was raised on the banks of the Saline River in Benton, Arkansas. My "home" was a stream where the water was just calm and shallow enough to settle in cozily. My "food" was giant sycamore leaves I called fish. It was where I learned to tread water. It was where I caught the winds of gusto on a rope swing. It was where my grandfather unearthed a 900-year-old dugout canoe, once belonging to the Caddo people of that region, a reminder of the sacred space the river represented to a people who no longer called it home. It was where moving water was the only thing that could be heard and the only thing that moved along: where time stood still. And it was the best entertainment that my twenty-nothing-year-old hippie parents could offer three restless children.

I'd wade in up to my belly button, and the shock of the cold would take my breath away. Like apple pie à la mode, the contrast was delicious. The smell of grilling meat and Budweiser original, the raw, earthy scent of clay and weeds, and the grinding of smooth rocks underfoot evoke nostalgic comfort in me to this day.

When we weren't at the Saline River, my brother and sister and I spent hours at a time wandering the woods near our house on Salt Creek Road, named after the creek that fed into the Saline River. Mama always said the creek and the river got their names from a French explorer who tasted the water and thought it was salty.

"Pretty sure he got a lick of his own sweat," she'd say.

The woods were both terrifying and comforting: a dichotomy of darkness and light. There was a sure presence that felt like a mysterious giant, partially concealed and unpredictable. My brother loved to tell us legends of ghosts said to be the souls of Confederate soldiers that illuminated the hills after the sun went down. The feeling of being watched pervaded us.

But most days, being in the woods felt like dwelling in the presence of a wise grandmother who wanted to gather us close and bless our sweet heads. She calmed us with bubbling sounds of the creek and nurtured us with the dappling light that danced through the trees, making mosaic patterns on the ground. Like most kids of the previous century, we were the glad recipients of benign neglect, and trees were guardians of our unsupervised adventures, witnesses to our deepest joys and childhood disappointments.

Sometimes Daddy accompanied us on our adventures in the woods. He had the soul of an ageless tree hugger, descending from a long line of hardy, bourbon-drinking Kentucky farm folk. After marrying right after high school, Mama nudged him to stop wearing bell-bottoms in the '80s. He eventually cut his long hair off after he started working at the bauxite mine because it'd get tangled under his helmet and caked with alum. A no-nonsense naturalist, he washed his hair with a bar of Zest soap, was obsessive about clipping fingernails, and knew more about trees than anyone. He loved hurling his body off cliffs in Olympic formation, plunging deep into cold water below. He had the spiritual gift of cultivation, growing everything from okra to marijuana in our backyard.

Daddy was one of nine kids from a devout Catholic family, so he felt weird going to the Southern Baptist church where Mama took us. He tried attending for a season to appease her, but he couldn't handle the informality and all the awkward chattiness afterward. He'd talk about the "hypocrites" with their self-righteous faces, the same ones he smoked pot with at the bauxite mine where he worked the night shift. He kept St. Christopher on his rearview mirror and prayed the Rosary when he remembered. It irritated Mama that he felt he could pray better when he was high. I used to think Daddy was "lost" because he didn't attend church with us or talk about his personal relationship with Jesus. His affinity for the saints perplexed Mama, but she softened to his traditions when he said, "Don't you ask your friends to pray for you? It's like that."

Daddy felt most alive and closest to God in nature, and he loved being with us in the woods near Salt Creek or the Saline River. A quiet-spirited mystic he was; the woods and the river were his sanctuaries, an escape from a mundane job.

Mama enjoyed the river too, despite her tendencies to be perfectly put together. She had also descended from the goody-two-shoes tribe. She smelled of good perfume, Equate Oil of Beauty face cream, and Aqua Net hairspray. She was naturally stunning and didn't need much help fixing up, but she loved to do it. My sister and I would tease her about her never-fail hair and makeup routine, even on the weekend.

"Mama, just what are you getting ready for?" we'd heckle her.

"Well, I'm getting ready for the *day*!" she loved to say.

Mama didn't have a smug bone in her body. If she saw somebody that she vaguely knew across the grocery store, she'd go out of her way to say hello while giving them an arm pat or a side squeeze.

Music was her refuge from the ordinary. She had a voice like Emmy Lou Harris, played guitar, sang specials at church and with a country group that met on Friday nights in my grandparents' basement. From the time we were babies, her lullabies were always soulful folk songs like Cat Stevens's "Moonshadow." It's a song about the shadows that come when the moon is so bright, but also about the inescapable and delicious present. It was the ultimate optimist's tune from the ultimate optimist herself.

When she'd get to the bridge, I didn't know what "faithful light" meant in reference to God, but she'd get loud and resonant on the high notes, and it was as if the heavy curtains of our lives had opened up and heaven was shining down.

Mama went to nursing school to become an RN when I was in the first grade. Those days were some of her hardest. She'd put us to bed and then brew a pot of coffee and stay up into the wee hours of the morning with her head buried in the books, lipstick long gone and mascara smeared. One time she stored a dead cat at the top of my brother's closet and took it out for dissection when we were sleeping. The formaldehyde smell never went away.

The day finally came for her to put on her crisp white lab coat and pin on her old-timey nursing cap to walk across the graduation stage, and that was one of our family's purest, proudest memories. She believed caring for the elderly was her true calling in life, and she did it well.

Mama is in the frame of most of my significant memories. She was the one who took us to church every time the doors were open, the one who took us to the softball fields and the dance classes before it got to be too expensive. The one who forced me to go underwater and who guided me around the roller-skating rink when I was afraid. The one who held me when I was sick and who pinched my jaws when I smart-mouthed or said something unkind.

My sister, Julie, was just two years older than I but tough and years beyond me in maturity. It was common for her to beat all of our older brother's friends in arm-wrestling matches or hit the softball over the fence. She was a paradox: tough as nails but tenderhearted and golden to the core. We'd spend hours playing in the yellow jasmine bushes that my dad planted in our backyard. She'd talk to me from her "house" via walkie talkie and we'd make plans to visit each other at our yellow houses. This would go on for hours until we'd nearly die from heat exhaustion and have to come inside to lie in front of the box fan with a cold rag.

My sister was my keeper, and everybody else's. She'd tie my older brother's roller skates, cook meals when Mama worked nights, and hold me when I cried. She's the big sister every soul on this earth needs, the friend everyone wishes they had. I've never doubted that Julie was a better person than I was, but at times I'd be envious of her likeability factor. I was air and fire—a little too weird, a little too awkward, a little too scatterbrained, and sometimes hot-tempered. Julie was pure earth and warmth, the anchoring presence needed in the room and the one we all leaned on.

My older brother, Jesse, was a natural storyteller and creative troublemaker. He was the ringleader of our grand adventures through the cow pastures or woods and loved to exaggerate our findings. Jesse and I butted heads. He delighted in aggravating me, and I wasn't wise enough not to take his bait. But despite all of our grumblings, I knew he'd always have my back. Like Daddy, he was and continues to be unconventional. Today he's a bachelor at forty, has never sent an email, barely has a cell phone, and thinks social media is ridiculous.

"If you want to talk to me, you can come to my house, knock on my door, and come on in," he'd tell us. And we knew that he truly meant it.

The older I get, the more I appreciate his kind of genius. As an adult struggling to live a life of contemplation and mindfulness, I find my thoughts are too fragmented by technology. Jesse's never had social-media brain like the rest of us, and that takes shape in beautiful ways of a forgotten era. When he tells stories, he makes people light up and forget the ticking clock. He's the tree firmly planted on the riverbanks watching all the crazy around him but resolute to stand still and take it all in.

As I grew lanky and self-conscious along the riverbanks, I felt pangs of resentment over our "river culture." Noticing how all my swimsuits turned brownish and how we had to swim in old shoes to protect our feet from any glass debris that a tornado might have brought in the water, I was embarrassed in front of my friends who all swam at Longhills Country Club. I longed to be a country-club girl too, but I knew there was no cash for frivolous things, especially when we had our own swimming hole down the road. I tried to make Mama feel guilty for taking us to the river instead of the clear, chlorinated square of concrete where the upper crust belonged. I'll never forget the first time I spent the night with Lainey Peterson. Not only did she have a club membership, but she also had her own underground pool in her backyard. I thought I had hit the jackpot swimming in that crystal-clear water.

* * *

Daddy eventually switched from nights to days at the bauxite plant, but the rickety rumbles of a train beginning to slip off track were felt long before then. From my earliest memories, I knew that I liked him better in the morning than at night. In the morning he was fresh and alert, always attentive. At night, he was goofy. He'd act silly and fall asleep in weird places—in his car, on the living room floor, on the toilet. Mama struggled to get him to bed most nights. We knew that if we wanted to do something that was against the rules, all we had to do was ask Daddy when he was still awake and in one of his silly moods.

Eventually I was old enough to realize it was all the Budweiser cans that piled up in our garbage that made him act funny. As the years wore on, Mama tried to hide it all from everyone in town, never allowing us to have friends spend the night. The times he was inebriated in public were mortifying. He'd trip and fall while walking with us down the sidewalk. Or fall asleep in movie theaters and snore so loudly that people would get antsy and ask us to leave.

Once he took me to a friend's birthday party at Bud's Roller Rink. Daddy was already lit up like a jack-o'-lantern when he drove me there, but instead of just dropping me off and disappearing, he decided it had been a while since he had had a good skate, and he stayed to "chaperone" the party. When the "Hokey Pokey" came on, I watched in horror as Daddy giddily skated center rink and then proceeded to dance the entire thing, a bedraggled bum on wheels: *you put your backside in, you put your backside . . .* on the floor.

Whenever things got really bad, we'd escape to my maternal grandparents' house for days or weeks at a time and sit at Mommama's round kitchen table to eat pie and talk about anything other than my drunk daddy. Daddy's drunkenness was always the elephant in the room, but I was lucky that at least it was a benign elephant. Neglectful, yes, but he wasn't violent or abusive. Still, my gauge for normalcy was never quite right.

I oscillated between indulging in a fantasy world and pursuing absolute perfection. I spent hours playing with bottles of nail polish, pretending they were children at Vacation Bible School, organizing them into classes and then dividing time for crafts, Bible study, and outdoor activities. Mama would find wads of Scotch tape under my bed; I was obsessed with the smell and texture of it.

I became a straight-A student, consumed with making perfect grades, mostly because I wanted approval from somebody, anybody, that I was lovely and smart and worthy. When the world around me was a swirling, unpredictable current, school was a fixture that I felt I could conquer and control. That frenetic, competitive sense of control carried over into church activities too. I was the lead in the children's musical and the Bible Drill Team blue-ribbon champion. Sometimes in the intensity of my childhood, I'd forget to have fun.

My siblings teased me for being the "fancy" child. I dreamed about fancy people in other lands. Charles and Diana wed the year before I was born, but I was *au courant* with everything British royal family by the time I was five, and fully abreast of Prince William's whereabouts, in particular, through my extensive collection of magazine articles and pictures. He was the object of my most deep-hearted affection—obsession, rather—so much that I wrote him a letter when I turned six. I was disappointed years later to learn from Mama that the letter actually didn't make it to Buckingham Palace. In fact, it didn't even navigate past our old steamer trunk.

One of my best years was fourth grade, when I got to play Dolly Parton in our school musical *The History of Country Music*. Mama took me to Gayla's costume shop, an old two-story yellow house full of dusty treasures, where Gayla decked me out in a billowy blonde wig and a red and white fringed cowgirl outfit, complete with a double-D-cup padded bra that nobody seemed to think was inappropriate for a nine-year-old. I shook my hips to the typewriter rhythm and then pranced around stage lip singing "Nine to Five." I didn't know it yet, but as I let that song get under my skin I was a feminist in the making in my most-conservative town.

Food was one of my earliest doors of curiosity. At home, we ate Southern favorites like barbecued chicken, fried chicken, greens, beans, fried potatoes, biscuits and gravy, and whatever vegetables were on hand from our backyard or from the garden of our old neighbor Tom Turbyfield. Tom was the only person I've ever known who was born in the 1800s. He'd show up at our back door in overalls and chewing tobacco running down his chin with a basketful of turnips or squash or tomatoes or sweet potatoes. "Whaddaya say, Tootsie Roll? Think these'll make a good supper tonight?"

Tom was a busybody who sat on his front porch waving at the cars that passed. He had a nickname for all the kids and elderly folks on our street. Most of them were cute and lovable, but anyone he was suspicious of or rubbed him the wrong way, we'd know it because they were simply *Whistle Britches.*

Mama penny-pinched and coupon-clipped as best she could, but I always knew we'd never go hungry, at least not as long as Tom Turbyfield was our neighbor. Sometimes we'd eat fast food for dinner. Or just a big bowl of homemade cornbread and milk. On special days, I was lucky to join my grandparents' square-dancing troupe and eat out at our local Ed & Kay's restaurant. They served up the best mile-high meringue pies in the South.

But when I was about eight, my culinary world was flipped upside down. I had watched a local TV news special series called *Taste of the Town.* Each week the show featured a restaurant in Little Rock, including up-close shots of the food, an interview with the chef, and locations and directions. I sat glued to the TV screen, salivating over the menu items at Bruno's Italian restaurant, somewhere in the "big city." Lasagna, pastas in crazy shapes I had never seen, something called veal, pizza topped with exotic toppings—all of it glowing and shiny and glorious. I scribbled down the address and directions, and for the following days, weeks, I begged Mama to take me to Little Rock and find Bruno's. To my surprise, she eventually did. Prior to this, I had never seen anything on a menu costing more than eight dollars, so when I took a gander at the Bruno's menu, I knew this was the most special and intense of occasions, and every second counted.

I ordered lasagna. Massive, debauched layers of slow-cooked sauce, foreign cheeses, and even the crunchy bitterness of caraway seeds—all new flavors to me—bewildered and bewitched my taste buds. In one culinary instant, I imagined that I had been transported to another place in the world, and it was exhilarating. I'm sure that Mama didn't realize at the time how this experience would be forever seared into my memory, but I am grateful that she obliged.

All this was more than being *fancy*. I didn't have the language for it then, but I was deeply afflicted with a prickly dissatisfaction with predictability and a yearning to belong in other places.

What I had was the *wanderlust woes*: the funny black magic in a person's DNA that keeps them perpetually curious and restless. It's equal parts live culture and magnetic force. I had never been anywhere outside of Arkansas other than to visit my great-grandma Bessie in Texas, but the need to chase authenticity elsewhere was as sure as my blue-green eyes, my bony elbows, and the bunions on my feet. It wasn't going anywhere, wasn't changing, and there wasn't even a surgery that could fix it. It was like an invisible cancer that only swelled with age. Its presence lingered always like an oversized, hexing black cat. I carried around a secret, heavy inevitability that someday it would awaken, rise up, and flee, carrying me along with it.

CHAPTER 4

Let It Be

From the time I learned to tie my shoelaces, I began hearing about the kingdom of heaven that Jesus talked about in the Gospels. The word *kingdom* carried weight for me, thanks to my fascination with royal families. I tried to imagine where this kingdom was. Was it somewhere in the vast starry sky? Was it under the earth or in another dimension? Was it an exclusive club? All I knew was, it was where Jesus ruled, and it was where I wanted to be.

When I was seven, I "accepted Jesus in my heart" at Vacation Bible School. Daddy was skeptical, but Mama was thrilled and took me to the preacher's office to talk about baptism.

"Natalie, do you know where Jesus lives now?" he quizzed me.

I looked down at the silver charmed heart around my neck and pointed to it shyly. "He lives in my heart," I gushed.

I sang songs of being washed as white as snow and eagerly told my friends that Jesus died for all of our sins. I wanted very much to believe Jesus did live in my heart. But at times, I'd get anxiety over not always feeling like he was there.

Did I do the prayer all right? I'd ask myself when I was alone.

Am I going to heaven when I die? Am I really in the kingdom? If God can't look at me because of my sin unless I have Jesus in my heart, then do I need to say the prayer again just to be sure? Confusing thoughts haunted me.

The starting place of my salvation experience came straight from the doctrine of original sin, which—interpreted through a Calvinistic lens—told me that what was deepest within me was dark, sinful, flawed, and against God. Like so many young people of this evangelical generation, we came to God through shame. God was introduced as the one who both *loved us more than we could imagine* but also the one who would allow us to be *punished forever in hell* if we didn't feel broken over our sins, repent, and "accept Christ" in just the right way.

That's a hell of a lot of weight for a seven-year-old to carry, but it sure worked for motivating kids to walk the aisle. My Southern Baptist conversion experience was supposed to bring me peace like a river, but it brought so much anxiety. That anxiety multiplied as I grappled with Daddy's drinking and his "unsaved" condition. One Halloween, I went to a dramatized walk-through production of heaven and hell at my church—a common salvation scare tactic for teens in the '90s. Instead of having peace about my future real estate past the pearly gates, what followed was traumatic nightmares of my dad being hauled into hell by angry-faced demons.

As I grew into my teen years, I doubled down on my faith choice, becoming ever more certain that the kingdom belonged to everyone who thought just like me—all of the believers who had got their fire insurance and also had Jesus in their hearts. This included everyone who subscribed to the same brand of Christianity I did. Everyone who was not in the club was an outsider. The kingdom of God didn't belong to them. When they died, they wouldn't make it there. This pattern of thinking taught me to immediately sift people out in conversation for evidence of whether they had Jesus in their hearts. Were they like me, or were they on a path to eternal damnation? As the turbulence in my house picked up and I was entering the tender, confusing years of adolescence, I obsessed even more about making sure I was really in the kingdom.

Meanwhile, Mama was growing bone weary of having a husband who checked out every night. Despite rehab attempts, ultimatums, and moving in and out of our grandparents' house, she ended their sixteen-year marriage in a heated flurry.

"It's time to take the boiling pot off the stove before it explodes," she'd say.

One of the few times I'd ever seen my dad cry was the day we said goodbye to the only place we'd ever called home. Mama dropped us off to see him at our little tan brick house on Salt Creek Road one last time. We did a loop around the backyard, gazed at the magnolia tree out front and the yellow jasmine bushes where my sister and I played house. Their colors were muted, and their limbs seemed to droop as if they were mourning our departure. We sat in silence and stared at the blank walls with nail marks. We noticed all the DIY projects left undone—the unfinished windowsills and missing tile squares. It felt like abandoning the path before we arrived at the destination. We laughed at the lingering formaldehyde stench in Jesse's closet. We grieved. Our hearts were black and blue from the feeling that *things didn't have to be this way.*

We threw away half of our belongings to move into a two-bedroom apartment while Mama figured out our next move. Daddy was unemployed, and Mama's bank account was resuscitated every month by her measly paycheck from her entry-level nursing job. She worked nights, which left us kids unsupervised and subsisting on ramen noodles half the time. Jesse threw some wild parties. Mama found a small house she could afford in another town within driving distance to her job. She needed to get away to a new town, and we mostly welcomed a fresh start with new friends. We needed to see new faces that were unaware of how our hearts had been pressed and squeezed and wrung out hard.

This was right before my twelfth birthday; my innocence and ignorance had been shattered long before, but the divorce imbued in me a new level of responsibility and maturity. I felt the heavy weight of *fixing Daddy* now sat squarely on my shoulders. It used to be Mama's job; now it was mine. It was a textbook case of codependency: I was desperately trying to control my surroundings—clinging to the slippery rocks as the river around me swooshed and flowed.

Daddy moved in with my grandmother, Mama Toon, who was in a state of shock over the first of her nine kids having gone through a divorce. The old-school Catholic in her was angry and hurt that Mama took such extreme measures.

"You can't be an alcoholic off of beer," she'd tell Mama as if she were just a Southern Baptist being squeamish about a little drink now and then.

But after several months of living with Daddy she saw just how dysfunctional he had become. She had a child to care for again.

Daddy lost his child-custody rights due to numerous DUIs, but we saw him on the weekends on our own. Julie kept tabs on his health and welfare—constantly checking to see if he was paying his bills on time, showing up to his new job at the highway department, and putting things in his mouth other than Slim Fast shakes and alcohol. Jesse grew closer to him during that time—they'd drink and smoke pot together at music festivals and camping trips. It was as if we had all entered the teenage years together.

* * *

Mama remarried by the time I was fourteen. I inherited two stepbrothers, also teenagers. Merging our families was dramatic at times, but Mama and my stepdad did their best to make it work.

Meanwhile, I poured myself into youth-group life at a little country church near our home. Like most evangelical youth groups of that decade, we rocked out to DC Talk and hung out in the church basement with mismatched couches and splatter-painted walls. We played chubby bunny and went to summer church camp at the biggest Baptist university in the state. We took mission trips to trailer parks in Mississippi and hosted backyard Bible clubs. We cried our eyes out singing soulful, emotional praise songs accompanied by acoustic guitars.

The church supported me on my first international mission trip. At seventeen, I got on an airplane for the first time and went to Peru for a month, doing pantomimed dramas in the foothills of the Andes Mountains. I was earnest about saving souls and sharing Jesus, but that trip was also an escape to a faraway land: a ticket to elsewhere. Mama and my stepdad thought it was a frivolous waste of a summer. "You should be working a summer job!" they argued. Remarkably, the church had my back and helped me come up with the money.

That trip had all the elements that made me light up: drama, travel, and Jesus. We'd hike from rural village to rural village, set up large speakers to project the narration and music, and then pantomime scenes of the "Gentle Ruler," the "Good Prince," the "Evil Knight," and the "People of the Land." In the end, the Good Prince rescues the people of the land from the Evil Knight. The spectators—mostly impoverished, indigenous mountain people—would cry and be seemingly touched by our performances. I was sure God had answered our prayers for their hearts to be softened and the *Word of God to fall on fertile ground*. They wanted to talk with us afterward, to stroke my blond hair and touch my face. I felt like a celebrity and was on a high over the numbers of people we "saved" on that trip. I slept soundly on the plane ride home, certain that I had just brought poor Peruvians access to the exclusive kingdom of God.

Misguided as I was in my young faith, that church and that mission trip gave me a sense of stability and belonging that I craved. My youth group was close-knit, and just in-my-business enough that I felt safe and loved and seen. I needed a secondary family outside of my family, and they took me in with arms wide open.

The Peru trip whetted my wanderlust appetite. I hungered for more. I wanted to know other countries and other cultures and I wanted to bring the kingdom of God to those places. I dreamed of being a missionary and riding the high of saving lost souls in the dark corners of the earth. I had the answers, the keys to life, and it was my duty to share them with others.

I carried on atop my sanctimonious high horse, well intentioned and eager to save the world, starting with my own father. I saw salvation and prayer as being mostly transactional. *If I only prayed hard enough . . . If I only tried hard enough . . .* I believed with all my heart that it was only a matter of time before Daddy repented and got help for his drinking. He would be restored—oh the faith I once had—he would be made whole again.

I sent recovering alcoholics I met from church to his door to try to stage interventions, but that only pissed him off. He drank more and more, and instead of Budweiser, it was whisky and gin. I'd try preaching to him myself—"You're sounding just like your mother!" he'd harp at me.

"Well maybe she was right!" I'd argue back.

"Don't worry about me! Worry about yourself," he'd say to deflect my efforts.

There were times when my sister and I would stop by for a visit. We'd see him through the upstairs window, flowers in the attic withering away in a cloud of cigarette smoke. "Come to the door, Daddy! *Please!*" we'd shout from down below. But he'd be too depressed to leave his room.

He tried sobering up on his own once without telling any of us, and that gave him a seizure on the side of the road where he was working with the highway department. He took a hard fall and severed his tongue from clamping down so hard. He tried rehab, but maintaining the habit of going to AA meetings afterward was too much. I think his introverted self felt phony trying to make new friends that would help him stay sober. Truth was, his closest friends—who had become his family—were all at Tom's Tavern getting drunk. Staying away from Tom's would be like divorcing his family all over again. And so, his sobriety never kept for more than several months at a time.

Meanwhile, his liver was failing. He asked a doctor for a transplant, but he was told there was no chance he'd make it on the waiting list. The hospital staff grew tired of seeing him return again and again, and the side-eye of disgust from some of his nurses was becoming all too familiar. The disease of alcoholism isn't extended the same levels of sympathy as other lifestyle diseases like type 2 diabetes, obesity, or heart disease.

I believed on some deep-rooted level that God was going to swoop down and perform a miracle at the last minute. At church camp I learned that if I had faith the size of a mustard seed, I could move a mountain, so why would God not intervene and heal my dad? I believed with all my heart that it was only a matter of time before he'd feel remorseful for all the drinking, see the light, ask Jesus to be his Lord, stop drinking, stop smoking, and get his act together. Then he'd be empowered by the Holy Ghost to go around preaching, teaching, and helping others do the same. Deliverance was just around the corner.

These were the stories I was told. Stories of people with great faith in the Bible. Testimonies people gave at church, from the pulpit, and in Sunday school. This was how things were supposed to turn out. This was the outcome of a righteous person who prayed and interceded on someone's behalf. It was only a matter of time, my young and simplistic faith informed me, that Daddy would be a part of the kingdom of God too. *It's time for my miracle, God. If I'll just pray hard enough and try hard enough . . .*

And underneath my certitudes, platitudes, and judgy facade was just a girl trying to keep her dad alive and seeing the clock running out of time.

* * *

Spring break of my junior year of college, my sister called to say she was really worried about Daddy. I made the hour-long drive to Mama Toon's house, praying for that miracle to come. Daddy was just forty-seven.

But he looked frailer than I had ever seen him. His thick, lustrous hair had thinned out, his eyes were yellow, and his cheeks were sunken in. I hugged him, and he held on longer than his weak legs would allow him to stand.

"Do you think you could take me to Wye Mountain?" he asked my sister and me. Wye Mountain is famous for its daffodils. Every spring, the mountain erupts into golden glory with every square foot covered in bright-yellow blossoms.

"Sure, Daddy, let's go right now."

Daddy sat silently in the passenger seat on the long, winding highway to get to the mountain. He wore his usual plaid flannel shirt, as if it were an ordinary day. But we knew he was dying, and he knew he was dying, and what else is there left to say really than hold hands and hold space for each other in the suffering? He was so weak that when he got out of the car, he could only walk a few steps in front of it, clutching his bottle of Gatorade. But when he saw the daffodil blossoms from a distance, he became emotional.

"Thank you for bringing me here. Thank you. Thank you for letting me see this," he kept repeating on the drive home.

The English Victorian-era poet Elizabeth Barrett Browning says,

. . . Earth's crammed with heaven,
And every common bush afire with God;
But only he who sees, takes off his shoes,
The rest sit around it and pluck blackberries.

To a dying person, the burning bushes are so much more obvious. The veil between heaven and earth is so thin that all the glory shines through, and the pettiness fades. There's a quiet stillness and a sense of clarity that takes over. The dying have eyes to see what we do not.

A supernatural sense of peace came over Daddy after that day as we went back to Mama Toon's to try to make him comfortable. We wanted to take him to the hospital for care, but he protested—"Not this time, I'm not going back there, not again."

We called all eight of his siblings to come in from around the country. My aunts and uncles took turns trying to get him to lie down—he paced the hallways writhing in pain. The hospice lady came with loads of morphine and an annoying cell-phone ringtone that disrupted the thin space of transition.

Daddy was always a huge Paul McCartney fan, and what helped him relax before the morphine kicked in was listening to "Let It Be" on repeat. Mother Mary had put him in a trance.

All that time I had been waiting for Daddy's dramatic repentance story to unfold, but it never happened. There was no teary altar call. No remorseful tales to tell. No sober days ahead to teach and preach.

I can't speak on his behalf of what it felt like to him, but it seemed *Mother Mary* was the feminine side of God that drew his eyes to beauty and rocked him and held him and hushed his spirit with a wave of sweet mercy. Perhaps he felt what the psalmist describes as a mother hen gathering her little ones up *in the shadow of her wings*.

On his deathbed, Daddy was comforted by a Mother God who said, *All is well, it's okay, my child.* Maybe he was like the worker at the vineyard in Jesus's famous parable who shows up at the final hour of the day and gets the same wages as those who had labored all day long. Such is the nature of a good mother—to give the same rewards and comforts to our wayward children as we do our industrious ones. To dole out even more compassion to the child who is ill. To snatch the kid up in her arms who can't seem to get it together.

Every wordy thing I had ever been taught about the transactional nature of repentance and salvation was muffled by thick, warm blankets of mercy that had no words—only rest. And in the upside-down kingdom of God, my sick, alcoholic Daddy pulled back the curtains for me to see that the kingdom of heaven was right there in front of me the whole time—there was nothing I could do to usher it in—it just was. There would be no miracle healing. No bright future of health and happiness and grandbabies. No colorful testimony to tell from the pulpit. But there was a loving God wrapping a warm blanket of mercy around a dying man, and the presence of Jesus overwhelmingly felt by our big family in my grandmother's living room as Daddy took his final breaths and we told him goodbye.

* * *

In the days that followed, I went back to school after spring break and had to take my finals. My academic scholarship could not be put on hold for me to slow down and grieve, and I was hit with a wall of anxiety. Per Daddy's request, we played "Let It Be" at his funeral, and I'd replay it again and again trying to find comfort in the lyrics. But I'd also replay ugly scenes of Daddy's frailty that I couldn't get out of my mind. I couldn't stop picturing the way he suffered—his darkening eyes that wouldn't close, his pain from his organs shutting down. The sound of his labored breathing haunted me every night.

Until one night, when I had a lucid dream. I was standing in a boat gently floating down the Saline River. The banks of the river were lined in yellow jasmine bushes—just like the ones he had planted in our backyard and the same shade of yellow as the daffodils on Wye Mountain. They were so bright they were shimmering in the sunlight as if they were on fire. The wind was at my back pushing my boat steadily along. I never saw Daddy's face, but I felt him touch my back and knew he was right behind me in the boat. We were rowing along together, and he was showing me this beautiful place.

The beauty of that dream replaced every dark image in my mind of his death. I can still see his handsome face on the riverbank with his young family. I still see him grilling chicken legs and swinging on the rope with his kids. I see him doing his best, despite his failures. I see all of his intentions rather than his shortcomings, and as the years go by, I only have more love and mercy for him. I have compassion for his condition and understanding for his failures. I see him through the eyes of a mother.

And I'm more aware of a mother-like God who has cast a moonshadow over me and quietly existed alongside us all without making a splash. It's never coerced or intruded, but it's never left my side. It's a faint echo of my innermost being, which happens to be made of light and not darkness: it's followed and carried me and comforted me.

My hand reaches out to that blanket of mercy and pulls it snugly inward and outward over every hard surface of my childhood.

In the words of Julian of Norwich: "All shall be well, and all shall be well, and all manner of thing shall be well."[2] And in the words of Paul McCartney: "Let it be."

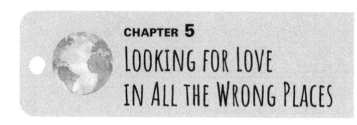

CHAPTER 5

Looking for Love in All the Wrong Places

I fell in love with the Brazilian exchange student in high school. He was a dark, handsome violinist with twinkly brown eyes and wild, wavy hair. We first met my junior year during our drama department's production of *Fame: The Musical.* I pranced onstage in '80s leotards and leg warmers, stealing glimpses of him in the orchestra pit. He was a senior then, and we became friends as he learned English.

My senior year, he returned to Arkansas to start college on a violin scholarship and began calling me. We fell fast and hard over long phone conversations into the night. He offered me everything I thought I needed: exotic mystery, excitement, passion, and neediness. As with my relationship with my dad, Carlos needed me to get through school and adapt to life in America, and that dynamic of caring for a man with a strong personality was intoxicatingly familiar.

On our best days, Carlos and I were just two kids blaring U2 songs on a road trip to the Memphis Blues Festival. We were sunshine and light and strumming songs on the guitar and river float trips. On our worst days, we were two broken souls learning how to survive in an anxious, demanding world.

Carlos was raised Baptist and came to my little country church with me, but he complained incessantly about the music. His trained musician's ear couldn't tolerate the distracting, out-of-tune hymn/praise-song combos. We made the decision to leave my church to go to one of the fancy-pants burgeoning megachurches in town.

Mountaintop Church was the shiny cupcake that caught our eye. It was technically Southern Baptist, but that tidbit was left out of the marketing materials. It had professional musicians, including a Grammy Award-winning singer-songwriter, theater-style seating, and lighting designed to make the pastors onstage with headset mics look like celebrities. It had beautiful facilities and social nights for college students. It offered short-term mission trips that piqued my wanderlust. It was a new start—*our* church rather than *my* church.

There were flashing red-light warning signs that I dismissed: an elders' board consisting of only White males, a denomination that didn't allow women to lead, a non-affirming LGBT stance, and overt teaching from the head pastor and his wife on eschewing birth control in favor of "letting God decide" how big your family should be. Because God couldn't possibly multiply his kingdom in any way other than through big, heteronormative families. When fundamentalism is served up in hipster clothing, groovy music, and beautiful people, it can be easy to miss. I kept going to the Mountaintop for reasons none other than it felt cool and I wanted to belong.

The more we went to Mountaintop Church, the more our relationship began to crumble. I had never dated anyone else before, and my instincts of what constituted a healthy relationship were already off. Carlos went from being the "carefree Brazilian" to being possessive and controlling. He wanted to know where I was at all times; he'd get mad if I stayed out too late with my friends; he'd correct my social skills; and he'd make me change outfits multiple times if he didn't like what I was wearing. I was always too much, not enough, not quite.

At the same time, I perpetuated the codependency and played my part in furthering our dysfunctional dynamic, ever ready to bend over backward to satisfy his compulsions, needs, and whims. He asked me to stop blow-drying my hair, and I did. If he thought my makeup was too much, I'd tone it down. If he needed help writing college papers, I'd stay up all night to do his work and mine. I went along with everything the boss wanted.

But he scratched my wanderlust itch by leading me to Brazil with him three summers. I got a study-abroad grant from my university's honors college and used it to study Portuguese and journalism at the state university of his hometown.

I adored his family, and they adored me. His mother and sisters, in particular, welcomed me with open hearts and *pão de queijo*—steamy cheese bread made from manioc flour. They took me all over Brazil—from the hot springs of Minas Gerais to the beaches of Rio de Janeiro and Bahia to the streets of São Paolo. But what I most enjoyed was just being a daughter in their house. I loved having big lunches around their table—the rice, black beans, eggplant, chuchu with cilantro, hearts of palm salad, guava with cheese, and freshly baked French bread. I loved the routine of rising early and heading to the college campus, stopping at the canteen for a freshly squeezed orange juice and *salgado*. I loved the thrill and challenge of writing papers in a foreign language and asking his sisters for help editing. I loved going to their Baptist church, singing in Portuguese hymns that were familiar to me. I loved watching *Mulheres Apaixonadas* around the family television in the evening. Those soap operas taught me the language more than anything else. I loved learning the words to songs by Gilberto Gil, Tom Jobin, and Marisa Monte and singing them aloud on road trips along the coast. I fell hard for Brazilian culture.

Graduation was approaching for us both, and Carlos would lose his student visa if we didn't make a move. I clung to our relationship because it was all that I had ever known, and the thought of ending it during the turbulent years of losing Daddy was unbearable.

So, we did what two hasty hooligans in heat would do: we secretly got married in order to get him a green card and started planning a wedding in Brazil. There was never an actual proposal or discussion with our families beforehand. We blitzed through the paperwork at the courthouse for the sake of keeping him in the country and staying together. After our big fat Brazilian wedding, we moved into a tiny apartment in Little Rock.

Then everything began to unravel. I had just got my first real job selling advertising at Fox. I always assumed he'd get a job once he got a green card, but that time never came. He was always looking for work, and when I'd offer him jobs at my aunt's restaurant or from other friends' connections it was never good enough. He'd blame me for not praying hard enough for the right job to come along. The only money we had was what I earned at my entry-level job, and he wanted to send it back to Brazil for "investments."

His fixation on my appearance only got worse. He'd chide me over my "thirteen-year-old-girl boobs," my big nose, which he affectionately called *industria tomada* (industrial outlet), and each morning at breakfast he'd point out what he imagined was a balding spot where my hair parted down the side.

The craziest part was that his gaslighting worked. My self-esteem suffered under the spell of his insecurities, and for a girl who saved herself for marriage only to be rejected, my body image and sense of self-worth was crushed in the process. Coming from a purity culture that prized abstinence before marriage, I was confused to finally arrive to the "promised land" of sexual liberation only to be scorned and rejected by the one who was supposed to love me.

I didn't drink in high school or college, but after being married to Carlos for a few months, I'd come home from work every day and feel compelled to pour myself an oversized glass of chardonnay just to soften the impact of whatever lecture was coming.

One of the most exhausting lectures came after getting ready to go to a church function. I was wearing a mauve-colored suede jacket, which he said looked cheap, and he asked me to change. The irony was lost on him that the jacket was cheap because he was unemployed, and we had no money. I had changed outfits three times, studying the full-length mirror propped against our bedroom wall each time to try to see what was so bad about my style. We argued for so long over my appearance that we didn't make it out in time and missed the function. The grand crescendo of the lecture came when he told me that he couldn't quite put his finger on how I could change my face or clothes or hair, but the painful truth was that *I just wasn't doing it for him.*

I did a bold thing and opened my own bank account, telling him I didn't want to send all my hard-earned money to Brazil. That set him into a violent tantrum. He'd scream, hold me down, throw things at me, and refuse to let me leave the house. We were not even a year into our marriage, and I wondered how bad it would get as the years went by. But the physical abuse was nothing compared to the trauma of rejection, the spiritual abuse, and the perpetual abashment of being labeled *almost but not quite good enough.*

We tried to get professional counseling, but it wasn't productive, and we couldn't afford it anyway. Most of the unstable behavior was a big secret that happened behind closed doors, but I slowly began to let the cat out of the bag, reaching out to friends, family, and a few people at church. I talked with them about being at my breaking point and possibly leaving Carlos.

My family was horrified but not surprised. Mama urged me to get out before I got pregnant and had to deal with an international custody battle—"Honey, you've made a big mistake. You're still young enough to have a do-over," she told me. "Get out now before it's too late."

But it wasn't that easy. I had been attending Mountaintop for four years and was heavily invested in their teaching and influence. Word got around the church that I was in and out of my mother's house, and the phone calls began to come in from men in the church. They'd speak in gentle tones as if they truly cared and then ask questions about the specifics of our problems. Then they'd salivate over the juicy details, and I could almost literally hear them retelling my junk to their wives. I'd tell them about the mental abuse and the beginnings of physical abuse. I'd tell them about the fear I had of staying with him. I'd tell them about his refusal to work but that I was one hundred percent in control of our money.

Then, after a long, bruised, swollen pause they would say, "Well . . ." and in the same scripted pattern, one by one they would come to the same close-grained conclusions:

Biblically speaking, you have *zero* grounds for divorce.

Submit to your husband.

Focus on doing your part.

Submit to him in whatever way necessary—your appearance, running the house, money, sex.

Pray for your husband and wait for God to move.

God will never bless you again if you leave him.

That last line felt like a curse over my life. Who were they other than the spokesperson for *God and his blessings committee*?

I pored over the Scriptures, reading the verses on divorce over and over again. The voices of people at church rang in my ears—"Clearly, the Bible says . . ."

The Mountaintop leaders' underlying message was that I had to stay in a toxic marriage and make it work in order to be whole. Marriage itself is the golden calf that is more important than the people in the marriage. Never mind that Paul said it was better to not even get married. This type of theology not only damages people trapped inside of toxic marriages but also isolates and alienates those in the church who are single by choice or not. There's no doubt that a healthy marriage is a reflection of the love of Christ. There's no doubt that unhealthy marriages can be healed and restored. But what's so damaging to women, especially in these closed systems, is a theology that declares that marriage is the end-all, be-all goal for fruitful Christian living. It's a theology that suggests women are disconnected from Christ if they disconnect from their husbands. And when you have a church as big as Mountaintop without any women leaders or elders, it's ripe for allowing the abuse of women to flourish.

Reflecting on this fourteen years later, I take full responsibility for the choices that I made to marry Carlos when I did and to get out when I did. But I've played the what-if game in regard to the crushing weight of damnation I got from my church at a time when I was overwhelmingly impressionable and wounded.

The fact is, they told me there was no choice. I felt trapped and pinned down, beaten up over what the Bible says. I wonder if, instead of trying to control me, they had just listened. What if they invited me to their homes for dinner and genuinely offered compassion and counsel that empowered me with choices? What if they had really seen me and loved me, rocky past, warts and all? The same folks who didn't show up to St. Theresa's Catholic Church in the ghetto side of town for Daddy's funeral suddenly cared about my spiritual state and sought to keep me within their control.

What if they didn't try to firmly direct my life, but sat with me in the woundedness? What if they offered words that built me up rather than generic, regurgitated talking points they'd heard at conferences? What if they honored and believed me rather than dismiss my concerns as trivial? At the very least, what if they acknowledged that *they could not live my life*, only I could? If I didn't feel so backed into a corner, bolted down by a life sentence of legalism—then maybe I could have found healing in my marriage or else walked away more gracefully.

***

Instead, I let the pendulum swing the other way. I rode it fast and hard and then did a round-off back tuck into a giant bowl of sugary numbness.

It started with the first man who told me I was beautiful. It was Clyde, my advertising client—a defense attorney fourteen years my senior with two young daughters and an ex-wife in town. He had played guitar for professional country-music artists, and he had a way with words that were smooth as honey butter on a biscuit. I was famished for words of affirmation, and they went down with sweet ease, numbing the deepest wounds of my heart. For the first time in my life, I felt loved exactly the way I was.

At first, I was embarrassed by our relationship and kept it a secret. I had moved back into my parents' house, and my divorce was still pending. It's safe to say I was cheating on my husband. But secrets are hard to keep in a small town, and I was plum exhausted from years of trying to maintain my good-girl status. It was a heavy mask that needed to come off, and the freedom of not being the people pleaser for the first time in my life was exhilarating. I gave myself permission to be something else. I was going off-brand, and I'd do it with wild abandon. After all, I was about to be a twenty-three-year-old divorcée. Did it even matter anymore?

Carlos contested the divorce, so it dragged on, despite not having children or property. He reached out to anyone at church who would listen, and they overwhelmingly took his side. He knew which words to say to gain sympathy, and since he was still unemployed, I would come to find out that he made it his full-time job to involve everyone. This must have been the basis of the certified letter that I received: the church elders saw him as the repentant, righteous head of our household with a wife who had gone astray into the arms of another man. Truth was, by this point we had both made mistakes, but we were in a patriarchal, complementarian church where women were not allowed to preach or lead. But he was the man, I was the woman, and by proxy he was right. I was wrong for not staying and submitting. I was the one who needed to be dismissed from the table.

For weeks I felt like I couldn't go anywhere in town without running into someone from church. Clyde and I continued to see each other as I brazenly wore my scarlet letter around town. A heavy-set guy from the Mountaintop began leaving Scripture about marriage on Clyde's doorstep. Clyde returned the favor by leaving Scripture about gluttony on his doorstep. Another girlfriend from the Mountaintop hacked into my email and Myspace accounts on a Friday night out of burning curiosity of the new sinful life I was leading. She confessed and apologized and then chided me for modeling for Cupids, the local lingerie shop, in a sexy-Halloween-costume fashion show that she learned about by reading my email.

The Cupids fashion show was a desperate attempt to patch together my tattered body image. I had padded and duct-taped my "thirteen-year-old-girl boobs" up to my chin and awkwardly strutted like a baby gazelle down a runway half-naked as sexy nurse, tin girl, and ladybug. It's not so much that I wanted to be seen as a desirable woman; I just wanted to be seen. On a wild whim, I got a boob job the same week as one of my childhood besties. We marveled at our new *grown sexiness*, at last with full bras and busty façades that boasted the image of our imaginations, the bodies we thought we were always meant to have.

But all the saline in Saline County couldn't fill the emptiness I still had over being cast out of God's kingdom. All I ever wanted was to be a child of God. The kingdom felt so far away, and I didn't know if I'd ever really find it. I grieved for the innocent girl I used to be, the girl that was no-longer. And for the first time in my life, I felt the slightest hint of what it's like to be the one on the outs. I had just a taste of what it is like to be the person not welcomed in a community, a church, a school—the one standing outside the city gates looking in. The one denied the table of God. The one sent out to pasture, alone in the wilderness and wandering in the dark woods.

For a time, I thought I'd found refuge in Clyde's family. I got along well with his parents, despite all the class and age differences. His family was old Southern money, and mine was blue-collar bumpkin. But the more time I spent with his people, the more obvious those differences were. For instance, I took him and his daughters to Ed & Kay's restaurant down in Saline County, and I grabbed a toothpick at the register on the way out (the way we've always done at Ed & Kay's), and his daughters each giddily grabbed one too before Clyde saw and snatched them out of their hands. I felt naively embarrassed, thinking he was taking them away because they might be an object of danger. Then he explained, "No, it's just incredibly tacky and uncouth to be seen with a toothpick hanging out of your mouth."

One Christmas morning, I showed up to his parents' house, gifts in hand for his whole family, only to be met by his ex-wife in pajamas at the door. They had apparently had one big happy family sleepover. Once again, that feeling of being *almost but not quite enough* came rushing back and the illusion of belonging was shattered. In hindsight, it was an incredible gift to his daughters that their parents spent holidays together. But at the time I felt like an intruder, the bimbo voyeur butting in on someone else's life. After we opened presents, Clyde's mother invited me to stay for Christmas lunch as an afterthought, but I couldn't handle any more awkwardness and politely told them I had somewhere else to be.

It was a lie.

I had no place to be. Clyde's parents lived several counties away, and I drove aimlessly down country roads in the pouring rain, slinging snot and sobbing all over the steering wheel as I tried to figure out where to go. My mother was spending Christmas with my stepdad, stepbrothers, and their families. My sister was with her in-laws. My brother was working.

It was too late to make any new plans with anyone else, and I was too embarrassed to call random aunts and uncles to see if I could crash one of their gatherings. I was hungry, and the only thing open was the Waffle House. I sat in the parking lot of the Waffle House but couldn't bring myself to go in. Instead, I threw myself a grand pity party before deciding it was time to swallow my pride and drive all the way to Saline County and see my Mommama.

Just like Mama had done when things got bad with Daddy, I took refuge at the altar of Mommama's little round kitchen table. Her table was equal parts therapy, self-care, and comfort. As long as she was home, she was never too busy to sit down over a cup of Constant Comment tea and listen to my woes.

My aunt, my mom's younger sister, came over as well. I told them what had just happened. My aunt put me in my place for getting upset: "You need to think about what's best for those girls if you're going to stay in this." She was right, but it still stung.

Mommama just listened. She listened while I processed it aloud. She didn't judge my feelings or try to tell me exactly what to do. She held space for me, being present in the pain.

For me, talking with grandparents is like prayer. There's an absolute freedom that comes from being able to cry out to a listening ear without any consequence or pushback. It's an unfiltered yearning that is the beginning of healing itself. The crushing weight I carried over, *what do I do next?* felt a little lighter that day.

It took longer than it needed to, but I ended things with Clyde. I was immature and unready to be a stepmother, and I didn't want to unfairly string him along. It was an abrupt ending, a quick snuffing out of a flame that never really burned independently. I couldn't put it into words at the time, but I knew in the deepest parts of my soul that my pursuit of wholeness needed to happen independent of a relationship. If I was searching for the place of my own resurrection, it wouldn't happen in the arms of a man.

CHAPTER 6
BAD COMPANY

The divorce was final. My ex-husband moved back to Brazil. And I was free to rebuild my life.

This was all what I wanted, but the permanence of it was a punch to the throat. For once, I understood why women stay in abusive situations for years. To forever walk away from a person who you once loved is soul-crushing, no matter how much easier your life becomes after the fact. It's the death of the life you thought you'd have.

On top of those heavy feelings to process, I still carried the weight of having been excommunicated from church. The certified letter wasn't enough punishment from Bob, the head pastor of Mountaintop. I called him to question why a formal condemnation was necessary when I would have stopped going there on my own so that Carlos and I wouldn't attend the same church. Why couldn't he let me leave with dignity? Is this the way he treats all women who initiate divorce at his church? My questioning of his "biblical authority" only pissed him off more. He couldn't just let me move on with my life; it seemed like ruining me was becoming an absurd obsession.

I began going to my mom's church. They had just hired the pastor I had grown up with, the one who baptized me. Shortly after, Bob from Mountaintop called my childhood pastor telling him all of the many reasons why he shouldn't let me attend his church. How did he even know I was going there? Was he going to stalk me my entire life to make sure I wasn't accepted in churches anymore? Thankfully, my childhood pastor, who already knew about my situation from my chatty mother, pushed back hard and I was never bothered by the folks at Mountaintop again.

Work was a wonderful distraction. I was the youngest salesperson at Fox 16 and stayed terrified and intimidated half of the time by some of Little Rock's brightest and best, most of them old enough to be my parents. I spent half the day chasing down existing and potential local advertising clients—shaking hands with used-car salesmen, having lunch with personal-injury lawyers, and popping into new boutiques to do a little shopping while figuring out a way to slyly suggest to the owner that they needed a commercial. The other half of the day was spent at my office cubicle making phone calls with national ad agencies and entering airtime into the computer system.

The best days were ones when we shot the commercials on location. There's something so very precious about the business guy or gal who is breaking out of their shell to be their own TV talent. My coworkers taught me grit, focus, and the art of simply carrying on. My boss later revealed that she watched each of us walking to our cars after our interviews and we were all hired, in part, based on our quick pace. I was sure that I just happened to be in a hurry that day and got lucky.

The first six months on the job, I flailed awkwardly, but my team cheered me on both personally and professionally, and I thrived. For the first time ever, I started making decent money. On the side, I acted in national TV commercials—all in the realm of cheesy money scams that ran during daytime trash TV. My family loved to mock my fabulous acting job in a JG Wentworth spot when I passionately hung out of the window yelling, "It's my money and I need it noooow!" I'm still waiting on the Academy to call me based on that stellar performance.

But the royalty checks added up, and I took absolute delight in not having to fork over my hard-earned money to a dissatisfied husband. I was also determined to prove wrong all the naysayers on the mountain who spoke for God that I'd "never be blessed again." I hoped and prayed that they were wrong, but part of me still lingered under that spell of paralyzing shame. This sense of shame became fear. A sense of dread that eventually the other shoe would drop, and I would fail and then wither into obscurity. I was broken on the inside, but by golly I had work I enjoyed and a growing bank account.

One day I spotted a red and white For Sale by Owner sign in the yard of a dilapidated house in an older part of town that I had driven by dozens of times. It was a faded pale brown box with a flat facade—

absent of trim, landscaping, or porches like the rest of the restored craftsman houses on the street. I learned later it was built in 1937 when the Great Depression made housing construction a little less fancy and a lot more modest.

The house was ugly as sin, but it called out to me like a wounded soulmate from the past. She had seen some hard times over the years, and nobody had ever given her any TLC, but she had bones that were good enough, gorgeous original hardwoods, and four spacious bedrooms that I dreamed of filling one day with guests and children. She was a blank slate with endless potential, and I needed her canvas.

A couple of scruffy house flippers were painting the front door when I stopped in one day to take a second look. "We have other projects happening and really need to get out of this house soon," they confessed.

"Well, you can just put down your paintbrushes right now. I'd like to buy it and renovate it myself," I said, my bold ignorance somehow convincing.

Before I could blink, I found myself with a big empty shell of the past and not a clue what to do with it. I had hoped that enough people in my family who knew how to paint things, saw things, and wire things would come to my rescue. Brother Jesse did my electrical, and I paid a few relatives in beer to get started on other things, but I soon realized that if I planned on having the house ready anytime in the next century, I needed another plan.

Enter Eddy. Was he a friend of a friend of a friend, or a fairy godfather who materialized out of nowhere? I don't remember. He was an old cabinet guy from Lowe's and loved to talk about cabinets and hunting. He wore flannel shirts and overalls and mumbled (usually about cabinets) with a deep, Southern drawl that reminded me of my old tobacco-chewing neighbor Tom Turbyfield. I had never met him before, yet he was deeply familiar to me, and that put me at ease. I didn't have the good sense to ask for his licensing credentials or references, but intuitively I knew he'd be no-nonsense and do good work. He lived far from Little Rock, in the town of Beebe—the sticks—but he assured me the commute wouldn't be a problem.

"What all can you do, and when could you start?" I asked him.

Eddy looked up to the side through his thick glasses as if he was remembering where he left his keys.

"Well . . . uh, I can do anything 'cept for your plumbin', and I can start today," he boasted.

"Okay, you're hired!" I beamed.

"Uncle Eddy" agreed to refinish my entire house for a mere ten thousand dollars. I didn't have the foresight to set a reasonable time goal, but I figured he'd work as fast as he could with a fixed price.

He got to work right away painting the interior and exterior. I pored over paint samples for days, agonizing over color wheels and interesting titles that reflected the exact mood I wanted for each room. Like a kid playing house, I picked out a strikingly different color for every room. The kitchen was Spanish orange. The dining room was a cool periwinkle. A metallic teal covered the master bath. The guest room was pale pink. Canary yellow streaked the front room where the sunrise glowed the brightest. The living room was a funky inchworm green. And the exterior was a cool mint that clashed accordingly. I was so hungry for color in my life again, and I was going to get it back, one loud and bold room at a time.

The colors of my life were flowing beautifully; I crushed it at work, felt like a Big Boss Lady with my own employee at home, and fell into a rhythm that seemed tidy and productive. I had achieved goals and direction, at last.

Then things got weird.

One day I was home alone admiring my new beautiful colors on the walls. Washing my hands in the kitchen sink, I heard a man's voice say, "Natalie," over my shoulder. I turned around quickly, startled and surprised that somebody was in my house. Panic set in when I realized I was completely alone. I walked around to every room and the house was empty. I shrugged it off as my imagination and was embarrassed to tell the story to anyone.

Not long into the paint job, Eddy showed up to work teary eyed, red-nosed, and frazzled. It was unusual for him to be emotional. I asked him if everything was okay before he broke down. "Shana done run off and left me," he blubbered.

His wife had just been there a few days prior with their two young sons in tow, helping apply painter's tape to the baseboards. He was totally blindsided.

"We had a fight. Then she took off with the boys and the car and I can't even get her to answer the phone! I reckon she's over at her mother's house." He sobbed. "We'll work it out eventually. I know we will 'cuz I can't live without her. She's my whole world and those boys too."

"I'm so sorry, Eddy. I'm afraid I'm not the one to give good marriage advice, considering my marriage only lasted a year, but I hope you can work it out."

I tried not to pry too hard into Eddy's business. For all I knew, his wife could be completely justified in leaving him. But several days passed, and it became increasingly hard for Eddy to find a ride into town every day. He suggested he could finish the job quicker if he lived on-site, and I had just moved back in with my mom to wait for the house to emerge, so there would be no awkward roommate situation. I put a small mattress on the floor and agreed to let Eddy stay until the house was complete.

After Eddy's first night in the house, I stopped by on my lunch break from work and noticed when I pulled into the driveway that Eddy's shotgun that usually hung across the back window of his pickup truck was missing. Eddy was busy rolling Inchworm Green onto the textured living room walls, but I could see the barrel of his shotgun sticking out from the covers of his bed.

"Everything okay, Ed?" I stammered.

Eddy stood up from a squat and wiped his sandy brow. "Yeah, uh, this house is haunted!"

"What?" I asked him, unable to reconcile this no-nonsense good old boy talking about the supernatural.

"Yeah, all night long I kept hearing things. At first, I thought somebody was tryin' to break in the back, so I ran and got my gun—thought I was 'bout to cap somebody. But then doors started openin' and shuttin' on their own. And that pile of two-by-fours that we had stacked in your bedroom windowsill? I could hear them bein' slung board by board till I went in there and turnt on the light and saw a big heapin' mess piled up in the floor. Every last one of 'em right there in the middle of the floor." He pointed at the two-by-fours.

"*Holy Crap*, Eddy."

"But don't worry 'bout me. I ain't 'fraid a no ghost. As long as it don't throw any of them boards at me, I'll be aw'right," he chuckled.

The next week I met Harry and Barb, the middle-aged couple with teenagers who lived next door. "Any idea who lived in my house before?" I queried.

"Oh yes we do," Barb trilled. "Charlie Bush. The only person to ever really live there. Grew up there with his family in the '40s, and then lived there until he died."

My heart hiccupped. I remembered seeing his name on mail that came to the house. "What happened to him?" I asked.

"He just got old, not sure exactly," she said. "He kept things going for a while, though. An old bachelor. Honey, remember that time . . ." Barb trailed off giggling.

"Oh yeah!" Harry roared. "Ever heard of Sweet Sweet Connie? Little Rock's infamous groupie that slept with all the big bands in the '70s?"

"We're an American Baaaaand!" I sang.

"Yeah, that Connie! Well, she was sweet on Charlie a couple years ago, and I guess you could say they were an item. Until one day she got wind that he had been cheatin' on her the whole time they were together. Imagine—a bachelor still having his cake and eating it too well into his seventies. Well, she went over there and tore him a good one right on his front porch. What a riot! The whole neighborhood got an earful of that fight. Don't mess with Sweet Connie!" they guffawed.

"Oh wow," I laughed nervously. "Well, was he at least a good neighbor?" I asked.

"He didn't hurt anybody, mostly kept to himself. But he was a stubborn old man, really set in his ways," Barb said.

"Like how?" I asked.

"He didn't want to change a single thing about his house. Was never touched since it was originally built. One time the city wanted to install a new water line through his backyard, but they would have had to tear down his shed to build it. The city offered to build him a brand-new one, and he didn't want to have any part of that. Absolutely refused. They had to route it elsewhere."

"Lord, have mercy." I swallowed.

I went back home, connecting the spooky dots: Here was a man who was the only one to call this place home. Here was a stubborn man who refused to change anything about his home. And here was Uncle Eddy and me slappin' loud colors on the wall and literally changing everything. Of course he was revolting! We were intruders in his house. He was royally pissed, and he wanted us to know it!

My childhood bestie, Britney, spent a lot of time at the house too. In high school, Britney was so tiny that her head rested under my chin. She didn't date boys. Then she went off to college, got a nursing degree, and grew into a tall supermodel's body with an Audrey Hepburn face overnight. The joke was on all the boys who hadn't given her a second glance before. Now she had no problem getting dates, but some of them turned stalkerish when she'd let them go. One night we were getting ready to go out, putting on makeup in my bathroom when we heard her name spoken in a breathy male voice. "Britneeeeey!" We both jumped, convinced that the Turkish anesthesiologist who she had just dumped had broken into my house to find her.

"Wait here. I'll tell him to leave now," I told her.

But after thorough examination of my house inside and out, I realized it was just Charlie at it once again, after the ladies.

"What have I done? I haven't even fully moved in yet!" I lamented.

"It's the curse from all those people up on the mountain!" my friends would tease. *You'll never be blessed again!*

So much for a blank canvas. Is there ever such a thing? It made me think of Faulkner's famous line: "The past is never dead. It's not even past."[3]

Maybe Charlie was hanging onto the house the way my past had hung onto me. Each of us struggling to turn over our soil in order to let new life emerge.

Eddy agreed not to tell me any other scary business that happened while he slept there. I didn't want to psych myself out too much and be afraid to move in when the time came.

* * *

One weekend when Eddy was away, my girlfriends came over for a sleepover, and I decided it was time for a good old-fashioned house anointing. That's like a séance, but the guilt-free Christian kind that's supposed to bless in the name of Jesus. After ordering pizza and watching *American Idol*, we turned off the TV, lit some candles, and sat crisscross applesauce in my living room floor.

My girlfriend Annie laughed.

"This is serious! Let's be serious, please!" I begged. And giggled.

"Okay, serious!" She closed one eye and snorted.

Jokes aside, I prayed an earnest prayer:

Dear Lord, I thank you so much for this beautiful house I can call my own. I love this house, and I don't want to be afraid to live in my house. Please remove any dark or dead spirits that may be living here. I don't know how the afterlife really works, God. I don't know if ghosts are real, or what this is all about. But I pray that if I have a ghost or an evil spirit, you'd have mercy on his soul and give him confidence to leave. In the name of Jesus—leave this house. In Jesus's name, Amen.

The ghost of Charlie Bush never fully materialized or let me know he was gone. But after that night, things changed. It wasn't the last time I would hear from Charlie Bush, but it was the last time I was afraid of him. I realized later that this prayer was for me. It made me feel a little less alone with a ghost and freed me to chase the thrill of restoring that old house to its full potential. I grew comfortable with the possibility of Charlie being there and sensed he was a misunderstood presence, an outcast like myself. I was convinced that once he got to know me, he enjoyed my company. I imagined that he started to like the changes I had made, the fixtures I had picked out, and the shiny hardwoods that he had no idea could be restored to such beauty.

Ghosts notwithstanding, my house project was the best therapy. Every paint can was a magic elixir of fresh possibilities. I loved the smeeeep sound of paint leaving the sponge roller and watching it glide across a wall—my bold colors contrasting nicely with the cool white trim. The sparkly teal and gold mosaic tile that I picked out for the master bath made my eyes twinkle as I took a bubble bath in my new Jacuzzi. I loved lying on the glossy restored pine floors, looking at their antique beauty close up and imagining all the holidays they'd witnessed over the years. I spoke good things to those floors and told them how happy I was to care for them. One of my advertising clients gifted me an at-cost landscaping makeover that was the jeweled crown of North Palm Street. Centered over the front walkway, he installed a beautiful antique English gate that made me feel like the Queen of England every time I walked through it.

The act of taking an old thing and making it new and beautiful again smoothed out all the dark, exhausted places of my heart and cultivated simple joy and childlike wonder. For the first time in a long time, I felt my heart beating again at a healthy, strong rhythm. As the house came back to life, I was animated again, seeing in color rather than black and white. It went beyond simply having a functional, beautiful house to live in. Rather, it was the process of creating something wonderful that healed a broken piece of my soul.

I lit candles and set up old pictures of my grandparents and great-grandparents on my restored fireplace mantle. My maternal Great-Grandma Bessie's famous side-eye and Mona Lisa smile looked at me approvingly, flanked by her husband who was a bauxite miner like Daddy and her barefoot children whom she could barely afford to feed during the Great Depression. She had nursed and co-slept with all four of them until they were more than a year old, and she stayed close with each one of them until her death. I could still hear her clear alto voice singing "Fairest Lord Jesus." Despite enduring poverty and losses, she left a legacy of love. I sensed that she, too, was part of the cloud of witnesses looking down on me with love and mercy, cheering me on to restored wholeness.

"Of course, it's not true. Of course not," I told myself when those cursed words *you'll never be blessed again* haunted me. If I couldn't imagine Great-Grandma Bessie withholding goodness over her children indefinitely for their mistakes, then how could a God who was infinitely loving and merciful not forgive the mistakes and misguidances from the few short years of my young life? Why would a petty, grudge-holding God even be worth believing in? Perhaps it took reaching rock bottom, and finding light and warmth instead of curses, that I began to imagine the immensity of God's unending love.

My past was not one that needed to be buried, but rather folded gently into the soil so that new life could come forth. Such is the nature of the universe: nothing is ever wasted, but every decaying thing gets turned over with time and mercy until new life emerges out of our rotting trash heaps.

The day finally came for Eddy to move out so I could move in. The house sparkled and shone from every angle—an absolute beauty inside and out. Moving out was hard on Eddy. The act of creating something beautiful had been just as therapeutic for him as it was for me, and he wasn't ready for it to end. He took ownership in his work, and it felt as if the rug had been pulled out from under him all over again when the project was finished. But it was time to drink one last Dr. Pepper with him, shake his hand on a job well done, and send him on his way.

Charlie, Eddy, and I were a team of misfits that turned something dull and forgotten into something remembered and glorious. I like to think that project restored us all in one way or another.

Charlie Bush's home soon became Grand Central Station for my group of faithful girlfriends, many of whom were wrestling with their own demons. All of my good little church-girl friends had completely disappeared from my life. Whether it was because they were instructed to "withdraw their fellowship" from me or simply stopped valuing my friendship, they vanished from my life one by one, like multiple deaths. I imagined that they were riding strong atop their sanctimonious high horses and didn't want to take a chance that bad company might bring them down.

It didn't matter anymore because I had a ragtag crew of almost-but-not-quites who liked to drink wine and had my back. We were a sisterhood united by daddy issues, failed relationships, and deep disappointments, and we had nothing to prove anymore. We had all washed out of life in one way or another, and we understood each other's shame. If the church had condemned us and failed to be our safe haven for honesty, my haunted house became a hospital that specialized in patching up wounds of the early twenties—the ones that marked the first real hard failures of life and the ones that shaped and refined who we are as women. We created a judgment-free zone where we felt at ease to take off our masks and expose all of our fears and failures without recourse. It was a place where we offered understanding, compassion, and at times commiseration. A place where church lady platitudes of "*just* what to do" about complex circumstances would be laughable.

Britney and I taught ourselves guitar in that house. Before, I had always dated the musician, but I was learning to make my own music. Those shiny floors witnessed countless impromptu dinner parties, wacky theme parties, game nights, and sleepovers. Those colorful walls reverberated real talk, laughter, music, tears, pain, and love. Those doors were ever open to anyone who needed a beer and a listening ear. The space that we cultivated in that house was beautiful and messy and sacred. We were so holy and didn't know it.

But it would prove to be the end of an era. In less than two years a For Sale sign would go up in the yard again and Charlie Bush would have a new family to scare the daylights out of.

I could never resolve a magnetic pull in my core that was forcing me out into the great unknown. That wanderlust that had plagued me since childhood had reared its frightful face again, and this time it was strong enough to lure me away from everything.

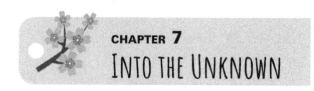

CHAPTER 7

INTO THE UNKNOWN

"I can't believe you're throwing away your life like this!" Mama chided from Mommama's round table.

"Why do you want to run away? You've got this job, this nice house that you've finally finished, and for once—a good boyfriend that we all like! Goodness, what about your future? If you want kids, those eggs don't keep."

"Yes, ma'am, sure don't," my Aunt Amy agreed while combing the ends of my niece's hair out to give them a snip.

I could always rely on the women in my family to spill their unfiltered opinions. Problem was, they were right in every conceivable way.

I liked my job and my friends. I had just become Facebook official with a young Air Force officer named Travis who was a hunk and a sweetheart. He was too good for me; I was sure of it. By every measure, I was happy.

I had met Travis eight months prior on a night out with Britney at my neighborhood bar and restaurant, Ciao Baci. It's a tight little space inside a 1920s bungalow in the historic Hillcrest District of Little Rock: the perfect setting to bump into someone. I was standing in line for the bathroom when in walked a magnetic force with an old Hollywood kind of face akin to Paul Newman or a young Elvis Presley. When he walked into the room, the center of gravity shifted, and I wondered if everyone else felt it too. It unbalanced me when he first saw me, and we locked eyes. He and his buddies had just returned from their first deployment to Iraq that very night, and they were out to celebrate their homecoming.

He meandered through the crowd to find me in the bathroom line and asked if I wanted a drink, and I was so stupefied that I said, "Sure, I'll take an appletini!" I don't even like appletinis, but

I pretended to enjoy the syrupy green sweetness all evening long as I got to know this dashing pilot. He was a little reserved, as he was dead tired, jetlagged, and it had been months since he had dated. But the more we talked, the more layers there were to unravel. He was a deep old book of mysteries, and I wanted to savor him page by page.

I had always sworn I would never date one of the pilots that came through Little Rock Air Force base. My impression of Air Force guys was that they were arrogant and blazed through the local girls as if they were dispensable playthings. But I gave him my number that night anyway, and after waiting a full three days to call me, Travis set out to prove me wrong—one Wednesday-night date at a time.

We bonded over our shared experience of being kicked out of religious institutions. I told him about the divorce and being excommunicated from church, and he told me about getting kicked out of private Christian high school his senior year for getting caught with alcohol on a Friday night at the empty football field.

"So much for the grace they preached," he lamented. "Football season was over, and they didn't need me anymore. I was just a pawn in their example-making agenda."

Travis and I understood each other to the core; he made me laugh constantly. He was the full sun to my partly cloudy skies. Our relationship was just so *easy.*

But my easy life couldn't scratch the persistent, bone-deep itch to leave it all behind. It couldn't be cured by the perfect relationship. And besides, Travis had barely said, "I love you," and I suspected he had finally said it because I was about to leave the country. The subject of marriage and future had never come up, and the old-fashioned girl in me sure as heck wasn't going to be the first to bring it up. The feminist in me overcompensated by running away.

I needed to make a peregrination. Not a trip, not a vacation, not a pilgrimage, but a peregrination to another world. The difference between a pilgrimage and a peregrination, according to Ant Grimley of the Yoke Movement is,

When you go on Pilgrimage,
You get someone to look after your dogs.
When you make your Peregrinate
You give away your dogs.[4]

I didn't have dogs, but I was giving away my safe, steady life. The door beckoned for me to walk away. Part of me was still missing. There were curious yearnings that needed to be satiated. There were things to know that my beloved Arkansas couldn't teach me. There were pieces of myself that were scattered around the globe and hidden in faraway lands. There was treasure to unearth and there were parts of me that needed to be reborn.

Maybe it was the lasting constraints of being shamed in a small town. Or maybe it was my Irish heritage that echoed this longing buried deep. Early Celtic Christians wandered as far as they could go to build island sanctuaries and monasteries in the most austere locations on rocky, windy landscapes where sea meets sky. The quest for "what lies beyond" was seen as holy. Leaving comfort, boundaries, familiarity, and security behind in order to experience new birth and "seeking the place of one's resurrection" was the essence of Celtic spirituality.[5] Like Abraham who was told, "Go from your country and your kindred and your father's house to the land that I will show you," I felt an irrational breath whispering, "Go," and nothing else.[6]

Where I was to go was still a mystery.

A month prior I had interviewed with a UK-based publishing firm we'll call Cambridge Reports that produced annual economic reports of emerging markets around the world. I stumbled on the company online, and I was ridiculously unqualified for the job. I had zero experience in print, knew nothing about "emerging markets," and couldn't find Abu Dhabi on a map. But by pure miracle or dumb luck I got an interview.

I took a week's vacation from my TV job and secretly flew across the ocean to meet a woman named Lorraine Dubois in a highfalutin hotel lobby in London. I wore my best black power suit and borrowed a friend's designer black patent leather shoes for the interview. They were the kind of shoes with red velvet bottoms that announced each step with a, "Watch out world, I'm on fire!" kind of pep. I felt like Carmen Sandiego in that outfit and needed the extra confidence because Lorraine Dubois was just as intimidating as her name implied. A French-American hybrid with a glossy dark brown bob and taut, polished skin, she met me with a half-smile and a dainty but firm handshake. She was a woman who knew her lane and swanned through it with power, poise, and purpose. Her shoes had red bottoms too to match her designer everything. She ordered a Diet Coke and went straight to business.

"So, what experience do you have doing sales pitches to foreigners?" she asked with a verbal fry as she surveyed my résumé up and down like the old girlfriend scrutinizing the new girl.

"Um, I sold a TV campaign to an Indian restaurant once," I replied. I couldn't think of anything else to say.

"Oh, how did that turn out for you?"

"It was great."

I lied. It was a disaster that ended in a multitude of angry Indian customers calling the TV station decrying false advertising. I had tried to patch things up with a friendly sit-down at the restaurant, but the meeting ended with the restaurant mom, dad, and eight-year-old son raising their voices in my face, as I struggled to understand their perspective and dialect. Something was lost in translation that I couldn't resolve. I wasn't exactly international business material. But it was on to the next question—

"Do you have any problems with working in the Middle East?" she asked.

"Well . . ." I stammered, "I prefer to work in any of the other places where the company operates—Eastern Europe, Latin America, Asia, or Africa. Really, I am fine with anywhere *except* the Middle East," I told her honestly.

I didn't have a good answer as to why I wasn't keen on uprooting my entire life to move to the Middle East alone. Truth be told, my opinions were largely informed by what I had seen and heard on Fox News, which was bad 99.9 percent of the time. I had no interest in the region, thought it might be dangerous, and couldn't see myself embracing the culture.

"You're applying for the position as Country Director," she said in a more salesy tone. "So, this means you *should be* driven by projects that are profitable. So, if it means the difference between a two hundred thousand-pound project in Eastern Europe and a two million-pound project in the Middle East, which would you choose?"

"I suppose I would choose the two million-pound project in the Middle East," I said.

"Well, okay then," she flashed a smile.

***

Lorraine called a month later and offered me the job. She couldn't tell me where I would be going, other than a week of training in Istanbul and then more training in a follow-on country to be determined. And then another country to be determined. And so on. After a training period, projects would range from three months to a year, and their locations weren't tied to anything other than the ill-defined idea of "emerging markets." By taking the job, I'd be entering into a nomadic lifestyle agreement in which I would go wherever the company sent me, for whatever length of time, in whatever hotel or apartment they provided, all while living out of a suitcase. The job was a huge gamble, a bright and shiny escape hatch, and an escape that came along with a paycheck. I said yes.

The word *yes* felt like a death and a birth, a suicide mission and a new pregnancy all rolled into one. I was expectant of *something*, without knowing what that something was. The unnamed territory that awaited me filled me with hope and fear and excitement of the unknown path before me.

I said my goodbyes to Travis early, as he left on another deployment to the Middle East. We agreed to continue our relationship long distance, but without saying it, both of us knew that my decision to leave would make us or break us.

I put my beloved house on the market, and within two weeks of my listing it, a young couple made an offer. I had never met them, but they happened to be cousins of my cousins. *Only in Arkansas*, I thought. I didn't tell them about Charlie Bush, and my real-estate agent kept his lips sealed too. I hoped that nothing spooky would happen between then and the closing day—which was also the very day I was to fly out to Istanbul. Thankfully, Charlie behaved himself.

My very last night in America was spent with pizza boxes sprawled out on my shiny floors one last time. Mama, sister Julie, and my girlfriends laughed at the absurdity of the whirlwind my house had been. Our laughter echoed off the bare, colorful walls, and the hollowness of it all made me grieve. The sudden realization that I could never again go back to that moment in time with *that* house and *those* friends made a lump in my throat. I wondered if that was how risk was supposed to feel. Was it always that unnerving? There would be no eject button in case it didn't work out. I could always come home, but I was rolling up the rug underneath me, and try as I might to unroll it again, it would never quite look the same.

Mama, Julie, Jesse, my grandparents, and my cousins met me with teary smiles at the Little Rock airport. I was the first in my family to leave Arkansas, and perhaps they didn't understand why I needed to leave. Mama held me tight and sobbed. I was still her baby—running away to East bejesus-God-Knows-Where. Quite literally, God knows where.

I held back my tears until the wheels were off the ground and Little Rock looked all the more little. That would be the beginning of a pattern for me—crying on airplanes. The captive stillness of sitting alone with myself without distraction while seeing the world whiz by me below, exorcised all my pent-up demons. All the joys and anxieties of my life would come rushing to the surface and overflow in an uncontrollable stream—leaving my seat neighbor awkwardly asking if everything was okay. The airplane catharsis was better than therapy; I'd walk away a new person every time.

And so, my peregrination began.

Dear Twenty-Nothing-Year-Old Self,

You are enough. You are good, you are holy, you bear the image of the divine just the way you are.

From your upturned nose, to your bunioned feet and your flat chest—you are beautiful head to toe—bearing the likeness of a good God whose love will stalk you like a good parent all the days of your life.

You don't need a man to be whole. You don't need a marriage to be whole. You don't need the support of a White megachurch to be whole. You can start being whole by getting up today, putting one foot in front of the other, breathing deeply and feeling alive.

That kingdom of God you want to be a part of so badly, let me let you in on a little secret . . . It's everywhere. Start with the valley you are in and look around you.

This kingdom is an upside-down one, so say hello to your fellow weirdos in the wilderness outside those city gates.

Yes, even the ones in the Waffle House. Blessed are the poor in spirit. The Spirit of God isn't limited to a four-walled church or a nice, neat family gathering on Christmas. Don't be afraid to have Christmas dinner with a new crowd. Folks at the Waffle House are holy too, and they might just have something to teach you. They know a thing or two about shame, disappointment, and deferred dreams. And yet they're doing a holy act: celebrating the simple joy of pecan pancakes because it's the best they can afford. Sometimes those who become our best friends and teachers are the ones you'd least expect.

And that holy ground you want to stand on? Look around you—it's everywhere. Mommama's little round table is a burning bush. Your home—wherever you land—is a sanctuary. A bustling market or a dank room at a hostel is an altar. The path you're on is sacred.

And finally, don't be afraid of your own curiosity. Keep searching, listening to your inner voice that comes from the great source of Love, the divine within you. She'll guide you and delight in every curious stone you turn over. You can trust her.

Sincerely,
Your Upper-Thirty-Something-Year-Old Self

PART II

THE Desert

If the desert is holy, it is because it is a forgotten place that allows us to remember the sacred. Perhaps that is why every pilgrimage to the desert is a pilgrimage to the self. There is no place to hide, and so we are found.

—Terry Tempest Williams, *Refuge*[7]

CHAPTER 8

WAYFARING STRANGER

Istanbul, Turkey

I checked my email during a layover. "Good luck. We all start this journey running away from something. Just get out before it's too late."

It was from a Dutch guy who worked in the same industry I was joining. We had connected online weeks prior, and up until then he had been encouraging.

What's that supposed to mean? His ambiguity made me pick my fingernails.

I swallowed his comment and got myself a late-afternoon cappuccino. Running away or not, I sought out adventure and found it—flying on a one-way ticket to Turkey—and I wasn't going to let a European naysayer rain on my wanderlust parade.

After a long, sleepless flight, I arrived in Istanbul just after dark. A company driver who didn't speak English picked me up and took me to the Taksim district in the heart of the city. My boutique hotel was hidden in a maze of narrow cobblestone alleys, so he took me as far as he could drive before the road was too narrow to pass and dropped me off. I dragged my oversized suitcases up and down the uneven stones in the alleys until I finally read the Turkish letters on the sign that matched my printed email. I was too tired to eat properly but lay awake pondering the absurdity of being alone in a strange bed. It was glorious and it was terrifying. I eventually counted enough sheep to pass out.

I awoke early the next day to give myself plenty of time to find the office in this new city. I zipped up my Carmen Sandiego skirt suit, smiled at myself in the mirror, and then burned the crap out of my hair with my flat iron. I screamed, yanked the cord out of the socket, and inspected my front fringe in the mirror. It was half gone, the rest of it a crinkled poof that smelled like burnt popcorn. I tried not to spoil my makeup with tears, pulled my hair into a sleek ponytail, then hair-sprayed my crispies down as best I could. I learned a valuable lesson that day: voltage converters do not work with heating devices.

But it was time to get on with it. Time to get over my vanity, put on my thinking cap, and face the new day. I was eager to learn, notebook in hand. The straight-A student in me still geeked out over the chance to take notes while practicing scripty fonts in colored ink.

The office was a small cubicle farm with several posh suites along the edges of the room, the glass shrines that housed Lorraine and her British husband Rupert, the founder of Cambridge Reports. She greeted me with a European double kiss, and I bent in awkwardly to reciprocate. How does an American girl from the South who is wired for hearty hugs convert to the double kiss? I could never figure out whether I was supposed to kiss the air or the actual face. I have even practiced this, and I end up clumsily leaning in while my rear end is sticking out. It is meant to be cordially elegant, but it's as awkward for me today as it was the first time I did it.

Lorraine introduced me to Gianna and Celeste, two women who would be in training with me. More double kisses with my scorched hair right in their noses. Gianna was a Persian Swiss beauty and Celeste a tall, striking Australian-French woman who could have easily passed as a glammed-up tennis star. Nationality hybrids would be a recurring theme in getting to know my new coworkers. They were all a gorgeous fusion of exotic yet familiar, spoke multiple languages, had attended fancy universities, and were worldly and well-traveled. Then there was me: a wide-eyed girl from Arkansas, fresh off the turnip truck and ignorant of most everything. I had a few travel experiences under my belt, but I felt very green knowing this was not a vacation—this was my life. I wondered if I was some experiment the company was doing in hiring novices—Prototype A for the Fresh Blood Project. Everyone else seemed to have at least some experience in the industry. Gianna and Celeste had come from competing companies and considered Cambridge a step up. The editors and writing team were mostly young but adept, having gone to Ivy League schools and written for sleek political and economic publications.

We were escorted to a small conference room, and our training began with Coco, an Afro-French-Haitian who had worked her way up in the company to regional director. More double kisses.

Coco pulled out a map of the world, color-coded with the different regions the company operated in—Africa, the Middle East, Eastern Europe, Asia, and South America. She dove right into the various projects, length of time for each, and budgets. The goal of each project was the production of an annual magazine or "report" with country business intelligence for potential investors.

"And there iz no project without ze money," she chirped cheerfully, eyebrows raised. "Where do we get ze money?" she asked us. "We get ze money from government partnerships and ze businesses that have ze money! Zis is your primary job. To get ze money."

Celeste nodded along. She was well acquainted with how this game was played and what her role was in it. After a morning of learning about the company and role-playing sales pitches, Coco told us they were still deciding where we would be sent for our in-country training—at the end of the week. I tried not to let the possibilities be too much of a distraction, but a number of the locations I had never even heard of—Brunei, Sharjah, and Ras al Khaimah might as well have been Whoville.

I inconspicuously wrote down their names so I could go back to my hotel, google them, and practice their pronunciations. For the first time in my life, I understood completely what it meant to *fake it till you make it.*

Gianna, Celeste, and I met up for dinner that night at a restaurant overlooking the sparkling Bosporus, the narrow channel connecting the Black Sea to the waters of the Mediterranean, the natural boundary between Europe and Asia. After a couple glasses of vino, Celeste pulled out an elegant little tin box and hand-rolled a sleek cigarette. "All right, let's debrief," she said while lighting up.

"Oh, would you like one?" She caught me ogling it.

"Oh, no, that's okay. I've just never seen this kind of cigarette before," I confessed.

"It tastes way better than the mass-produced ones. Homemade is always better, right?" she said.

Truth was, I had never tried the regular kind either.

Celeste whipped out her notebook with her Cambridge Reports contract stamped "confidential." "Let's compare our contracts, shall we?" she said.

Gianna and I hadn't thought to bring ours, but we studied hers and realized we were all given three very different contracts. We'd be doing the same job, but there were strengths and weaknesses to the different contracts we were given. "They have to know we'd do this, right?" Gianna asked. "I mean, why wouldn't they just give us the same contract?" she said.

"Because in this industry, they will screw with you if you let them," Celeste divulged while pouting her lips and blowing a stream of sweet tobacco smoke upward.

"You really have to look out for yourself. There's a lot of money to be made, but they will push you around, work you like a dog, and squeeze you for every dime you're worth. Only you will look out for you," she warned us. "I'm going to renegotiate my contract before they send me afield. I advise you girls do the same."

"She's right," Gianna said joining in. "It's tough to do, but we have to do it before leaving Istanbul."

My heart palpitated. The thought of getting screwed after all I had walked away from—my life, my boyfriend, my house, my job— made the fried crispies on my head stand on end. Sure, I had tasted corporate nonsense in the television industry, but I had mostly trusted my immediate management. This was new territory, and I felt inclined to trust Gianna and Celeste's experience in showing me the ropes. We agreed that we'd bond together and have each other's backs in our initiation process. They had already flown us to Istanbul for training and took a chance on us; together we had the upper hand.

"One more thing you must know right away," Celeste continued while rolling another cigarette. "You need to learn how to say, 'F— off!'"

"Oh yes!" Gianna laughed while clapping.

"What? Why?!" I was confused. My naïveté was written across my forehead.

"The men you will encounter on this job will try to take advantage of you. 'F— off' is universally understood, and they get the point."

So I practiced it boldly, and we all three giggled.

***

Training week continued with more learning and more role-playing. But I explored the city with every pocket of time I could steal away. Gianna and Celeste were more interested in sleeping than sightseeing. Istanbul was an old, familiar friend to them. But to me, she was a new, alluring acquaintance, a big, beautiful mystery and an East-meets-West riddle to crack. In many ways, it reminded me of what I'd seen in Europe on a high school trip with my English class: Western architecture, cobblestone streets, outdoor cafés, and plazas filled with fashionable women drinking Aperol spritzes and businessmen in fine suits.

But it was also Europe's exotic distant cousin. It was a door to a new household—the East—and with that carried new flavors and cultures and assumptions that were strikingly different from those of the West. There was the Muslim call to prayer that was new to my ears, minarets that studded the skyline, shisha cafés with languid men drinking tea while debating the facts of life, and magnetic faces with darker eyes and higher cheekbones.

A stroll through the Grand Bazaar, or *Kapalıçarşı*, was a roaring echo of the Ottoman legacy. For centuries, Istanbul had been known as Constantinople, the seat of the Eastern Orthodox Church, and the epicenter of the Byzantine Empire. But when the Ottoman Turks took over in 1453, they turned churches into mosques, overhauled the culture, and began construction of what would evolve to be one of the largest covered markets in the world. For centuries that followed, the market continued to be an economic powerhouse offering fine textiles, jewels, spices, and more. It had also been a hub for slave trade. An ancient shopping mall of sorts, it offered treasures from the Far East to the Mediterranean and beyond.

As I walked through the bazaar, vendors shouted at me in various languages, taking a gamble on my nationality: "Hello!" "Bonjour!" "Hola!" "Marhaba!" The pathway was illuminated with hundreds of hanging lanterns made from tiny shards of glass soldered together in mosaic patterns. Pregnant mounds of spices neatly packed and smoothed over caught my eye. All the colors of the earth's palate gloried in bright yellow curries, orange Turkish saffron, red chilies, and purple sumac. A vibrant potpourri of teas perfumed rows of green jasmine buds, baby roses, dried pomegranate, chamomile, and hibiscus flowers.

I felt like Pollyanna at the country bazaar; I wanted to taste and drink it all in at once. I became flushed with the realization that I didn't have a home anymore to which I might bring any of these treasures. My nomadic lifestyle and overstuffed suitcases allowed for nothing extra, and there was nobody to share it with anyhow. This would be my first of countless markets, so I established a new practice that day of storing up treasures in my memory without actually buying anything. And that would be enough.

Before I knew it, I was lost. The colorful maze and roaring crowd made me dizzy and disoriented. At first, I wanted to run, but I felt the pull of something else: a new season of wandering had begun.

In my people-pleasing past, I had spent my entire life yielding to others. What happens when you get pulled into a million different directions by other people is that you wind up drowning out your own inner voice. You learn not to trust it because you don't even hear it. I needed to wander for the sake of wandering—not for my pocketbook, my social status, or my performance abilities, but for me as a whole person who was willing to get lost in order to find myself.

Instead of panicking, I took a deep breath and slowly wandered. I recognized the look of earnestness on the shopkeepers' faces as they sold their wares, and I saw myself in them. I noticed the children of the shopkeepers, chasing one another and weaving in and out of stalls, and I saw my inner child in them. I saw the fat American tourists and young European backpackers alike in wide-eyed wonder and curiosity, and I saw myself in them too. I began to pay attention.

I liked what I saw. In a city that I had been told was so "dark" and "lost," how could it be that I could see so much brightness already? I felt so small—just a beating heart swallowed up by an ancient market that was a living, breathing, luminous, rhythmic drum. I was a part of it somehow, a witness to its present glory. *Could this energy I feel and this light I see be part of the kingdom of God too?* I wondered as I wandered.

The crazy labyrinth eventually spit me out on the main road. The gray sky peeled over into a cold mist. Without an umbrella, I skittered eastward with my face nestled in my coat collar before spotting the famous domed Hagia Sophia in the distance. A giant Byzantine church turned mosque turned museum, and recently reclassified as a mosque, Hagia Sophia means "holy wisdom." I wasn't sure what wisdom she could offer me, but I thought she'd at least be a refuge from the cold.

She was warm and dreamy. The dark skies prevented much natural light from illuminating the ancient cathedral-turned-mosque, but the circular candle chandeliers cast a gauzy glow that stilled me. A plump cat slept curled up next to a marble pillar, and I took a seat next to him, basking in the quiet, a delicious contrast from the bustling bazaar. A shoeless man with a prayer mat was against one wall. Other than my high school bestie, who was Jewish, it was the first time I had seen any non-Christian pray. I watched him genuflect and touch his face to the ground several times. He was alone, and I gathered that he was sincere and specific in his requests. I wondered if maybe his child was sick, or his business was in jeopardy, or perhaps he was thankful for finding love or had just been healed. I later learned that Muslims pray five times a day, not to submit their grocery lists to God, but in order to maintain their connection to the divine.

O God, do you hear his prayers? I wanted to know. Opening that door of curiosity and even posing the question made me uncomfortable.

In the American evangelicalism I grew up in, it was always implied that God only heard prayers said in the name of Jesus. Without the blood sacrifice of Christ covering us, God couldn't look at us in our sinful state. But somehow, being in proximity to the Muslim man with a heartfelt prayer made me sad to think for even a second that God didn't hear his prayer too.

I looked up at the massive dome. My eyes couldn't even take in the full expanse of it. I wondered how many prayers had been lifted to heaven in that very space. How many anguished cries, how many whispers of gratitude, how many wholehearted petitions had been offered there by Christians and Muslims over the centuries? How many doubters too had stumbled in out of desperation? The feeling of being small came over me again as I pondered the vastness of the answer. And so, I felt the least I could do was join the choir of voices over the years and offer my own earnest prayer.

O God, give me wisdom.

It seemed only fitting to ask for wisdom in the space called holy wisdom, and I didn't have anything else to ask for. My future as a ramblin' woman was as opaque as the Turkish air that day. I didn't know whom I could trust, or even which country I would be living in the following week. I recalled the passage in the book of James that says, "If any of you is lacking in wisdom, ask God, who gives to all generously and ungrudgingly, and it will be given you."[8]

O God, give me wisdom.

The afternoon light was almost entirely gone, and I was getting hungry, so I wandered into a decent-looking restaurant across the street. I had just put in my order for an Efes beer and kebab when a middle-aged man sauntered up to my table. Yes, the freedom to roam was euphoric, but a woman wandering the world alone had a cost: the unsolicited company of men. "Hi, how are you?" he asked in a heavy accent.

"Fffff . . . fine," I couldn't bring myself to say it. I had just practiced with Celeste the day before, but the friendly Arkansas girl was still in the driver's seat.

My politeness gave him the impression that I was okay with his presence at my table, so he pulled out a chair and sat down right across from me. He told me he was Kurdish and looking for a girlfriend. He talked about his family. I told him I had a family too, a boyfriend back home, but "no, I'm not on vacation." It didn't even make sense to me to try to understand where home was these days, let alone explain that to a Kurdish stranger sitting at my table. The painful realization began to set in that I had to be smug and joyless in order to end our awkward conversation. It felt like a betrayal to my identity to be so rude. Like a conservative woman trying on leather pants for the first time—it wasn't exactly "me," but I had to learn to move in a new light if I was going to survive life abroad and alone.

The next day, Gianna, Celeste, and I talked with management individually about renegotiating our contracts. I did my best to hide my shaky voice in my face-to-face confrontation with Lorraine. But to my surprise, she readily renegotiated my contract. We all three walked away with higher commission percentages and better work terms. I felt emboldened but also a little sheepish for making such a brazen move as the new, inexperienced girl.

We had our final training session with Coco before she gave us details about which country we were headed for. Gianna was going to Algeria, Celeste was headed for Malaysia, and I would be going to Jordan.

"Oh, Jordan!" I tried to act happily surprised. I knew it was in the Middle East and had an Americanish name—and that was pretty much it.

Coco reassured me: "You're lucky to have Jordan. And ze current country director, Hillary, iz American—you'll get along great!"

CHAPTER 9

DANCING WITH MYSELF

Jordan

I was never meant to stay in Jordan for more than two months. At least, that is what Coco told me in my final briefing.

On my way out of Istanbul, I snagged a Jordanian guidebook at the airport and read as much as I could on the short flight to Amman. Jordan is an absolute monarchy, ruled by King Abdullah and his drop-dead-gorgeous wife, Queen Rania. Abdullah is the son of the late King Hussein whose wife, Queen Noor, is American. (She was Hussein's fourth wife and not Abdullah's mother.) Both King Hussein and King Abdullah are beloved by most of their people and the region. But beyond their being attractive figureheads, Jordan's stability depends on benevolent ruling. Unlike most of the Middle East, Jordan doesn't have large reserves of oil or lucrative industries. There has been poverty, a growing middle class, and a continuous influx of refugees from Palestine, Lebanon, Syria, and Iraq in recent decades. Natural resources are few, and water is often scarce.

Upon final descent, the landscape looked like fried chicken. For miles and miles, it was nothing but crunchy brown rock patterns and desert. Then a jagged sea of pale-colored buildings. So much beige. Amman is a jumble of modern architecture, ancient Roman ruins, and countless mosques situated across seven hills.

I hailed a cab and headed to the Shmeisani business district to find the Al Qasr Hotel, my new home. Most women in Shmeisani were wearing the hijab to cover their hair. I didn't know whether I was supposed to wear one, so I wandered to the Vinaigrette rooftop restaurant of the Al Qasr Hotel for dinner with my scarf loosely draped over my hair. If anything, blending in is not always a bad thing. Surprisingly, the restaurant was full of secularly dressed women too—expats and locals, as I discovered, some covered and some not.

The next morning, I was eager to meet my new boss, Hillary, for breakfast and start learning the ropes. I was hungry for a girlfriend, and already craving familiarity. She didn't know it, but I had already cast her as my American bestie in Jordan.

We recognized each other right away, as two American girls in a foreign country would. She had a delicate face and wide smile, with brown eyes and blond hair swept neatly into a bun. She was from Idaho but introduced herself as Dutch too, a dual citizen. Like everyone else in the company, she had that alluring duplicity, both familiar and elusive. It had been fewer than four years since she graduated from college and left the United States, but she used British expressions instead of American ones such as "going on holiday" and "in hospital."

We chatted over coffee and avocado toast about our work history, educational background, and the job in Jordan. Then I veered into the more personal realms, mentioning my amazing boyfriend Travis and how he'd probably be visiting me in Jordan after his deployment in Iraq.

"Oh, that's sweet. I have a Jordanian fiancé. So, about our government partnerships here . . . ," she condescended coolly. Alas, Hillary would not be a girl's girl or my friend, not even for the sake of being two single American girls in the Middle East. She was technically my boss for the time being, and she wanted that dynamic to be firmly cemented.

The next day I met our editorial manager, Stanislaw, a Russian Canadian with a buzz cut, steely blue eyes, and a poker face. His eyebrows didn't move up or down but stayed unnervingly motionless at all times. Just when I thought there could not be a thicker barrier than what I had encountered with Hillary, Stanislaw was Fort Knox with the key buried deep underground. He had the same look on his face staring into his laptop, watching the news, eating lunch, having a drink with a client, or—one would imagine—winning the lottery or finding out his mom has cancer. When he wasn't looking, I studied those eyes for the slightest hint of vulnerability, but it was nowhere to be found. I was convinced he had to be a spy or an automaton.

I didn't get open hugs and warm reception from Team Jordan, but it wasn't Hillary or Stanislaw's fault. The fact is: we Southerners are books in a chronic state of openness. What you see is what you get, and we put it all out there for the taking. This is true in business, in life, and in the comings and goings of everyday encounters. A grocery cashier can become your prayer partner. A hairdresser can become your therapist. Your aunt's best friend might give you unsolicited advice on how to snag a good man or make the best salad dressing. We consider people who have a smug bone to be untrustworthy or snooty. We put each other at ease when we have nothing to hide (or at least the appearance of such). As a result, we make friends easily, even if some of those friendships seem shallow to outsiders. Mama never taught me how to hold my cards close to the chest or that it would even be necessary to do so.

I ate dinner alone at my hotel's rooftop restaurant every night. The bartenders felt like my only friends. Beyond chitchat, I had considered myself an introvert, but without friends a part of me was dying a slow and ugly death.

Despite my Southern charm, I struck out attracting and securing friends, but I was determined not to let that liability keep me from getting to know Jordan. On a free weekend, I hired a driver for the day and set out to explore Mount Nebo, the mountain where God showed Moses the Promised Land, which he could only view but not enter due to his momentary lapse of faith during forty years in the wilderness.

My driver Sufiyan was a petite Jordanian man with snow-white hair and a beard, twinkly eyes, a little potbelly, and rosy cheeks. In other words, Arabian Santa Claus. I hopped in the front seat of the cab to avoid carsickness, and the feeling of being so alone in the world. Sufiyan and I hit it off—he didn't seem threatening, and we chatted about our families and life in Jordan as we bounced along the dusty highway. We stopped at a rest stop that had souvenir booths. He got a kick out of dressing me up as a "Bedouin lady" in a red and white dishdasha on my head, native to the tribes of Jordan. As we were leaving, a flock of sheep and their shepherd were crossing the street. Sufiyan chased the sheep and pinched their bottoms, making them clumsily trot away. Then he scooped up a baby goat and placed him in my arms. We took pictures of our "baby" and had a Coke before hitting the road again.

Not five minutes on the road, there was a moment of silence before Sufiyan reached over and put his hand on my leg while cutting me a wide-eyed hungry look. Once again, my Southern friendliness had been misunderstood, and the opportunist at the wheel was seizing a moment.

"F— off!" I yelled, slapping his hand away. I made him pull over and then switched to the backseat. We were in the middle of nowhere, so there would be no hailing another cab. I was stuck with him, and my only defense was to put him in his place. Thankfully that was the end of Sufiyan's advances that day. He apologized, and I considered my ability to use the F-word a small victory.

We reached the top of Mount Nebo by midday. The blue sky contrasted with the burnt orange land that unfurled just a short distance before a greener patch rolled into Israel. Moses had climbed Mount Nebo in search of the land that God promised his descendants on oath to Abraham, Isaac, and Jacob. How close he was! The border to Israel was just a stone's throw away—on top of that mountain it looked like it was right underfoot.

Is this it? I thought to myself.

It was glorious, but it was also underwhelming. It was hard to imagine that such a small piece of real estate had become the subject of so much spilled blood over the centuries.

The conflict was first lit a couple thousand years ago, but in the twentieth century it sparked after thousands of persecuted European Jews returned to their ancestral lands, a movement known as Zionism. The Arabs of Palestine didn't welcome the Zionist attempt to establish a national homeland since Arabs already claimed it as home and were well established there. After two bloody wars in 1948 and 1967, the land is now controlled by Israel, including the formerly Jordanian-controlled West Bank. Today, there are seven million Palestinian refugees and their descendants that have fled or were forced out of homes in Israel. Jordan took in so many Palestinian refugees over the years that Palestinians have eclipsed the Jordanians—three-fourths of the country's population is Palestinian.

I thought about my tribe back home who loves to romanticize Israel and the land itself as being for God's "chosen" people. Bizarrely, American evangelicals overwhelmingly support the Israeli occupation of the West Bank and Gaza in the name of "Israel is for Jews!" They have not been shy about pitting one group of people against another— Jews over Arabs, most of whom are Muslims, but many of whom are Christians.

American Evangelicals get this biblical interpretation from *dispensationalism*, a theology crafted from nineteenth-century English minister John Nelson Darby and popularized in the United States by a number of prominent Protestant theologians and evangelists of the nineteenth and twentieth centuries. Dispensationalists assert that Christ's return to Jerusalem will occur after the pre-ordained process of the Jews returning to Palestine. Israel's seizure of the land is a grand fulfillment of prophecy, and any violence that has occurred or will occur is inevitable tribulation—a "sign of the times" and an end justified by the means.

It's a curious thing. Jesus never talked about the actual land. In the Gospels, the land is irrelevant. Jesus talked about his kingdom that transcends time, space, race, gender, class, and religious affiliation. His parables are filled with stories in which outsiders are the heroes (Luke 10), and where Jews, Gentiles, slaves, free men, male and female are set on equal ground (Galatians 3:28). Where the peacemakers are called "children of God." Where the meek inherit the earth. Where the poor in spirit obtain the kingdom (Matthew 5).

On top of Mount Nebo, I didn't feel so close to God. As I looked out over the Kingdom of Jordan and Abraham's Promised Land, I realized part of me had expected to have a grand mountaintop experience, the kind of "thin place" we seek where we feel drenched in divine mystery and gain clarity on our life's path. But I could not find comfort in Abraham's bosom, not even on his old stomping grounds. It didn't seem very long since I had been kicked off the mountain of my church back home. At the summit of a beautiful mountain deemed holy by Christendom, all I felt was alone, both in a physical and spiritual wilderness.

As I kept my distance from Sufiyan and felt the cold breeze whip my hair, I ached for unity with the God who made it all, whose still, small voice was faintly heard despite my estrangement from "God's people." I still believed in a Jesus who loved all of the land and its people the same, who looked at the crowds with compassion, sheep without a shepherd. I wanted to know what it meant to pray, "your kingdom come, your will be done." What was God's will for my life alone, abroad? What was my place in the kingdom? Was I even still in the kingdom? I might have been living out of two suitcases, but I carried around a heavy load of questions that constantly weighed down my thoughts.

* * *

Lorraine called to let me know that my time in Jordan would be extended "indefinitely." They weren't yet sure when I'd be relocated or to where, but I was to move out of the Al Qasr Hotel at the end of the month and move in with Stanislaw in the company apartment.

This was a huge blow; I was ready to move on and couldn't see myself in Jordan much longer. Sharing a living space with a Russian spy was sure to be dreadfully awkward, not to mention inappropriate considering I had a boyfriend back home. I'd have my own bedroom, but we'd share a bathroom and a kitchen. Lorraine said the company needed to save on costs. Hillary was about to get married and had her own living arrangements. Stanislaw and I would share an apartment and a car, and that was that.

Stan was already settled in the master bedroom, so I moved my things to the second bedroom and began to unpack while overhearing him talk to his mother on the phone in Russian. It was the most I had ever heard him talk, and I couldn't help but wonder what exactly they were talking about. The dumb American roommate who was crashing his life circumstances, perhaps?

The fridge was empty, so we needed to get groceries. Together. We'd get hungry after work and need to figure out dinner. Together. In the evening, we'd sit in silence watching BBC News on our one TV in the shared living room. Together. The daily grind is an intimate thing, when done with a close family member or lover. But with a silent stranger, it is the strangest thing on earth. I'd retreat to my bedroom and Skype Travis, attempting to explain my odd life with a secret agent. Travis was at least happy that I wasn't cozying up to Silent Stranger Stan. He reminded me that he'd be visiting in a few months, and to hang on in the meantime.

The project dragged on—our days packed with meetings. Hillary, Stan, and I went to most every meeting together. Anyone and everyone who had money or power was at the top of our agenda: cabinet members, the royal family, the most prominent business owners and investors in the country. Our job was essentially to sift Jordan for all it was worth, until there was nobody else to ask. The company taught us a set formula of three meetings, or "pointers." The first pointer was a meet and greet. The second was an interview. Third was a sales pitch in which we asked for their money to support the publication. Often the person would feel a little hoodwinked, disappointed that we wanted more than just their intelligent answers to our questions. The illusion of flattery was shattered by the presentation of a customized contract with the bottom line embellished by the sign of a swirly, loopy British pound. But often they would say yes. And by the time we'd get to a third pointer, we knew how much they were worth, how much they were capable of giving, and how much to ask.

Our biggest interview was with a prominent businessman in town whom I'll call Omar. Omar was the largest shareholder of a multi-billion-dollar international company. Omar invited us to interview him and his son, Faisal, also a prominent business owner, in their family compound. Faisal had a Bobby Kennedy-like gravitas about him: short, but dark, handsome, and exuding power. During our initial meet and greet, Omar asked where I was from and then lit up when I said Arkansas. He went on regular business trips to Arkansas and was familiar with the culture. I didn't know it yet, but Arkansas is the center of the universe. Time and time again I would meet people around the world with some strange connection to the Natural State. Though small and forgotten we are, between big companies like Wal-Mart, JB Hunt, Tyson, and the diaspora of artists, Arkansans leave sneaky footprints that cover the whole earth. At the end of the interview, Omar turned to his son Faisal and said, "You should have gone to school in Arkansas."

The next day Faisal started sending me text messages asking when the interview edits would be complete. He must have got my number from my business card. I casually mentioned it in the office, and Hillary flew off the handle.

"*I* am the country director!" she fumed. "Why is he texting you and not me?"

I caught Stan rolling his eyes from behind his laptop screen, a rare sign of emotion. She was right, of course. I regretted opening my big mouth to Hillary. Old habits die hard.

"Natalie, I want you to stay here for tomorrow's meeting. It's too big of a deal for you to potentially wreck it," she said.

Later that evening over Indian food takeout, Stan broke his silent streak and took it upon himself to coach me. "You do not have to tell Hillary any more information than she needs to know. She's only going to use it against you. Trust me on this: be quiet when it comes to Hillary."

As an extended punishment, Hillary began excluding me from all the important interviews and sales pitches. I hated getting sent to the corner, but it was a consolation that someone had taken my side over Hillary's jealous retaliation. And from the tight-lipped Russian, no less.

In the days that followed, I stayed in the office with Lydia, our sweet young Jordanian secretary, and Ahmed, one of the interns from the Jordan Investment Board. Ahmed technically didn't work with us, but he was such a chronic chain smoker that he'd saunter through our office to exit the building multiple times an hour. He was never short on jokes or small talk, and I never imagined my introverted heart would be so delighted to hear from the lazy office guy. "Send an email, take a smoke break. Send an email, take a smoke break," was Ahmed's mantra. I thanked God for Ahmed's smoke breaks if only to have the presence of a human being to disrupt the boredom.

One weekend Stan left for a weekend trip to Dubai. I was left with an empty apartment and the car all to myself. The fridge was empty, and I decided it was time: I would learn to drive in Jordan. Up until then I had relied on the silent stranger to be my chauffeur. Driving in Amman was like being in a pinball machine. There are so many roundabouts, unclear lane placement, aggressive motorists, speeding sports cars, pedestrians, sheep, and goats all on the same road. Figuring out how to adjust to it would be like learning a new language. The horn is an absolute necessity—you must "announce" your presence through every intersection as if to say, "Please follow the law this time and don't hit me!"

It had been several years since I had driven a stick shift and several months since I had even been behind the wheel. By the time I got to the first roundabout, I whirled through it while screaming at the top of my lungs. I was trapped in a whirlpool. Getting out seemed impossible— the inner lane had the right of way, and cars were continuously cutting in front of me. After several dizzying loops, and all the adrenaline coursing through my body, I finally escaped the death wheel, and the spell was broken. I was able to drive in Jordan, and I sped away like the Queen of Sheba on horseback.

While I was sitting in the parking lot of the grocery store, my phone rang, startling me. Nobody ever called it. "Hi Natalie, it's Faisal!"

"Oh, Faisal. Hello!" I was speechless, the deer in the headlights trying to avoid telling him he was the reason why my boss hated my guts.

Faisal was really good at small talk, somehow bringing up everything from indie music to the best restaurants in New Orleans. "Reason why I'm calling is because I would like to invite you to our polo party. In the English countryside," he said. "It's a gorgeous time of year in the UK, and it's going to be a fun group."

"Oh wow. Who's we? Is your family hosting it?" I sputtered.

"No, Dad's not coming. And I'm actually separated from my wife right now. So, it's just a few polo friends and a few members of the Jordanian royal family. Don't worry about the expense—I'll get your airfare and hotel," he insisted.

"Oh goodness. I'm not sure I can get away from work. And I don't think I'll know anybody there," I objected.

"It'll be a long weekend. And feel free to invite a few girlfriends. Could be from the States if you wish—will get their airfare and hotel too," he boasted.

"Oh, that's very generous, but I'm not sure. Let me think about it," I quickly said, and then hung up. I drove home thinking there was no way I would get away with going. Especially after Hillary's raging disapproval of me. Plus, I had a man I loved who was at war. What would he think about me going to an overnight party in another country, invited by another man?

But I was chronically lonely, and the opportunity to have a free rendezvous with my best friends made my heart leap. I mentioned it to Travis over Skype that night. His response was the most gracious I could imagine. "You should definitely go! That sounds like a blast!"

When it came to the question, To go or not to go, Travis was always on Team Go, no matter the circumstances.

Stan returned to Amman, and I divulged the conundrum to him too. "Oh, this is easy: go! It will be epic. Why not?" he asked.

"Because, Hillary," I responded.

"Hillary? Wait . . . what? Why does Hillary even have to know about it?" he asked. "Who cares about the project? This is your life, your business. Explore whenever you can and leave no regrets," he reassured me.

In one solidifying conversation about rebellion, Stanislaw became my partner in crime and my friend. I began to pick up on his dry sense of humor and enjoy it, and I think he learned to tolerate my scattered idiosyncrasies as well. Whether it was our shared frustration over Hillary or the fact that we lived under the same roof, we didn't have to spell it out but understood clearly that he'd have my back, and I'd have his.

It would still be some years before I realized that I didn't have to ask permission from men to make decisions. Learning to trust my own desires and instincts was a long time coming; a confident womanhood does not happen overnight. But my years of always striving to be the good girl were coming to an end as I began to walk comfortably in my own free skin. I began to see failure as the gift that freed me from a self-righteous prison. It also didn't hurt that I had a boyfriend who was secure in himself and not prone to jealousy. Travis didn't have a toxic bone in his body, and he gave me the space I needed to spread my wings and figure out who I was in this world.

As I counted down the days to my getaway, my delicious secret was the fuel that kept me going. I'd be rebelling against my superiors, but I reveled in the joy of being carried by my own curiosity, rather than by what everyone else expected of me.

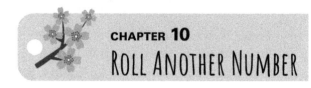

Hampshire Hills, England

The Hampshire Four Seasons in the English countryside was a tall, cool glass of water for a parched soul. The hotel was a converted Georgian manor house set on five hundred acres of rolling green fields and wildflowers. The spring air was as fresh as a sugar snap, and the afternoon sun glistened off thick locks of grass. It was a little piece of heaven on earth. I meandered through the grounds slowly and aimlessly. Coming from the dusty, dry landscape of Jordan, I found the fragrant green ripeness in the month of May to be a feast for my senses. By afternoon, I drank tea in the parlor while waiting for Britney and Betsy, my two besties from Arkansas, to arrive. The old wavy windowpanes made the scenery outside look like a Monet painting.

Britney and Betsy arrived before nightfall. We squealed and hugged and then caught up on all that we had missed over the months while lying on our pristine princess beds in the fluffiest bathrobes we had ever felt. It was the first time any of us had stayed anywhere that fancy, and our uncontainable giddiness was over-the-top inappropriate. At least I wasn't alone in my inability to keep a stiff upper lip. Clearly, we were the Beverly Hillbillies that had come to crash the British aristocracy.

As I would discover, the ruling classes of Jordan were practically British. As an old vestige of colonialism, the elites and those with power and wealth were influenced by English aristocratic sensibilities. They spoke the Queen's English, grew up in British boarding schools, learned proper etiquette, and played polo instead of soccer.

The girls and I met up with Faisal and some of his friends after breakfast the next day. Faisal was accompanied by a Jordanian prince named Ambrose. Prince Ambrose was tall with stiff shoulders and a heavy brow and jawline akin to Frankenstein. He carried himself like a dignitary on a mission, but beneath his hazel eyes was a man who reveled in turning injustices into trivialities. He'd casually toss out phrases like "The whole world is built on lies" and "The number-one aphrodisiac is power." It took me a few beats to realize he didn't see those things as negative. When we'd pull out our cameras to snap a photo, he'd make sure he and Faisal were out of frame and then quote Shakespeare. "Remember: discretion is the better part of valor." It was a way of ensuring their privacy without openly threatening us. Perhaps he saw life as a game—a sport to be played—and each of his subordinates were pieces of a puzzle to be used and discarded at will.

The first order of business for us girls was learning how to sit on a horse while holding a polo stick. We suited up in chaps, strapped on polo helmets, and were hoisted onto shiny thoroughbred polo horses. We all had a case of the giggles, which made it impossible to actually learn anything. It could have been a scene from *The Bachelor*. Our Southern accents and complete ignorance of English pomp and circumstance was a sideshow spectacle for these experienced UK, Jordanian, and Argentinian polo players.

Giddy and naive as we were, we weren't oblivious to the fact that we had been cast as the entertainment. Faisal had carefully picked us for this role, believing we'd be the flirty, easy girls that their company of characters deserved. And the game had just begun. They gave us nicknames and guffawed at our ridiculousness on horses. My gaping wound of loneliness and that part of me that thrived off being a showboater enjoyed the attention, but the deeper part of me that just wanted to be known and understood recoiled at their objectification of us. It was partly what I had expected, but it stung. I had played the performer my entire life, succumbing to whatever part I was expected to play. But those days were dwindling. After our dog and pony show, we sat on the sidelines and watched the real deal played out on the field.

Later that day we found ourselves listening to indie music in someone's hotel suite. The girls and I danced while the guys watched us. In that moment we were on full display, a human commodity for the taking. I could see them paying close attention to long-legged Britney who, unbeknownst to them, was the consummate beautiful girl at the party who coolly rejects unwanted male advances. It didn't matter that they had money and power; she'd never budge, and that made me proud.

Then Betsy broke the spell. She stood on the bed and began unashamedly belting out lyrics to the song. Wide-mouthed and passionate, she sang for her own thrill. She sang for the girls. The guys were visibly irritated, as if she was ruining their curated moment of lust. It was as if her own soulful voice filling the air was an insistence of her dignity, a declaration: *I'm not here to perform for you. I'm here to enjoy myself.*

* * *

The next day, the polo weekend continued at the historic Spread Eagle Hotel in Chichester. The hotel was an old coaching inn that dated to the fifteenth century. It was quaint and cozy. Britney, Betsy, and I continued to dance the dance of being friendly and attentive to our hosts without offending them, but also stealing away whatever fun we could for ourselves. We escaped the polo crowd for a shopping trip in town and an afternoon at the pub.

In the evening, Faisal and Prince Ambrose invited us for tea in the hotel lobby. As we arrived, Faisal held up a little yellow shopping bag and grinned like the Cheshire cat. "I have a surprise for us!" he beamed.

But Britney and Betsy recognized the yellow bag and already suspected what was in store. Upon their arrival in London, Faisal had me ask them to swing by a London address to pick up a package from the porter and courier it to Hampshire. The stench of weed was faint but obvious, and they had the good sense to say no to being drug mules in a foreign country. Apparently, Faisal had figured out another way to get the goods.

"Follow me." He and Prince Ambrose motioned toward the back lawn of the hotel property. It was hard to say no to Faisal. He possessed the powers of persuasion and influence, while also appearing to be the fun-loving, unassuming schoolboy. He used that to his advantage to charm his way through life. When he said jump, everybody in the room would ask how high without resenting it.

It was getting dark, and streaks of Byzantium purple streaked the sky behind the silhouette of a giant oak tree. We sat in a circle in the cool grass under the tree, and for the first time in my life I actually contemplated smoking pot. My own thoughts were making my eye twitch in surprise of myself. It wasn't that I had never been exposed to marijuana. The smell of weed was strangely comforting; it smelled like home. But even having been around it so much, I had managed to avoid any peer-pressure attempts to try it. I never told anyone that my dad grew it in our backyard. I had been judgy of the potheads in my hometown. I wanted nothing to do with their ungodly culture, their unsanctified ways. Their grungy clothes and saggy britches repulsed me, and I looked down on them for being lazy and ambitionless. When my brother was arrested for smoking weed in high school and sent to a court-ordered boot camp, I was ashamed and embarrassed. *Good girls don't smoke*, I had always told myself.

But my good stamp had already been ripped off like a Band-Aid, which freed me up to chase curiosity. I wanted to know what all the fuss was about—just one time. Plus, I missed my daddy and wanted to experience the thing that brought him comfort and made him feel more connected with God. *It's now or never*, I told myself.

Faisal lit the first blunt, took a deep toke, and passed it around the circle. "Oh yeah, this is the really good stuff," he bragged.

Prince Ambrose took a puff and passed it to Betsy.

When it came around to me, it felt like a foreign object. How do you hold it? I had only seen women holding cigarettes between their index and middle finger, but that felt wrong. There is no ladylike way to hold a joint. I wished Celeste were around to show me how to make it look glamorous.

I held the papery roll up to my mouth and took a deep inhale. The burning sensation in my throat made me cough, and everyone chuckled. I switched to a thumb-and-index-finger grip and tried again; the second time was a little smoother. The pungent herbal taste swirled around my mouth, and I liked it. Inhaling the flavor of weed was like drinking coffee for the first time after smelling it my entire life. I passed the blunt around again, and we took turns until we had burned down several into nubs. I felt calm, but not much more.

"I don't feel anything at all! I don't think weed has any effect on me," I complained out loud.

"It hasn't been that long, gotta wait for it," Faisal told me.

It was getting dark and chilly, so we moved the party inside for tea. I had a hard time understanding how Faisal and friends could smoke marijuana when their strict adherence to Islam forbade them from drinking alcohol. But it wasn't a bad thing that nobody was drunk on top of being high, and our spirits were good.

We found a table next to a crackling fire in the lounge bar. I could see my reflection in the copper kettles adorning the mantle, and I felt like Keira Knightly in *Pride and Prejudice*. All the tension of the world mattered not when everything in our country inn was so shiny and beautiful. My girlfriends glowed like angels, and I was ever grateful for their presence. We nestled ourselves in pillowy armchairs and stared wistfully at the fire.

Then Faisal broke our trance: "Guys, James here has an announcement to make."

I looked up to see a tall, husky Afro-British man dressed in an Edwardian suit hovering. In a hot second, all of my warm fuzzies unraveled into frenzied paranoia: *He is about to announce to us that he knows what we did, he has called the authorities, and hence we are about to be kicked out of the Spread Eagle and sent to a cold and dank English jail.*

"I have Ceylon, Earl Grey, Darjeeling, Chinese Green, Oolong, and Chamomile," he said in Queen's English.

The relief was hysterical. I went into uncontrollable laughter, doubled over by his polite and proper delivery of the unexpected. In an instant, my paranoia flipped upside down, shifting like one of those rabbit-or-duck mind pictures, and everything turned funny. All my dignity was steamrolled by barrels of belly laughs, and every eye that met mine sent me into stiches. Even ominous Prince Ambrose was just a funny little harmless bird. All the paranoia had melted into a blissful silliness that lasted a couple of hours.

As I sat drinking Darjeeling, I saw Faisal and friends in a more compassionate light. Rich, powerful, and entitled as they were, I could see their humanity. I could see the same vulnerabilities that lurk under the surface of all of us, and I could see them a little more how God sees them: his beloved children of Abraham. I wondered how this natural, earthy thing was illegal. Imagine warring adversaries smoking out together instead of dropping bombs on each other. Could there be peace on earth? Probably not, but maybe there'd be a lot more laughter. Indigenous peoples of the Americas knew this, with their use of ceremonial pipes to make peace treaties.

One smoke-out was all I wanted, and I haven't felt the urge to try it again. But that one gave me heaps of understanding for people who choose to smoke it—whether for recreational reasons or those suffering from anxiety, cancer, or chronic pain. It also made me sad knowing that, as a White woman, I'd never face the same sort of punishment for possession as Black people.

As I would continue to learn on my peregrination: proximity breeds understanding. We can imagine what it's like to walk in someone else's shoes or contemplate what makes them tick, but imagining is not the same as doing. There are plenty of times when we should take a stand to not do what the crowd is doing, and yet there are other times when we need to figure out why the crowd acts as they do. Or perhaps stop taking ourselves too seriously long enough to be human. Sometimes it is necessary to taste and see what other people taste to begin to understand them. I had lots of preconceived notions of Jordanians, Arabs, and Muslims, but the closer I got to people, tasting what they tasted and seeing what they saw, the better I understood. I realized sometimes I just needed to live and not overanalyze. In the English countryside, I needed to just take a drag. It had me wondering: What other forbidden fruit was out there waiting to be sampled? What other new tastes would be good for me?

Jordan

I went back to Amman in a melancholic haze. I was leaving my good friends to return to a lonely and bizarre life in Jordan. I had fun with Faisal and the Jordanian royals, but I did not kid myself into thinking they would become my friends. Faisal was friendly at first, but eventually he wanted more from me than I was willing to give: secret intimacy. He lied when he said he was separated from his wife. "Separation," come to find out, meant "she's not in the room with me right now." He was in the market for a mistress. His fun-loving company had helped stave off my dark side of lonely, but I knew that a continued friendship would come at a price. He was a puppet master looking for a pretty little malleable thing, and I wasn't about to be it.

Stan, Ahmed (the lazy, chain-smoking intern), and I went out for drinks shortly after my trip. I was over trying to force friendships, but Stan was no longer the silent stranger to me; he was steadily becoming my trustworthy friend. They wanted to know all about my "lifestyles of the rich and famous" escapade, and I needed to debrief with people who understood the culture better than I did.

Stan listened to my wild weekend on parade, lit a cigarette, then reached for a bar napkin. "I'm going to explain to you what was explained to me on a bar napkin by an Emirati businessman. Are you ready for this?" he asked, setting his cigarette in the ash tray. He began scribbling a complicated-looking chart on the napkin.

"Male-female relationships are complicated around here," he explained. "You see, there are a lot of good men. But there are also barriers to love and others who abuse Islam and think since they are allowed to have four wives that they can 'always be shopping.' So herein we have five categories of male-female relationships." He wrote them down on the napkin:

1. *The Project*. This is usually the wife or long-term girlfriend. The relationship mom and dad approved of or even arranged themselves. She's usually of the same class and religion; the mother of the children. But she may or not be loved in a deeply romantic way.

2. *The Lover*. This is the one true love. The soulmate. Often, she's the forbidden fruit that mom and dad didn't approve of. For whatever reason, they're not allowed to be together. Maybe she's Jewish and he's Palestinian. Or she's Christian and he's Muslim. She's wealthy and he's poor. The classic Montague/Capulet scenario. The Lover hardly ever becomes the Project.

3. *The Mistress*. This one is primarily for sex. It's not real love for the man, and he is okay with that, but the woman often gets confused and expects real love and commitment in return. Things usually don't end well with the Mistress scenario, but it still persists over and over again.

4. *The Dancer*. This is the arm candy. She makes the man look good and many might think the two are sexually involved, but the relationship is mutual platonic fun. This is often the older man with the younger woman. They enjoy each other's company and that's as far as it goes.

5. *The Partner in Crime*. This is the best friend, the sidekick, the woman who can hang with the guys. There is no physical intimacy. She's the only woman who knows about all the other women, and she's loyal not to tell.

"And that's it," he said coldly. "You were probably seen as a potential mistress for Faisal and nothing else."

"Is this really how it is here?" I asked, hoping for a different answer.

"I can't speak for all Jordanian or Arab men, but for some it's sad but true," he said.

"This is the most depressing thing I've ever seen," I lamented. "But I think these categories are universal. I've seen these scenarios in America too."

Although we came from very diverse backgrounds, we concluded that there are good men all over this world, and in every culture, there are men who see women as objects to collect, treasures for plundering, existing only for pleasure and appearances.

Misogyny needs to be dismantled, but I wondered how all human relationships are weighed down by layers of selfish expectations. How often do we really *see* others? When we first meet people, we tend to sift them into a category. We stick a label on them without trying to see who they truly are. We decide quickly whether they're somebody we can jibe with, and we reject them if they can't offer anything to make our lives better—friendship, business, money, sex, conversation, or pride. Sometimes we help people less fortunate just to absolve our own guilt or stroke our egos. When it comes down to our naked bones, most of us have an underlying agenda when it comes to the compassion we choose to dole out or withhold.

I began to think about my tacit list of expectations. I had expected Hillary to become my American bestie in Jordan without understanding what her capacity was to nurture a new friendship during her hectic season: planning a wedding and driving the train for a big work project. I had expected Faisal to be a friend who would entertain me and keep me from dying of boredom. I had expected Stanislaw to become someone he was not in order to make me feel more comfortable living with a stranger. Sure, Hillary could have been a little kinder and Faisal a little less womanizing, but ultimately, they disappointed me by not meeting *my* expectations, and consequentially, I struggled to see their wildly beautiful and independent humanity.

I didn't see the Christ in them because I didn't look for it.

It is a rare thing when we see people—truly *see them*—and love without expecting anything in return. Being honest with myself, I realized how many strings I had attached to people in my life. And it made me sad to think how these strings are bonds that keep wounds from healing and shalom from happening.

I still believed in a Jesus who embodied a radical love that welcomed people from all walks of life. What made it so radical was that it was no-strings-attached generosity.

The Gospel of Luke tells the story of a dinner banquet at the home of a wealthy Pharisee. He was a powerful and influential man in a hierarchical culture, not unlike present-day Jordan. If the story were told in modern times, it could have been at the home of Faisal or one of his Jordanian royal cohorts. Jesus is a guest at the banquet, and Scripture says he is being carefully watched. A lot of bold things happen at this banquet, including Jesus healing a sick man on the Sabbath and a discussion about who should sit where. Jesus tells the guests not to be the ones to seat themselves at the seat of honor. Then he gives some advice to the host as well, brazenly telling him,

> When you give a luncheon or a dinner, do not invite your friends or your brothers or your relatives or rich neighbors, in case they may invite you in return, and you would be repaid. But when you give a banquet, invite the poor, the crippled, the lame, and the blind. And you will be blessed, because they cannot repay you, for you will be repaid at the resurrection of the righteous.[9]

Jesus strips away all of our layers of expectations that we put on people to simply say: love. Love people without expecting anything in return. By seeking out those who cannot reciprocate our good deeds, we learn to do this. We learn to see the light of Christ in people and love them because of it. They cannot offer us anything in return, so there's no other reason to love them other than because they have the image of God in them. Even knowing about this in theory, practicing it is so much harder. I suppose this is why love is a practice, not a feeling. We're clumsy at it, but yet we can try again and again.

I wasn't seeking out the types of people that Jesus said I should invite to my dinner party. Perhaps the paralyzing fear of failure got in the way. I worked in an industry that taught me to sniff out money and power like a drug-sniffing dog. And I was getting really good at it; I took pride in being able to size people up for their financial worth in a matter of minutes. So, I kept on swimming fast and hard in the glittery waters of success in order to prove to myself and others that I was worthy. My arms flailed and my feet paddled earnestly as the sad performer, chasing wealth and succumbing to whatever part anybody expected me to play.

* * *

Travis finally made it for a visit. I picked him up from the airport and kissed his scruffy face, tawny and toned from the desert sun of his deployment in Iraq. His hands were firmer, and he looked leaner, perhaps from being completely sober the past few months. But his smile made me feel, at least temporarily, that everything was right with the world.

We spent two weeks floating in the Dead Sea and exploring the ruins of Petra. We made a side trip to Beirut, where we got lost in old Lebanese neighborhoods, hunted down the best falafel in the world, and collected sea glass on the shores of the old Phoenician town of Byblos. Travis was always up for the next adventure; there was nothing he didn't want to experience for himself.

Before he left, we went camping in the Jordanian Wadi Rum desert. I'm not really a camping kind of girl, but Wadi Rum is magic. Intoxicating, like rum itself, and the perfect backdrop to fall in love. Wadi Rum is as red as the surface of Mars with intricate rock formations popping up all over the desert like a sculpture park. *Lawrence of Arabia* was filmed there.

A thin Bedouin man in a tattered T-shirt, baseball cap, and aviator sunglasses picked us up in the town nearest the desert to take us to our campsite. In his beat-up pickup truck he drove us through a sea of dunes before dumping us in the middle of austere nowhere with our Bedouin guides, a few other campers, and a small cluster of tents. Once the truck drove away, the only sound we heard was the occasional gust of wind rustling through the twisty rock formations.

We took off our shoes and walked barefoot across the warm sand, which retained its heat into the evening as the temperatures dropped. The round orange bulb of the sun in the distance did a disappearing act, tucking itself into the horizon, and then seemed to explode into millions of shards of bright light that spewed across the night sky.

We ate Bedouin stew and rice at a table set with candles held up by sand in plastic cups. After dinner, we were served sage tea, and I reclined into Travis's arms around a fire. It felt like we were swimming in the Milky Way as we waited for the evening entertainment. A Bedouin man plucking black-magic melodies on his ancient stringed instrument called an oud put me into a trance. It felt so viscerally *familiar*—a nostalgia that didn't make sense for a setting so far removed.

The next morning, we set off on a two-and-half-hour camel ride back to town. Travis's camel had a funny-looking face and hairy ears, and we named him Charlie. I somehow missed the luggage call for the campers' bags to be hauled in a pickup truck, so my suitcase had to be tied to the side of my camel, Chester. It wasn't long into our lumbering trek across the sands that our Bedouin guide realized that Chester was most unbalanced by my suitcase. The only solution was to weigh his other side down with rocks to balance him out, and then cut us loose from the pack. Chester and I wandered further and further and then further from the group before I realized it was just the two of us alone in the desert heat. It seemed Chester knew where he was going, so I tried to trust the furry beast. But as I looked at the silhouette of a beautiful man and his camel in the distance, I could also feel the sadness and longing of knowing that he would soon leave me.

I knew that I was walking a path that needed to be walked alone, but at the same time my loneliness was eating me alive. I didn't have the courage to ask the tough questions out loud. Everything with Travis was so light and fun. I didn't have the emotional energy to say out loud the deep feelings I was developing for him. If I was the first to broach the subject of "what are we doing here?" then I was afraid my cumbersome, complicated feelings might weigh us down like an unbalanced camel. As we held each other close and said our goodbyes, I had a lump in my throat, wondering whether our love was too tenuous and fragile or if our long-distance relationship could survive the test of time.

CHAPTER 12

DAYLIGHT AND DARKNESS

Still in Jordan

I wanted to learn Arabic, but certainly not for the fun of it. I was bewitched by the way it looked with all of its dramatic swirls and dots like Arabian sands. But I had a hard time imitating the harsh, chunky sounds and guttural, nasally tones. It was nothing like the beautiful, flowy Portuguese I had learned years prior. But I wanted to communicate and see below the cultural iceberg. I wanted to get the inside jokes at the office and hold my own at the market.

Stanislaw was still mostly silent, but he wanted to learn Arabic too, so we found a class taught by a beautiful stay-at-home Jordanian mother named Farah. Each week, we'd go to her house for private lessons at her kitchen table. She'd get her kids settled with homework or television before serving us a cookie and ginger tea as a sweet way to soften the trauma of having our vision blurred and our brains pressed and stretched for two hours.

Our days were filled with sales meetings, and we'd go out with work friends on the weekends. But Stan and I had an unspoken rule that whoever woke up first on Saturday morning had to go fetch the manakish for breakfast. Manakish is a Levantine dough cooked in a brick oven, topped with *zaatar* (thyme), cheese, or meats. My favorite shop in our neighborhood had a manakish with turkey, cheese, and pickles. I was usually the one to make the manakish runs, and it was the only time that I felt confident enough to practice Arabic. Knowing just a teeny bit of the language gave me a dose of confidence to make friends outside work. It's a universal truth that restaurant people are the coolest, most forgiving subculture in the entire world. If you need help finding kind, interesting people in a new city, find the local food peeps and stay in their corner.

One of those food people was Wael Karachi. I don't even remember how I first met Wael, but he had one of those unforgettable faces that was warm and magnetic. His complexion was the color of the Jordanian desert—a dark tannish red with deep crevices carved out by decades of laughter. His eyes were bulging and blue, vibrant as the Jordanian sky. Something about his gaze reminded me of my father, and I loved studying his expressions. But his best feature was his long, curly eyebrows that kissed in the middle and then danced off his face as if trying to celebrate life as much as he did. Wael had had a repertoire of random, impressive jobs throughout his life. He was a best friend with the former Queen Alia before she married King Hussein (and tragically died in a helicopter crash). He was once the Jordanian Ambassador to Nigeria in the '70s. And he owned a successful restaurant called Grappa in the heart of Amman's Second Circle Rainbow Street district.

"Will you be my guest today?" was Wael's favorite question for his friends. His resonant voice was akin to Topol as Teyve in *Fiddler on the Roof*, full of spark and wonder of an old man kept alive by sheer exuberance. Wael loved hosting big groups of friends in his garden at Grappa, and he began inviting me to his outrageous dinner parties. It was a mystery how he actually made a living because it seemed he gave everything away.

His table was a revolving scene of *mezza* platters, spilling over with grilled meats, hummus, baba ghanoush, and pita bread. The second course was usually pasta, followed by fruit or a decadent chocolate soufflé. Drinks were always aplenty. His eyes would twinkle when he'd bring rounds of what he called the Karadsheh special, made of vodka, fresh-squeezed lemon juice, and pureed mint. In Jordan, Christians are the only ones allowed to make and sell alcohol.

Wael was proud to talk about his heritage. The Karadshehs were one of three Christian families that settled in Madaba, the ancient Moabite city nearest Mount Nebo. As early as the second century, Madaba was an important Byzantine Christian center for culture and trade. It is most famous for its mosaic map of ancient Jerusalem discovered on the floor of an Orthodox Christian church. The Madabians often fought with the local Bedouins, but history suggests that the Madabians earned their respect, in part, because of their generous hospitality. Wael lived up to that reputation.

His guests would discuss everything from politics and history to art. After the dessert course, he would serve us tea and roll out the shisha pipes. Shisha, also known as hookah, is flavored tobacco filtered through an intricately designed hourglass-shaped waterpipe. Watermelon-mint shisha was my favorite, and in that magical garden under a Mediterranean starry sky, I felt like Alice in Wonderland after she had joined forces with the caterpillar that turned out to be a kind soul. Instead of being perplexed by his question, "Whoooo are Youuu," she brushed off her existential crisis, took a puff, and decided to feel at home in Wonderland.

The night would always end in a champagne toast and dancing.

"I have just the song for you!" Wael beamed. It was the famous Lebanese song "Natalie" that he loved to play while twirling me around. With Wael, I might very well have been the Dancer, but I didn't mind; I reveled in it. He offered his friendship and wanted nothing in return, only my presence.

By day, he was just as fun. He often invited me to join him for Rotary Club lunches, and it felt a lot like going with my grandparents to square-dancing parties. The food was delicious and the coffee strong. Wael's larger-than-life personality lifted my spirits, and that old man became the best friend I had in Jordan. For the first time in a strange land, I felt loved and seen.

One night, Wael had a dinner party at Grappa with various people he had met and several artists from the city. After the main course was served, the man to my right, a new acquaintance, raised his hand to get the table's attention.

"Natalie, please give me your hand," he began. I stuck my right hand out cautiously over the table as everyone watched. He put one hand above my hand and one hand below without touching them. He held his hands steady and waved them over my hand as if he were performing an x-ray. A dull ache hit my spine and stomach at the same time, as I could literally feel him touching my hands without actually making contact. I started to get embarrassed as the table caught on to my sense of surprise.

"Can I tell you something about yourself?" this stranger asked me.

"Sure," I responded in curiosity. But this was weird.

"Your father. He died because of a liquid substance, didn't he?" the man said.

"Yes," I responded awkwardly. I hadn't told them about my father's death or his alcoholism. *Where was this coming from?*

"And your mother. She really, *really* hurt your father badly, didn't she?" he jeered. His eyes were piercing me, and he was snickering as he tried to humiliate and shame me in front of people I barely knew.

I sat silently stunned before the words finally came out. "Okay, that's enough now."

I looked up at Wael, and he looked sad and confused about what just happened with one of his guests. Just minutes before, the mood had been cheerful and welcoming. But after that weird stunt, the colors of the party melted like birthday candles and all the air was sucked from my lungs. It wasn't that this stranger was using psychic talents or intuition or call it what you will. It was that he was using his abilities to gleefully poke an old wound. He saw a crack in me, and he sought to pry it open and put it on full display.

* * *

I saw how good and evil dance in tandem in Jordan as much as they do in Arkansas. It's easy to call a ridiculing psychic from the Middle East "dark," but as the years have gone by, I've thought about my own demons and the potential to harm other people as a result of my unresolved pain. In the words of Richard Rohr, "If we do not transform our pain, we will most assuredly transmit it."[10] Passing on our pain is a human game of hot potato in which we—usually unwittingly—shove our trauma onto others.

The stories we create about ourselves form grooves in our brains as old as time. They have the power to heal or the power to destroy. Two stories wrestled within me: On the one hand, I was unworthy, unlovable, just waiting for the other shoe to drop and things to completely fall apart. On the other hand, I was a beloved child of God perfectly *good enough* just the way I was, wandering in the wilderness with a Jesus who never left me. Miles from home, stripped from all familiarity, I found these competing stories even more naked and pronounced.

Out of pure curiosity and boredom, I visited the English-speaking expat church in town where diplomats and missionaries worshiped. At the entrance, I shook hands with the greeters and was given a bulletin with their announcements and an outline of the sermon. I settled into a pew, and it felt right. We stood to sing the first praise song and my shoulders sagged involuntarily. The whole set was the same basic praise songs that I used to hear at the Mountaintop. Musical nostalgia is a beast to reckon with. In a good sense, it can take us back to mix-tape road trips, young summer love, or our mother's breast. In a bad sense, an old melody can leave us in a fetal position on the bathroom floor. For people who have had traumatic experiences with church, church music no longer sounds comforting or uplifting. Old-fashioned hymns were still soothing to me, but praise songs were triggers that conjured up feelings of shame and rejection.

English-speaking churches in non-English-speaking countries are heavily colonized by American culture. More specifically: White evangelical culture. While the congregation may be ethnically and racially diverse, the services are very American. The pastor is usually American. His jokes are American. The music is American. So much of what I thought was Christianity was actually just White American culture. And how much of that culture was so easily conflated with *the way* Jesus taught. I longed for expressions of the gospel that were decolonized and independent. Be it African drumbeats, Celtic prayer circles, or Eastern Orthodox liturgies: I needed to see Jesus in other places to restore my dying faith.

One day I wandered into a local church with services in Arabic. It was largely underground—a number of its congregants belonged to Muslim families and wanted to keep their participation a secret. The pastor's wife, Sunny, was a ray of sunshine. She and her husband were Palestinian refugees who had come to Jordan from Israel after losing their home. She was warm and welcoming and seemed to be the glue that held the tiny congregation together. There were no bulletins with announcements, no bells and whistles. No stained-glass windows or fancy acoustic bands. Just a couple of people singing Arabic songs and a brief sermon with discussion. Despite my Arabic studies, I didn't understand a nibble of it. But I was witnessing an entirely different expression of the gospel, in ways more ancient than my own culture. The services were always at night, and I found myself returning whenever I had a free moment. Just a year prior, my Fox News-informed mind would not have imagined a group of Arabs gathering to read from Bibles and sing about Jesus.

Then, at Easter, my Arabic teacher Farah invited Stanislaw and me to the local Eastern Orthodox celebration. "I'm a Baptist, but if you're going to celebrate Easter in Jordan, you *have* to go Eastern Orthodox. It's the only way!" she boasted.

I couldn't imagine the equivalent in America—it would be like Baptists in Arkansas going to the Catholic Church on Easter. Most would not deviate from their sanctioned denomination for a single Sunday. In some circles, it'd be pure heresy. But the Eastern Orthodox Church is the oldest Christian tradition in the Middle East, and it is common for Jordanian Christians to unify during their most important holiday.

The service was at midnight. The streets surrounding the church were filled with worshipers waiting for the procession leading to the church. Stanislaw, Farah, and I could hear the deep rumble of a bass drum in the distance. The throbbing beat grew closer and closer until the procession of drummers, clergy, and laypeople paraded in front of us. Behind the drummers, a bearded priest in a tall, black, cylindrical hat carried a lantern with a burning flame. He held it with such care, as if it were the ark of the covenant.

"That's the fire taken from Jesus's empty tomb in Jerusalem," Farah told me. "The flame is passed on from one church to the next, all over the Holy Land."

The crowds followed the priest into the temple until it was packed. We squeezed into a pew in one of the upper balconies, but there were crowds standing in the aisles and spilling out the door. Even at such a late hour, there were wide-eyed children and bundled babies asleep on their mothers' shoulders. I couldn't understand the Arabic of the liturgy, but I was struck by the celebratory mood of the service. There were no shame-driven altar calls or evangelistic motives.

Afterward, the kids ran wild, and the crowds passed around Easter bread. It felt more like a street fair than a church service. The Light was breaking, Christ was risen, and how else to express the Good News than a loud-and-proud street party in the middle of the night?

Even Muslims sometimes take part in these services. After a string of terrorist bombings in Egyptian churches over the last decade, Jordanian Muslim youth groups have started turning up at Easter services to guard Christian worshipers from harm and stand in solidarity on their most sacred holiday. It's a nod to the ancient past when Christians, Muslims, and Jews sometimes shared the same houses of worship. Celebrations tend to bring people together like that.

"So, what'd you think?" Farah asked me after the service.

"That was different from anything I've ever experienced. I can't quite explain how, but it's so refreshing," I told her. I couldn't recall an Easter service that didn't focus on how *wretched* we all are, in need of saving. How we *deserved* the punishment, being *sinful* and *depraved*, but God had a plan to rescue us by sending Jesus to take our place by dying on the cross. Theologians call this substitutionary atonement.

I'll make no claims to be a theologian, but I can certainly testify to the damage that comes from religious teaching that leads by guilt and shame. It does not bear good fruit, only fear, paranoia, judgment, and punitive character. Fear and shame become big, hairy gatekeepers that keep people from participating in the household of God. What struck me about Easter service in Jordan was that it didn't tell people what to believe but was a celebration that served what they already knew in their souls.

John Philip Newell tells the story of a similar experience he had at the Cathedral of St. John the Divine in New York City. Every year on the Sunday closest to St. Francis's feast day, on October 4, they have the "Blessing of the Creatures" to honor the sacredness of the earth and all of creation. For many New Yorkers, it's the only time of year they attend church; the cathedral is more packed than on Easter or Christmas. The music is interlaced with wolf and whale sounds. New Yorkers and their pets are welcomed into the sanctuary. Parakeets and macaws squawk along with the choir, perched on people's shoulders. The liturgy finishes with the Silent Procession of the Creatures. The big doors open, and the congregation falls silent as a parade of animals big and small comes down the wide aisle—a camel followed by a boa constrictor, followed by a pig and a goat and all creatures exotic and domestic. As with Easter in Jordan, the church doesn't tell people what to believe:

> The Church's role was to serve that deep knowing and to help translate it into how we live together with the earth. Too often in the past our approach to truth has been to assume that we have it and others do not. Consequently, we have thought that our role is to tell people what to believe. We are being invited instead into a new humility, to serve the holy wisdom that is already stirring in the hearts of people everywhere, the growing awareness of earth's interrelatedness and sacredness. An essential feature of rebirthing within the Christian household will be to remember that the well of truth is not ours. It is deep within the earth and deep within the heart of humanity. Our role is to be a servant of that well.[11]

The deep knowing that comes from celebration is an awareness that I am held, you are held, and we are all held in the arms of a loving God. We do things that hurt each other, and we pass our own pain on to others, but there's healing at the table of God, where all are invited. The table of God is wide and welcoming and available to all who want to eat and drink—not just to those who think and look just like me, pray just like me, or love just like me.

Jordan was, for me, an ancient gateway into seeing the church in a more expansive light. I saw the body of Christ as humanity—or even more expansively—to include all of creation. I saw the light of humanity as beautiful and multifaceted, dancing and refracting in all directions. As every color we see is a different wavelength of light reflected back to our eyes, so the different colors of our lights make up pieces of the One Light, born out of love.

Damascus, Syria

"What if we drove to Syria?" Stanislaw and I mused. As I had learned, Stan was plagued by the same wanderlust itch as I was, and we were getting bored driving around Jordan. We had already driven to the Iraqi border twice, hoping to cross over—just to say we did it. But the war was still raging, so we chickened out both times, making a U-turn to head back to Amman before ever reaching the border.

A road trip from Jordan to Syria was a mythological creature, even to curious people like me who signed up for sales projects in the Middle East without much thought. The stories sounded like tall tales. Friends of friends had tried it. Some had succeeded, some hadn't. The border between Jordan and Syria was the Wild West, unpredictable and volatile, especially for American passport holders.

Stan and I had an interview with a savvy Jordanian businessman who brought it up at random—"I've got a guy. Want to go?" he asked.

By *guy* he meant a professional middleman who could bribe us across the border. "All you have to do is stay in the car or wait at the rest stop. American passport, no problem. He'll handle everything."

Next thing we knew, Stanislaw and I were planning a trip. This was 2009, so the Arab Spring had not yet sprung, and ISIS didn't yet have a foothold. After our English countryside rendezvous, Betsy was itching for more adventure, and my cousin Hazel was coming from London with her. They were just as wild-eyed and spontaneous as we were, so we planned the trip around their visit.

Ali, our *guy*, floated into our driveway bright and early in a boat-like black sedan akin to a Lincoln Town Car. It was immaculate, with shiny black leather interior and bottles of water in the cup holders. Slick seats and a nice-car smell can instill so much trust, and I wouldn't expect anything less from a professional briber. It put my naive heart at ease that our plan was a brilliant one.

Uncle Ali had well-manicured, bushy hair, a colossal, cartoon-like nose, and a bright smile that made the bottom half of his face look bigger than the top. He radiated positive energy, but not in a flaky, bullshitting kind of way. He was a fun-loving, protective teddy bear. We called him our driver, but he was more of a glorified chaperone to keep us out of trouble. With Amman in our rear-view mirror, we bounced through the desert northward, singing along to Ali's quirky and diverse mixed tape. When Ray Stevens's "Ahab the Arab" came on, it was as if my Arkansas past and Middle Eastern present had collided and had a love child.

By afternoon we reached the border. It was a series of simple arches with Arabic scribble. Ali parked the boat, and we idled at the rest-stop café for what seemed like several hours. Canadian Stanislaw coolly smoked his cigarettes, untroubled by the high stakes for the Americans. Betsy, Hazel, and I got buzzed on sweet juice and bitter Arabic coffee while holding our breath and watching Ali hustle among various customer service desks, our passports in hand. Just when we started to wonder whether we'd have to turn around and drive back to Amman, Ali came bouncing toward us with a smile, fanning our passports in the air.

"Done!" he beamed.

It felt like getting away with a crime. We drove through the entry gate that had a peculiar water-spraying tunnel. Was it an anthrax wash or a complimentary carwash? We'd never know, but we were relieved to be in Syria at last. The setting sun cast an amber glow in our car as we drove toward Damascus, windows down, music up, and hair whipping in the breeze. Florence and the Machine had just come on the scene, and in that lucky twilight hour, Syria was treated to the Border Bandit Babes' cover of "Dog Days Are Over" howled out the windows at the top of our lungs. Stan pretended he wasn't enjoying our song, while Ali smiled at our off-key rendition in the rearview mirror. There was nothing like leaving all our cares to the dust and the wind while unashamedly laying our souls bare on that desert highway.

Damascus is a vibrant, bustling city of just under two million. It's thought to be the oldest inhabited city on earth; driving through town we could see evidence of layer upon layer of architecture and history fused through the ages like a game of Tetris. The face of Assad was everywhere—on billboards, the center of roundabouts, and on storefronts. He liked to pose with a suit, sunglasses, and a smirk—as if the city were advertising a movie about the least sexy cast member of *Miami Vice* ever to audition.

After traveling down a very long road to get to Damascus, the next morning it seemed fitting that our first stop would be Straight Street, where Paul received his sight again after his long, hair-raising trip to Damascus. As the book of Acts recounts, Paul (at that time called Saul) was on a tirade of terror rounding up Christians to be murdered. He had written letters to the synagogue in Damascus, asking for any hot tips on men and women belonging to the Way, as followers of Jesus were first called. As he neared Damascus, he saw a blinding light and heard a voice that said, "Saul, Saul, why do you persecute me?"

Saul was stunned and fell to the ground. "Who are you?" he asked.

"I am Jesus, whom you are persecuting. But get up and enter the city, and you will be told what you are to do."

Saul was in shock. He couldn't see and couldn't eat or drink for three days. His comrades led him into town, where he crashed at the home of a man named Judas. Meanwhile, Jesus appeared to a disciple named Ananias and told him to head straight to Straight Street and heal a blind man, Saul of Tarsus. Ananias was well aware of Saul the terrorist, and he was afraid to go. He argued with Jesus about it until Jesus said, "Go!" Ananias met Saul and laid hands on his eyes, saying, "Brother Saul, the Lord Jesus, who appeared to you on your way here, has sent me so that you may regain your sight and be filled with the Holy Spirit."

"Immediately something like scales fell from his eyes," and he could see again. He got up and was baptized, ate a meal, regained his strength, and began his ministry preaching in the synagogues that Jesus was the Son of God.[12]

At the very end of the street called Straight, Uncle Ali led us to a tall, black iron gate festooned with red Syriac Maronite crosses. It was the House of Saint Ananias, and it was the only early Christian church of the first century to survive in Damascus. We walked through the gate and descended a staircase underground to the church. It was a small stone cellar of a room with a modest altar and small pews with pilgrims praying. In one corner there was a metal grate on the ceiling with little offerings left by visitors: prayers written on tiny scrolls and small portrait photographs tucked under the netting. Christian pilgrims believe this is a place where John the Baptist, the one who would baptize Jesus, had prayed.

John the Baptist was always one of my favorite characters of the Bible. I imagined him with his camel hair clothes and diet of locusts and wild honey to be the kind of nonconformist that set the religious elites' hair on fire and made uppity women clutch their pearls. But John the Baptist was the prophetic voice crying out in the wilderness, declaring that the kingdom of heaven was at hand. Such is the way of Christ to choose the Rastafarian hippy type to be his spokesperson announcing the coming kingdom.

As I wandered through my own figurative wilderness, still struggling to understand what and where this kingdom was, I took out a passport photo from my wallet and tucked it in into the ceiling. *John the Baptist, pray for me.*

Leaving the House of St. Ananias, we wandered through narrow streets, passing swirling vines, stray dogs, and alley cats. They seemed to be the only ones out and about—Damascus was largely a ghost town on Friday, the Muslim day of rest. Friday was the equivalent of Sundays in the Deep South when everything shuts down for a day of forced stillness.

Despite all the shops being closed, we meandered through the ancient souk until we happened on a row of peculiar stalls that were open. Vendors were selling turtle shells, starfish, snakes coiled up in jars, alligator tails, and creepy-crawly things like scorpions and centipedes. Animal bones (or were they human?) dangled from the awning, crackling in the breeze like a shaman's wind chimes.

"Only the black-magic shops are open on Fridays," Ali told us.

I was imagining all of these elements going into a big black caldron for a gnarly witch's brew.

"Creepy!" Betsy, Hazel, and I winced.

"Is this a common practice here?" Stanislaw asked Ali.

"This is the oldest living city. There were other religions before Islam, Christianity, and Judaism. You still see indigenous practice going back to the Iron Age. But the real black magic you're about to see . . . are you guys ready to go to a four-hundred-year-old restaurant?" said Ali.

Al Khawali Restaurant opened up to a dimly lit entry lounge, with fine filigreed wooden walls and antique furniture with mother-of-pearl inlay. The parlor opened into a grand atrium surrounded by arched windows. Higher up, a second row of window balconies crowned the room with swinging shutters and plant boxes, spilling over with dangling moneywort vines. The restaurant was a subtle nod to French colonialism but was still Old-World Arabian. For better or worse, the combined cultures made it exquisitely beautiful.

Ali began ordering all of their most famous dishes, starting with the thyme salad. I would have never imagined that an herb could be the base for a salad, but it was pure witchcraft when combined with balsamic glaze, olives, tomatoes, and grilled haloumi cheese. Next was a rusty red muhammara, a Levantine ground-red-pepper dip mixed with walnuts and pomegranate molasses. Then the staples: hummus, baba ghanoush, mounds of pita, and grilled meats. We washed it all down with lemon-mint shakes.

What is it about war-torn places that crank out exquisite food? The most turbulent hotbeds of contention serve the food of the gods. Colliding kingdoms and cultural clashes act like a pressure cooker for amazing flavor combinations. Perhaps it's because when turmoil strikes and only the present is certain, people stop all their meaningless planning and plotting to focus instead on the daily bread. Syria is one of those places.

We finished our meal with hand-churned Arabic ice cream topped with salted pistachios. And I realized that just like Southern Baptist potlucks, the desserts served in non-drinking places are usually superior. I had not felt a stronger sugar hug since eating Mommama's banana pudding on Thanksgiving. Nostalgia that made no sense at all washed over me again. When it comes to loving people through food, we're all eating from the same table.

The servers brought us little cups of strong coffee which were gone after a few sips, and then Ali taught us the Syrian superstition of interpreting each other's coffee grounds at the bottom of the cup. Like cloud gazing, we gave each other a fortune based on pictures we saw with the leftover grounds. A food coma rolled over us, leaving us no option but a nap back at the hotel.

When we awoke, Ali took us to a restaurant on a giant hill, overlooking the city's twinkling green minaret lights. The hilltop restaurant was a real locals' place, abuzz with Muslim families sharing their special Friday meal al fresco. The menu was only in Arabic, serving traditional dishes like lamb stew and citrus-laced salads. We might have been the only tourists present that night.

Just as we were finishing our final course of Mediterranean fruits and tea, while paying the bill, I heard a high-pitched voice calling my name. The sound got louder and louder as I began to realize it was coming from all the way down the paved path that circled the hilltop.

An old lady in a wheelchair was rolling toward us. She was dressed in a black cloak and wore big, round, black sunglasses like an elderly movie star or an escapee from an insane asylum. *Was she a witch?*

At first I thought she was saying something else that sounded like my name, until she got closer and turned her head to face me, cackling loudly, "Natalieeeeee ha ha ha ha! Naaataaalieeee!"

Hazel, Betsy, Stan, and I stared at each other in shock. "Is she saying your name?"

Quickly, it became clear that she was saying my name and trying to taunt me. Ali turned white as a turnip and his eyes bugged out of his head. "Let's get out of here," he said, getting up from the table.

We all scrambled past the mystery woman, making a beeline for the car.

"Ali, open the door!" Stan shouted while Hazel jiggled the door handle. The witch woman kept her face fixed in our direction, continuing to call out my name while gleefully mocking our fear and howling over our discomfort. Ali unlocked the door and we piled in like bank robbers in a getaway car. Ali peeled out and sped away, as the cloaked woman was still pointing and laughing at us—mouth agape and eyes shielded from the moon.

"What was that all about?!" I laughed nervously.

"I don't know," said Ali. "But these things are normal in Syria."

I would soon learn that curses were common here.

We then headed back to old Damascus. We had nowhere specific to go, but Ali let us out to wander the timeworn streets that projected a different kind of magic at night. Some people were just getting off work, shuffling along hazy-eyed with backpacks and briefcases. Others were dressed for dinner; couples sauntered arm in arm. We turned a corner and bumped into an older man carrying a box of tomatoes. He could have been a professor on his way home from work—pleated khaki pants, a pastel plaid button-down shirt with a pen and notebook in his front pocket. He was mostly bald with snow-white tufts of hair fringing his temples.

"Well, helloooo there!" he said in a crisp, Arabic accent.

"Hi! Hello!" we smiled back, delighted at such a friendly face after our encounter with darkness.

"Where are you good-looking kids off to tonight?" the man asked.

"We don't really know yet. Just wandering mostly," I told him.

The man put down his box of tomatoes against a wall and took out the notebook from his front pocket. "May I have your name, please, Miss?" he asked.

After having just had my name snatched from me against my will by a witch, I was glad to offer it freely to a friendly face who politely asked for it.

"Na-ta-lie," he repeated, scribbling it down in what looked like gibberish. Was it Hebrew or hieroglyphics?

"This is your name in Aramaic. Now let me just do a little calculation here . . ." He rested his index finger under his bottom lip while trailing off into an internal dialogue with adding, subtracting, and numerological decoding.

"Ah-ha! Yes! Here it is! A small fortune for you." He proudly handed me the paper using both hands as if it were an exquisite gift.

I was dumbfounded by the mysterious chicken-scratch cryptogram. *Dear God, is this illuminati?* My judgy evangelical side clapped back.

"Your name is strong. It's a good one. You'll have a very blessed life, indeed. Be blessed!" he said.

The wacky professor offered Hazel, Betsy, and Stan the same service. We waited in suspense as he transcribed and decoded the Aramaic numerical value of our names, to reveal a small, auspicious fortune.

"What are you doing, exactly?" Betsy inquired.

"Oh, I am a philologist. My name is Christopher," he said.

"What's a philologist do?" I asked.

"I study languages of the ancient Near East, and I can do mathematical formulations based on words," he said. Christopher might have been one crazy cat, but he buoyantly delighted in our spontaneous encounter, and offered his quirky blessing over us without asking for anything in return. He wrapped his arms around our shoulders and gave us a tight squeeze, and then disappeared into the dark alley with his tomato box hoisted on one shoulder.

"Ali, what was that all about?" Hazel asked.

"Oh, I don't know. But this is normal in Damascus." He shrugged.

In one hour, I had received both a blessing and a curse on my name. Back home, everyday blessings and curses are more easily disguised. But their nature is still the same. Nobody asks for a curse. Curses come rolling out of nowhere—in this case, a witch in a wheelchair—but they come just as easily from seemingly innocuous sources: the discouraging teacher, the toxic friend, or the abusive relative. Curses don't ask for our permission. They come in for the plunder, invasive and coercive. They shame and shun, embarrass, terrorize, and destroy. They summon the parts of us that are weak, scared, and dying and then stomp on them. The goal of the curse is to shatter; it is the opposite of shalom.

Blessings, on the other hand, involve our participation. The giver of the blessing—whether a philologist in the alley or the Holy Spirit herself—first asks for our permission. Blessings are gentle and noncoercive, but they're always an invitation into a "divine dance" as Franciscan friar Richard Rohr puts it.[13] Jesus healed a blind man by spitting in mud and putting it on his eyes. That wasn't enough for the healing, though. He asked the blind man to go to the pool of Siloam and wash it out in order to see. Jesus invited the blind man to participate in his own healing.[14]

Such is the nature of our interaction with the divine. We have tried so hard through the ages—with some hefty help from the Greeks—to objectify God, to make "him" into a tamable, controllable, predictable being. But it is only through our participation in this glorious life that we can begin to understand the nature of our Creator's blessings. Rohr says,

All authentic knowledge of God is *participatory knowledge* . . . . We have sacrificed our unique telescope for a very inadequate microscope. Divine knowing—some would call it spiritual intuition—is actually an allowing of someone else to know in us, through us, for us, and even as us. It demands what I often call an "identity transplant."[15]

Barbara Brown Taylor, too, writes about the common wisdom surrounding the practice of pronouncing blessing: "Blessing does not confer holiness. The holiness is already there, embedded in the very givenness of the thing. Because God made these beings, they share in God's own holiness, whether or not they meet your minimum requirements for a blessing."[16]

* * *

With our good fortunes in hand from Christopher the philologist, we turned a corner and stumbled down another fanciful rabbit hole.

It was a nightclub called Zodiac. Laser lights beamed through the swirly smoke of shisha pipes. Spicy Latin music reverberated off the walls. The dance floor was a sizzling salsa scene. Gorgeous, red-lipped women twirled and clapped with suave, suited men at their fingertips. We couldn't help but stay; we wanted to be enmeshed in this gorgeous party, this painfully beautiful scene. We found our place in a cozy tufted booth. The waiter hustled to our table with a big smile.

"Hello! Where are you all from?" he asked.

"I'm Canadian, but they're all American," Stanislaw told him.

"American? Wow!" he sputtered. "What are you doing in Damascus?" he asked.

"Just for vacation," we told him.

"Vacation? I can't remember the last time I met an American here for vacation," he said. "So, what do you think about Syria?"

"We're actually loving it. We really love Syria," I told him. Stan and the others nodded in agreement. Ali sat silently in the corner of the booth with a subtle grin on his face.

The next thing we knew, big platters of food started arriving at our table.

"We didn't order these," Stan said.

"Oh no, but you are our guests here," the waiter beamed. "For our new friends, the Americans!"

"Ali, what's this all about?" we asked him.

"I don't know," Ali said smiling. "But this is normal in Syria."

The party enfolded us like a big velvety creature, claiming us as one of its own. We didn't have the smooth moves of our Syrian brothers and sisters, but we got caught up in their dance nonetheless. Latin beats blended with Western pop, African drums, and Arabian riffs, and it sounded like the exotic heartbeat of God. Eating their food and dancing their dance and being on the receiving end of love from a globally marginalized group felt like a divine celebration and kingdom come.

Delicious food kept coming, and the drinks kept flowing, and the bill never came. Was it because of their stark surprise-turned-delight over seeing American tourists? Was it because they saw their country's enemies as new friends? Was it because of Arab culture, which is known for its radical acts of hospitality? Perhaps all of the above.

We went to sleep that night on a happy high. We had just attended the kind of party Jesus said we should all throw—the kind where we invite people who can't give us anything in return, and we were the glad recipients of that kind of divine inclusion.

I found myself contemplating the hazy worlds of two dueling kingdoms: one of light and one of darkness. One of welcome, the other rejection. One of creation, the other of destruction. One of blessing, the other a curse. These diabolical kingdoms are present everywhere, in all places. Clean or unclean, foreign or familiar, rich or poor, religious or secular.

Either we're participating in the kingdom of God and the ongoing creation of the world, restoring and redeeming all things to wholeness and shalom, or we are playing a part in the kingdom of darkness, which keeps people from flourishing, pins them down by oppression, or riddles them with shame. For every moment in time, we can be gatekeepers of welcome or gatekeepers of rejection.

For me, the surprising thing was finding Jesus in the places he wasn't supposed to be. A nightclub in Syria would be the least likely place I'd expect to see unhinged hospitality and a radical, Christlike welcome. Sadly, I felt more accepted there than in a lot of churches back home. In a political sense, we were their enemies descending on the streets of Damascus. Some would say we weren't even supposed to be there. But instead of booting us out or decrying the wicked ways of our government, the good saints at Zodiac showed us love and a warm welcome without expecting anything in return.

Everything about my American Christian identity was shattered in the territory of the "other." These experiences had confirmed the very thing that I was most afraid of being true: we are not special. We are not the shining city on the hill, the chosen, nor the righteous. We are not better. The idea of American exceptionalism was once a fact in my mind, a promise, like those God made to Abraham. In time it had been reduced to a hope, and as I ventured further, American exceptionalism was a dream, one I had a hard time remembering. But in Syria, the idea revealed itself as a myth.

The Calvinist teaching that what is deepest within us is ugly and sinful distorted the way I saw people of other faiths. It's the kind of dangerous belief that can make an ugly leap from who's righteous or condemned to who deserves to live or die. It made me ashamed that I had once ascribed to a belief system that was directly tied to the denial of the image of God in Muslims and the suffering of so many.

My time in Syria shone a light on what I already knew was true: The hidden longing that dances between each heartbeat is the same everywhere. It's a longing we can trace all the way to our childhood—the desire for love and unity, peace and wholeness, freedom and unbridled joy. These are the same desires that existed at our mother's breast, before there were words—only raw connection. It is the same spark and light of our innermost being that over time gets tarnished and smudged over with layers of fear and shame. But underneath it all is a deep well of love that is birthed out of the heart of God.

Author John Philip Newell calls it our "forgotten tune." He tells us that St. Paul's Letter to the Galatians that says we need "adoption as children" has been misinterpreted. [17] It is not that we need to be adopted by some divine entity, but rather, we need to adopt our divine nature that already exists. In other words, we need to come into possession of what is already ours.

"This is the song at the heart of the human soul, not a foreign tune that leads us to seek admission into a family that is not ours."[18] We already belong in the family because we exist. And so, in relation to those most different from us, in culture and religion especially, if we believe that they also have the same deep longing in their hearts as we do for love and shalom, we will be able to look for the "light that completes the truths we hold most dear rather than competing with them."[19]

The irony wasn't lost on me that it took Syrians treating me like family to realize that Syrians were in the family too. I had just scratched the surface of something that would forever change the way I saw the kingdom of God.

CHAPTER 14

MORNING HAS BROKEN

Still in Damascus

On our final morning in Damascus, Ali insisted that we visit the Umayyad Mosque. I didn't feel like going; I had seen my fair share of mosques by then. But Ali had not steered us wrong, so we obliged.

Before we were allowed to go in, we had to first pass through the putting-on-special-clothes room. Stan was fine to enter wearing his T-shirt and shorts, but we girls were dressed up in long, gray hooded cloaks reminiscent of the grim reaper. We giggled, took selfies, and admired our ridiculous get-ups before entering the main courtyard.

A vast stretch of marble floor was surrounded by walls of Corinthian pillars and a blue sky overhead with flocks of birds passing above. The ground I was standing on was a site of worship going back to the Iron Age. The temple was first erected for the Aramaean god of thunderstorms and rain, Hadad-Ramman or Ba'al. When the Romans moved in, they naturally converted it to a temple to honor their own god of thunder, Jupiter. By the fourth century, the temple was converted to a Byzantine Christian cathedral under Emperor Theodosius I. Then in 634, Damascus was conquered by Muslim Arab forces, thus beginning the Umayyad dynasty.

For seventy years, the site was a shared space of worship for both Christians and Muslims. Later it was converted to a mosque in a compromise, which meant some other sites, once Muslim, would become Christian churches. But the mosque remains a place of pilgrimage for Christians and Muslims—Shia, Sunni, and Sufi.

We walked inside through the stretch of burgundy Arabian carpets to see a large square shrine, lit up by green lights and surrounded by narrow Corinthian columns. "What's in there?" I asked Ali. It was obviously a point of importance.

"It's the head of John the Baptist," he said solemnly.

"Wait, what?!" I was confused. What does John the Baptist mean to Muslims? My Southern Baptist roots were twitching.

"John the Baptist is known as the prophet Yahya in Islam. His birth to Zechariah and his barren wife in old age was miraculous. He came to announce a coming kingdom; this is all in the Qur'an," he said.

Now I was really tripping. But sure enough, I looked closer and both Christians and Muslims surrounded the shrine, slowly walking around it while praying. Two separate religions had converged—each seeking the divine while paying reverence to the same person.

We walked outside toward the center of the prayer courtyard and found a spot in the center of the shiny marble floors. Stan and Hazel snapped photos, stretching out their fancy zoom lenses to capture every angle of the mosque's beauty. Betsy and I stretched out like lazy cats in the midday sun. Some pilgrims were milling about, others prostrate in prayer. My attention was drawn to all of the unaccompanied children running wild. A pair of identical twin girls dressed in matching black and yellow checked dresses skipped hand in hand. A pack of barefooted boys jostled each other against a wall. One put his arm around another and told him a secret while the other laughed loudly, then took a puff off a cigarette. They couldn't have been older than ten.

Ali directed our attention to the tallest minaret in front of us. "See that? That's the Madhanat Isa. Damascene tradition holds that on that minaret Jesus will descend when he returns to earth," he said. "It is there that he will confront the antichrist."

Again, I was confused. The fact that Muslims not only believed that Jesus would return but had an exact spot where they believed it would happen made my heart beat to a strange rhythm. I wanted to laugh and ridicule the idea, but it also gave me pause. Most Christians have no idea that many Muslims believe this. American Christians love to obsess over our end-times theology. It's a lucrative business with the *Left Behind* book series and the ultimate comeuppance story told in churches across America. The book of Revelation is not read allegorically, but rather as a literal foretelling of Jesus's return to Jerusalem to reward Christians and all of the fresh Jewish-Christian converts, and punish everyone else.

But the more I pondered it then and over the years since, the more I've considered the thought: If Jesus happened to have a literal return to the earth, *wouldn't it be just like him to return to the most subversive place imaginable? At a Muslim mosque in a country that's the so-called enemy of Christendom. A country whose refugees have been rejected by the United States. Likely or not, our Jesus could very well show up anywhere he pleases.*

The call to prayer began. It reverberated loudly off the surrounding walls. The sound waves sent paralyzing currents through our bodies that stilled us on those cool marble floors. I don't know what it's like for a Muslim to hear it, but to me that wailing prayer sounded like heartfelt cries and a primordial longing for wholeness. It's a yearning as ancient as time itself. In the religious site that weathered countless storms over the centuries, the prayer sounded like echoes of the heart of humanity, each one clambering for understanding and seeking the divine in the best way they know how.

Much like my earlier experience in Istanbul's Hagia Sophia, a magnificent space that was once the largest church in the Byzantine Empire until it was converted into a mosque in the fifteenth century, I wondered how many human hearts had stood in that same spot seeking the face of God. All of us clinging to our holy books and believing with ironclad certainty that our way is the only sure path to God. Yet the morning had broken, the sun had shone down, and the gentle breeze had blown over all of us that day the same.

I felt a hushed wave of mercy roll over all of us. The mercy of Christ was present in that courtyard. I felt mercy for all of the desperate times we plead the favor of God, for all of the unseen forces that have left us damaged and neglected, and for all of the ways in which our theology is imperfect. No words or judgment, only mercy. Mercy for the Christian pilgrims, the Muslim pilgrims, the self-righteous, and the humble. Mercy for the oppressed who took refuge in that space centuries prior. Mercy for all of us in pursuit of truth, despite our spiritual heritage.

Mercy for the curse-bearers and the afflicted. Mercy for the quirky academics and the seekers of knowledge. Mercy for the grief-stricken and miserable. Mercy for the children who would soon be disrupted by violence and bloodshed. Mercy for those who would become refugees and lose everything in a few short years. And mercy for us too: our young, adventurous hearts were only trying to figure out the world. And mercy for me, recovering from past trauma and learning to see Christ in all the earth.

My mind could not form words to describe what my heart knew: the mercy of God was upon us at the Umayyad Mosque. We were standing on holy ground, born of the one light. Each of us in our spiritual journey thinks we've cornered the market on God, but I like to believe we all felt the same sweet currents of grace that day. It was the same unexpected mercy that fell on my dad before his death. The kind of mercy that defied everything I had ever been taught about faith. It was the kind of mercy that led the psalmist to write, "The LORD is good to all; and his compassion is over all that he has made."[20]

It was the kind of luminous mercy written about by the Sufi mystics in the Islamic tradition:

> God has proscribed upon Himself:
> "Indeed My mercy comes before,
> goes after,
> and takes over My wrath"[21]

Mercy laughs at our expectations and then throws a blanket around our bruised egos. Mercy sneaks up on us, catches us by surprise, and then hugs us tightly. Mercy delights without shaming. Mercy subverts over and over and over again. Mercy is an endless folding and unfolding, a self-emptying cycle. Mercy is always an invitation to love and be loved.

I couldn't come up with any response other than to lie on my back across the cold tiled floor of the courtyard, watching a flock of birds flying low overhead, fluttering past the Jesus minaret, high into the sky.

CHAPTER 15

Bridge Over Troubled Water

Jerusalem

Time dragged on in Jordan, slow and battered like my overstuffed suitcase with a busted seam. My workdays with Hillary were awkward and tense, but I was learning how to hustle while keeping my big nose in my own business and my loose lips sealed.

My saving grace was nights with Wael and friends at Grappa and weekends at the Dead Sea. Together with Ahmed, the lazy office guy, Stanislaw and I gleefully took full advantage of our company's barter agreement with some of the seaside resorts. We gave them a page of advertisement in the report in exchange for free rooms.

Relishing the chance to live luxuriously for a stint, we looked like the cat that killed the canary stretching out in our individual private suites in some of the nicest resorts in the Middle East. We were classy enough to empty the mini fridge upon departure, stocking up on free goodies for the house.

Shenanigans always abounded at the Dead Sea. Ahmed smoked like a chimney and didn't hold his alcohol well. One time after watching a concert at a neighboring resort, we took a golf-cart ride back to our resort. The resort driveways are long, steeply winding slopes. Ahmed was so lightheaded that he relaxed a little too hard going around a swift curve and flopped out of the golf cart *Weekend at Bernie's* style. We gasped in horror watching him tumble down the hill like a rag doll before his body came to a stop and he sat up and shrugged.

For dinners we'd wind up a mountain to a restaurant called Panorama. From there, we had a full view of the Dead Sea, smudged and hazy around the edges, like a giant mirage melting into the sunset. There was always a gentle breeze and an old man playing Arabian melodies on the oud. It was an escape in time, and I was Cleopatra atop her buttressed lookout.

The Dead Sea is so salty that the densest of bodies can float blissfully buoyant on top of the water. It's the lowest elevation point on earth, and the saltiness makes it impossible for any living thing to survive in its waters—hence the name.

It amazed me how something so dead could make me feel so alive. I'd slather myself from head to toe in the thick black clay on the shore and then float in the sparkling waters, baking in the sun like drying asphalt. The minerals in the mud are believed to have healing properties. Herod the Great is said to have had a health resort on the Dead Sea. Cosmetics companies have been using its salt and mineral mud in their products for decades.

But I wonder how much of the believed healing properties are just the benefits of connecting deeply with the earth—1,412 feet below sea level, to be exact. Bathing in a hole deep in the ground is a reminder of our humanness. The word *human* comes from *humus*, meaning earth or ground. The word *Adam* comes from the Hebrew word *adamah*, which means "ground" or "earth." In the biblical story of Genesis, God tells Adam, "You are dust, and to dust you will return."[22] Perhaps bathing in dirt massages our subconscious and sharpens our intuition. Or maybe it takes going that low to understand that soul care and body care are one and the same. The precise combination of dirt and stardust that makes up our being is held together by divine animation.

The Dead Sea is also shrouded in dark mysteries of the ancient past. Some scholars believe it to be the biblical site of Sodom and Gomorrah. Ahmed told us that some of his older relatives had dishes and artifacts that they found at the Dead Sea when they were young, evidence of a civilization that was wiped out.

On one lazy afternoon, Ahmed took Stan and me on a drive to explore the winding roads surrounding the sea. He played loud Lebanese music and kept the windows down so he could smoke one cigarette after another. At a random curve in the road, he pulled over abruptly and jerked the car into park. "See that tall rock right there, the one that looks like a lady," he said, pointing to a rocky pillar that towered high above the road, glowing red in the late afternoon light.

In the biblical story, Lot's wife leaves the city with him and turns into a pillar of salt when she turns back to look at the city.

The story of Lot is also in the Qur'an. In the Qur'anic version, Lot is called a prophet. It doesn't say that his wife leaves with him, but rather he is told by the angels that his wife will be one to turn back and be destroyed with the city. It was fascinating to hear this story retold slightly differently by a Muslim man with a local legend as a visual aid.

I knew the Dead Sea from the Jordanian side, but on the other side was Jerusalem. To Palestinians living in Jordan, Jerusalem was often a painful topic. Too many people had lost their homes and livelihoods and became refugees after the 1948 Arab-Israeli War and follow-on Six-Day War of 1967. Some still wore their former house keys on strings around their necks, remembering their homes, now forever off-limits.

I had gone my entire life having a glorified idea of Israel being a land for the Jews, God's "chosen people," but when it came down to it, my first introduction to Jerusalem was from the perspective of those who don't call it Jerusalem. To Palestinians, it is called Al-Quds. I didn't take the irony lightly, bobbing in the Dead Sea looking at the bright lights just on the other side of the waters.

I was beginning to see the God of Abraham being the God of the detour and the God in the margins. The God who was with Hagar in the wilderness, cast away with her son Ishmael, rejected by Abraham and Sarah, but promised a nation and a future by the same God. The God of Moses and his people, lost in the desert for decades. The God who was with the Hebrews exiled to Babylon. The God of Jesus of Nazareth, as a young boy made a refugee in Egypt. Time and again, God was shown to be on the side of the oppressed and rejected. The God of the Bible was the God of the underdog, the meek, and the humble.

I was still a privileged White girl, but I had just been the girl outside the city gates, cast out of my tribe, and so when it came to approaching Jerusalem, I more easily identified with the Palestinians removed from their ancestral homeland. "The brothers kicked out of the family," Jordanian Palestinians called themselves.

Al-Quds would be a part of my peregrination that needed to happen alone. Well, that, and I couldn't convince anyone in Jordan to come with me.

* * *

My driver dropped me off at the King Hussein Bridge, which straddles the Jordan River and connects Jordan to Israel. Israelis call this same bridge the Allenby Bridge, named after a colonial-era British colonel. That Israel and Jordan couldn't agree on a name for their bridge seemed to be a symbol for how the two nations were inextricably connected but yet so different.

I stamped out of Jordan easily and then walked the dusty road of no-man's land to stamp into Israel. I had expected the process of getting into Israel to be a slam dunk. The United States provides more military aid to Israel than any other country and guarantees billions in loans that provide it with the lowest possible interest rates, like a parent who can't bear to cut off her grown children's allowance. For the last decade, America has given over three billion dollars a year in no-strings-attached foreign aid.[23] Not to mention US politicians tripping over themselves to get in front of a camera to make pro-Israel statements. In a time that seems to require a left-or-right talking point for every news item, over the last couple of decades support of Israel has been mostly nonpartisan.

But I was the last person to leave the border that day. The border agents were skeptical of my motives—was I a journalist reporting on the violence in Gaza? A tall female guard with short, choppy red hair pressed me hard. Why was I living in Jordan? Why was I alone? What could a young woman traveling alone possibly be doing in the Middle East? Why did I come on land and not by plane? The interrogation went on. I didn't fit into any easy categories for the border agents, so they didn't know what to do with me. At one point, I casually joked, "I thought our countries were friends!" Getting into Syria had been way easier.

The female agent finally decided I was low risk enough to enter Israel and stamped me in well after dark. I caught a cab to my hostel in the Arab quarter of old Jerusalem. The city was quiet, the streets were calm, and after my exhausting tango with the Israeli border patrol, I was relieved to be staying at a place run by a welcoming Palestinian family. I had a bowl of hot *foul* for dinner (fava beans) and turned in snugly in my tiny cot with a hard mattress.

As I fell asleep, I was caught off guard by waves of familiarity. The feeling I had in the hostel was inexplicably nostalgic. I imagined that I was sleeping on a palette in Mommama's living-room floor—a simple egg-crate mattress wrapped in old sheets worn thin and soft from years of washing. The ceiling fan overhead bobbled loosely and wildly when turned up too high. *Sha-thunk, sha-thunk, sha-thunk*, it would say, like the rhythms of the ocean, lulling me to slumber. I thought of the purr of a box fan set right beside my bed, cooling my skin in the humid Arkansas summers. The most comforting things are really the simplest.

The next day, I set out to explore all of the holy sites. I was in search of the thin places where heaven and earth would collide. I had big expectations to encounter the spirit of God in the footsteps of Jesus, starting with the Via Dolorosa, the street in old Jerusalem believed to be the path Jesus took to Calvary. Via Dolorosa is literally "the painful way" or "way of suffering." I wandered through the fourteen Stations of the Cross, surrounded by huddles of tourists, local merchants, and various bearded religious people. I got caught behind a group of Spanish pilgrims who stopped at each station to belt out passionate melodies accompanied by Spanish guitar. I ended my tour at the Church of the Holy Sepulchre, believed to be built over the actual hill of Golgotha where Jesus was crucified and the alleged site of Christ's tomb where he was buried and resurrected. For Christian tourism and pilgrimages, the Church of the Holy Sepulchre is supposed to be the epicenter of holy places. There isn't a site more important than the actual location of death, burial, and resurrection of Jesus, and I was standing in the midst of it (along with hundreds of my closest smelly tourist friends).

I waited and watched for something profound to happen. I contemplated the suffering of Christ, the death of Christ, and the resurrection of Christ, which happened on the holy ground where I stood. But I didn't feel much except my growling stomach. I don't know if I was waiting for some giant mystical thing to transpire or to feel the presence of God by my side, but of all the churches, mosques, and temples I had seen on my peregrination—it just felt like a crowded tourist trap. It wasn't a thin place for me; it was the thickest. There was an awful lot of pushing and shoving going on around the site of his tomb. People had come from miles afar to feel *just a little bit closer* to Christ (myself included), but all I could feel was claustrophobia.

After a short while, I had had enough of the frenetic crowd and left sad and underwhelmed. I found a good shawarma stand for lunch, and I imagined that if Jesus were there that day, the pushy crowd might have missed him as he slipped out the side door to have a shawarma with the Arab merchant's angsty teenage son in the alley.

At nightfall, I stumbled on a hip Jewish neighborhood. For a change of scenery, I found myself in a laid-back rooftop bar full of beautiful hippie-chic youngsters with grungy hair and Bohemian threads. It was worlds apart from the Arab quarter where I stayed; I felt as if I had gone to another country. I could have been at a funky café in Paris or a ruin bar in Budapest. The guy on the barstool next to me introduced himself as Aaron. He had shoulder-length hair, olive skin, and sea-green eyes. He talked slowly and misty-eyed like a sunbaked surfer or a Jewish Matthew McConaughey. We talked about travel and all the places we'd been and would like to go. Aaron was emotional talking about India; apparently there are a lot of Israeli youth who have a love affair with Hindu culture, which partially explained the Boho vibes I was getting from the scene. I told him I was working in Amman, Jordan.

"Have you ever been to Jordan?" I asked him.

"Oh no, of course not!" he shuddered.

"Really? Like, never? It's literally right there." I pointed to the direction just across the Dead Sea.

"Nope. It's way too dangerous to go there," he said.

"Dangerous? I've never felt unsafe there," I said nudging him.

"But you're American. They don't like people *like me*," he said.

"They look just like you over there," I told him. "How would they even know you're Jewish? Besides, I don't think they'd really even care if they did."

Just then I felt an excruciating thud on my shin. The hard slap of metal would surely leave an ugly bruise. It was the barrel of an M16 that had slipped out of his lap and struck my leg before hitting the ground.

"Oh, my Lord, I didn't even know you had a gun under there!" I tried to hide how much it hurt. He was embarrassed and grabbed his gun, propping it up against the wall of the bar like an umbrella.

"What if people are afraid of you? I mean, in civilian clothes with that big gun! I don't see that in Jordan," I told him.

"Yeah, I'm a soldier. Right now, just an escort for these guys," he said.

"These guys" referred to a group of Americans on a birthright tour who had just filled up the bar. Birthright Israel is a nonprofit that gives American Jewish young people free ten-day trips to Israel to reconnect with their heritage. Some call it a form of indoctrination, but these kids seemed to be reveling in the chance for a free summer trip. Noah, the guy to my other side, was an American FSO in the State Department who had come from his first post in Saudi Arabia but wanted to take advantage of Birthright before his twenty-seventh birthday, when he'd be too old for the program. I was fascinated by the fact that Noah, an American Jew, didn't feel afraid to live among Saudi Muslims, and even spoke Arabic fluently, while Aaron, an Israeli Jew, saw peaceful Amman as being "too scary and dangerous" but dreamed of the day when he could trek across India.

Aren't we most afraid of the other that is our closest neighbor? How many Americans won't go to *that ghetto neighborhood* but revel in flying to Uganda, where they'll feel heroic for treading through *dangerous* territory and share Insta stories of all the cute African babies they helped *rescue*? How many Southern White women won't set a pretty painted foot in a Black or Latinx business or even dare venture to that side of town, but would jump at the chance to take an exotic trip to Central or South America? Israeli Jews and Arabs avoiding each other's neighborhoods are no different.

In recent history, American evangelicals overwhelmingly backed a presidency that demonized asylum seekers at the border, characterizing an entire group of people as dangerous and a threat to national security. But those same groups would take summer mission trips to Guatemala and Honduras to "help" those same people. In the act of crossing our Southern border, they go from being "sweet precious poor people who just need to be loved on and saved" to "dangerous intruders that deserve to be jailed and have their kids taken away."

We don't have a problem loving the other, as long as they keep a distance far enough for us to romanticize them. But once they encroach too closely to our own holy huddles, we turn up our noses and declare them the enemy. We disguise our bigotry by calling for the preservation of our "way of life" or "belief systems." But the only thing we're really preserving is our own comfort levels.

* * *

For a girl raised in church, traipsing around the Holy Land has a way of making Bible stories come floating to the surface. I thought about the Samaritan woman at the well whom Jesus encountered in the Gospel of John. In Jesus's day, the Samaritans and Jews were similar. They had shared ancestry. They believed in one God, YHWH. They shared traditions. They read what Jews call the Torah, which is what Christians usually call the Pentateuch, the first five books of the Bible. They followed the law. But they differed on this: which mountain was the chosen place of worship? Jews held to Mount Zion and Samaritans clung to Mount Gerizim. Which mountain is the holy one? That was the question.

When Jesus approached the Samaritan woman, he was already committing a major social taboo: speaking to a woman. And the fact that it was a Samaritan woman made it all the more scandalous. But in the longest recorded conversation Jesus has with anyone in the Bible, he engages her, asking her for a drink of water. She calls him out on his breaking of cultural and religious norms.

He responds by saying, "If you knew the gift of God, and who it is that is saying to you, 'Give me a drink,' you would have asked him, and he would have given you living water."

The woman is confused by his riddle. What does it mean to have living water? Is he greater than Jacob, who gave their ancestors that well?

Jesus continues, "Everyone who drinks of this water will be thirsty again, but those who drink of the water that I will give them will never be thirsty. The water that I will give will become in them a spring of water gushing up to eternal life."

They continue their playful conversation. She sees that he's at least a prophet, for he knows that she's had five husbands and her current man isn't even her husband. He doesn't shame her or get spun up over who might see their inappropriate encounter, but rather takes his time with her and treats her with dignity and care. She brings up the fact that they worship on two different mountains.

And he tells her, "The hour is coming when you will worship the Father neither on this mountain nor in Jerusalem. . . . The hour is coming and is now here, when the true worshipers will worship the Father in spirit and in truth."

She says she knows the Messiah is coming and more things will be revealed.

Jesus tells her, "I am he, the one who is speaking to you."

The woman leaves her jar at the well and runs to the town, ecstatically telling everyone she sees that she's found the Messiah. Her town is quick to believe in Jesus, perhaps because he meets them right where they are—in the margins. They are seen and loved just as they are.[24]

It isn't the first time Samaritans and the subject of eternal life are brought up in the Gospels. The Gospel of Luke tells a story about an expert in the law who asks what to do to inherit eternal life. Jesus asks him, in return, what is written in the law. The expert replies, "You shall love the Lord your God with all your heart, and with all your soul, and with all your strength, and with all your mind; and your neighbor as yourself."

Jesus responds, "You have given the right answer; do this, and you will live."

But then the man asks, "And who is my neighbor?"

Jesus tells him a story about a man who is robbed, stripped of his clothing, badly beaten, and left half dead on the side of the road. The man clearly needs help, but one by one, the religious people pass him by. Eventually a Samaritan picks him up, bandages his wounds, and puts the man up in an inn. He tells the innkeeper that he'll be returning to pay for any expenses needed to look after the man. Jesus then asks which of the passersby was a neighbor to the beaten man. Jesus asks again, "Which of these was a neighbor?" And the expert of the law could not bring himself to even say the word *Samaritan*, but rather "the one who showed him mercy."[25]

I had once interpreted "love your neighbor as yourself" in a self-righteous, condescending kind of way. The neighbors were surely unruly or unrighteous, perhaps heathen and hell bound. As in many of his parables, Jesus subverts what we know about religion. He flips the script on who's in and who's out by making the closest "other" the hero. He doesn't tell them a story about how to act around the neighbors with their twisted theology and unwholesome ways. It's not a story about how people who have the right answers should go "loving on" the lost. This story had to have made his followers uncomfortable, as the Samaritans were the most despised "other" in their own backyard. In a sense, Jesus is saying, *Love your neighbors who are different from you but who are marvelous, wonderful people. Learn from them.*

How hard it is to learn to love those who worship on different mountains.

* * *

Again, I went back to my hostel to tuck myself in. That feeling of being at Mommama's house returned with the sha-thunking ceiling fan and simple cot. I missed home, I missed Travis, and I missed my friends, but I felt strangely at home where I was. The flood of nostalgia mixed with love and connectivity took my breath away. I really was completely at home.

My expectation of encountering a thin place at a sanctioned holy site didn't deliver. I had crossed the Allenby / King Hussein Bridge and headed to Jerusalem; I had walked the Via Dolorosa; and I had wandered through the Church of the Holy Sepulchre; and I hadn't felt much of anything. But there in my scruffy Arab hostel I felt there wasn't a holier ground in the land than the cold floors under my bare feet.

CHAPTER 16

CANDLE IN THE WIND

Somewhere over the ocean at 35,000 feet

The day came to leave Jordan for good, and I was shaken. The plane reached altitude and the captive stillness rolled over me in hot waves of grief as I shot tears and slung snot. I still feel bad for the poor stranger next to me who was subjected to my strange seven-mile-high catharsis.

To make things even more emotional, I was reading the last chapter of Queen Noor's memoir, in which she writes about the final days of her husband's life, the late King Hussein. As he lay on his deathbed, someone in the family brought him a cup of water to drink that had been brought from Hagar's well.

The Bible and Qur'an recount the story of Hagar. She was Sarah's Egyptian slave and the mother of Ishmael, Abraham's first son. We get the name Hagar from the Hebrew writers who first told the story. It means "foreign thing"—basically a racial slur instead of her actual name.

After years of trying to conceive a child without success, Sarah gets desperate and hands over her slave, Hagar, to be impregnated by her husband in order to conceive a child on her behalf. Hagar has a son, Ishmael.

But a few years later, Sarah has her miracle baby, Isaac. When Isaac starts to grow up, Ishmael is a pesky older brother. Sarah catches Ishmael making fun of Isaac, and it sets her hair on fire. She sends Hagar and Ishmael away for good, cast out of the family into the wilderness to die. In the account in Genesis, an angel of the Lord appears to Hagar, and according to the Qur'an, the angel hits the ground with his wing or heel to miraculously make a well of water to save them.

Unbeknownst to me, the well is an actual place in Saudi Arabia that has never dried up. Muslims regard the water as holy and bottle it up to bring home after making their hajj to Mecca.

We'll never know what Hagar's real name was, but it's ironic that the one who was denied the dignity of being named was the first in Scripture to name God, *El Roi*, the "God Who Sees." *El Roi* saw Hagar in her distress in the wild wilderness and cared for her.

Of all the characters in the Bible, I felt a bond with Hagar in my desert days. Good little church girls love to talk about the faith of Sarah or Ruth or Esther or Mary or the elusive Proverbs 31 woman, but Hagar gets lost in the shadows of history as nothing more than the mother of Ishmael, the illegitimate. The one who was dismissed from the table and robbed of an inheritance. The one who was told by her mistress, "Sweetheart, you might have thought you were *in*, but there's no place for you here and you'll never be blessed by God."

Hagar was my girl. She was the queen of the original Almost But Not Quite Enough Club, and she wore the shame like an ugly garment. She was used, abused, rejected, and then sent out to pasture. She wandered through the desert asking where God was in all of it. And God saw all of it and met her where she was. I felt every part of Hagar in my bones.

The late, beloved writer Rachel Held Evans wrote a midrash-styled monologue in the imagined voice of Hagar in her final book, *Inspired*:

My faith, like Abraham's, was tested. But my faith, unlike the patriarchs, was not immortalized in Caravaggio's reds or Chagall's blues for later generations to view, nor was it remembered in the litany of Hebrews or in the genealogies of your New Testament. Yet just one person in all your sacred scripture dared to name God, and it wasn't a priest, prophet, warrior, or king. It was I, Hagar—foreigner, woman, slave. Don't you dare forget.[26]

In Jordan, I encountered the God who sees. The God who didn't look on me with shame, but with love. The God who hadn't abandoned me the way my evangelical community had. The God who was with me in the wild wilderness. The God who was still present in the dark alleys of my doubt. The God who saw my twisted mix of sinner and saint and wasn't out to smite me. The God who was big enough to tolerate and engage all of my questions. The God who pulled back the curtains to show me glory and flashes of a beautiful kingdom and sweet mercy in unlikely places.

Reading Queen Noor's words while leaving the first place other than my country that I had called home, I felt the collective grief that I imagine Jordanians felt when King Hussein died. I felt the sadness that I imagine Palestinian, Syrian, and Lebanese refugees who had resettled in Jordan felt over losing a leader who was known to be so generous.

I was aware of the ways that Arabs and Muslims in particular have felt unseen and unloved. I saw how Hagar's trauma had been passed down from generation to generation. I saw how Christians were keeping this wound open every time they reminded Arabs—through actions or harmful policies—that they're not the chosen ones. I felt a respect, a kinship even, to their beautiful Muslim faith. I felt they too had a place in the household of God. I wanted them to be part of the family too. I wondered how I would explain all of this to my friends and family back home.

I felt a loss of friends and a community that I wouldn't return to for many years to come. I sobbed remembering Wael's wrinkled-up eyes that turned a lighter shade of green when he cried and hugged me goodbye one last time.

* * *

So there I was.

The earth below turned from brown to red to yellow and then finally green as I headed eastward. My new home would be Brunei, a tiny country on the island of Borneo that was split among nations. If Borneo resembled a man on a recliner, Malaysia was the man, Indonesia the recliner, and Brunei the TV dinner resting high on the man's chest. Known as the "Kuwait of the Far East," Brunei is an oil-rich sultanate with no drinking and virtually no poverty. Before taking this job, I had never heard of it and had to google it to know what part of the world I was headed for. I would be finishing my training with a Turkish woman named Azra and her American editor and also boyfriend, James.

Azra and James were the quintessential editorial power couple. Folks in the company had warned me about Azra. They told me how many women she made cry who trained under her. Even Hillary made a point to tell me what a bear she could be. She was apparently the star of the company, and Brunei was the highest-grossing project, so I'd be learning from a real sales shark.

Remembering how long it took me to adjust to life in Jordan, I wasn't looking forward to starting over. But as I saw the treetops below, I felt wildly hopeful. I longed for a greener scene. Having spent so long in the desert, I missed the sound and the smell of rain like a person whose water has been shut off misses taking a shower. There were still parts of my soul that were bone dry and needed watering too.

I walked into the balmy Brunei airport with wide eyes and an open heart, ready for the next adventure.

Bandar Seri Begawan, Brunei Darussalam

Bandar Seri Begawan was smaller than Little Rock, Arkansas, the entire country being less than half a million people. Like any capital city, it had a few tall buildings and a tidy business district—with manicured greenery and a wave of humidity that reminded me I wasn't in the Levant anymore. Cutesy lampposts aligning the roads made the highway look like the tram path into Disney World. The predominantly Muslim population was dressed similarly to people in the Middle East, only the fabrics were bright and colorful. If you got a postcard from Brunei, it would most likely feature the Omar Ali Saifudden Mosque with its white minarets and large golden dome. Set against an artificial lagoon that acts as a reflecting mirror, it's a strikingly beautiful sight all lit up at night. My hotel was in the business district, connected to a giant shopping mall that smelled of the pungent scent of shrimp paste from the food court.

I was a nervous wreck the first time Azra and James invited me over to their place for dinner. They sent the company driver to pick me up: Ludo, a smiley Filipino man with a can-do attitude. Azra and James lived in a fancy compound on the edge of town that had its own beach and a golf course and lots of oil-tycoon expats. The city quickly turned into dense forest, and I admired all the new outlandish trees that looked like they belonged in a Dr. Seuss book while rehearsing in my mind things I'd say that wouldn't make me sound like a total stooge. I'd earned a few notches on my belt in Middle East foreign affairs, but I was starting over with Brunei and hadn't moved farther beyond the casual Google search.

We arrived, and I saw that their house looked like something out of a *Condé Nast Traveler* magazine or an old black and white sketch from British colonial times in the Far East. I could hardly believe the company put them up so nicely considering the humble Jordanian abode where Stanislaw and I shared a bathroom. But, then, considering how much the Brunei project was worth, it made more sense that they got the tropical McMansion.

Azra met me at the door with tanned skin and a perfect sales-pitch smile. "Helllooooo!" she beamed and then hugged me tight.

"Hi, I'm James," her editor boyfriend said as he came out of the kitchen.

"Can I fix you a gin and tonic?" Azra asked warmly.

All the PTSD from working with Hillary and my self-coaching to be more guarded this time quickly slipped from memory as Azra, James, and I sat on their back porch talking about everything from life in Southeast Asia to American indie music.

Azra fixed us another round of gin and tonics, and the subject of the sultan came up. The sultan of Brunei had absolute ruling authority. His full name was His Majesty Sultan Haji Hassanal Bolkiah Mu'Izzaddin Waddaulah ibni Al-Marhoun Sultan Haji Omar Ali Saifuddien Sa'adul Khairi Waddien Sultan and Yang Di-Pertuan of Brunei. I had no aspirations to remember the full name, but the man intrigued me nonetheless. He was known to be the wealthiest monarch in the world. He lived in the world's largest residential palace and owned thousands of Rolls Royces, Ferraris, and Lamborghinis. He had enough money to prop up the economies of neighboring countries when times were tough, and he had enough money to satisfy his every whim, be it a new collection of polo ponies, private concerts with Elton John and Diana Ross, or the acquisition of the Beverly Hills Hotel and Queen Elizabeth's Jeweler, Asprey.

His younger brother Jefri was said to have sent emissaries around the world to hunt down the most beautiful women to bring back to his harem. American writer Jillian Lauren wrote about her experience with the royal family in her 2010 memoir, *Some Girls: My Life in a Harem*. She thought she was being hired for a modeling gig but soon found herself locked in the palace with dozens of women from around the world just waiting to have sex with Prince Jefri. At one point, Jefri squandered away one-fourth of the sultan's money before the sultan exiled him from Brunei. Some say Prince Jefri has been secretly allowed to return.

"We might get to meet the sultan before the project is finished," Azra said.

Fantastic.

I didn't know whether to be excited or afraid.

But excitement, I'd learn after a few weeks in Brunei, seemed nonexistent in this austere country. If there's one place in the world that's so slow and still you can hear the trees growing, it's Brunei. How can a capital city be so quiet? I had grown accustomed to the high-frequency whizzing and whirring of Jordan, but Brunei felt more like Arkansas again. The laid-back, low-frequency vibe hums over the lush rain forests and permeates the culture as well. It's evident in the way Bruneians drive without honking (perhaps for fear of upsetting the royal family), the way they speak in quiet tones, and the way they feel at leisure to take long pauses between sentences, filling the air with even more silence. I was bored and uncomfortable by what I perceived as a mundane and uninspiring culture.

"These people have zero ambition because their government gives them everything," I howled at Travis over Skype. "They are just so boring!"

* * *

If I had any fun, it was with Azra and James. They were easygoing and straightforward as could be. Having been warned, I waited for the other shoe to drop and their true colors to come through. But that moment never came. We spent countless evenings on their back porch catching up on paperwork, sometimes to the tune of James's acoustic guitar. He was smart and funny and spoke my Southern American lingo. We found out that his parents were friends with one of my aunts. He was a Southern Catholic boy who could have well been one of my Toon cousins.

Azra was a polished gem with a warm center. She possessed a special kind of magic that's the stuff of legend in the sales world. She had that uncanny ability to sweetly cajole even the most stubborn business guy into signing on the dotted line the very first time. She'd flash her smile, cast a spell, and then suavely strong-arm the unsuspecting person into handing over thousands of British pounds. But then at the end of a high-stakes day, we'd go back to their compound, drink gin and tonics, and cry our eyes out watching *The Biggest Loser*. She had worked for the company for years and yet surprisingly wasn't cynical or jaded. At her core, Azra was a sincere and tender old soul that longed for goodness.

What seemed like a recipe for disaster wasn't a problem at all, as the two of them miraculously let me be a working third wheel in their love-work dynamic. Whether we were just bored in a country with no nightlife, or were destined to be friends, we clicked as if we had known each other for years.

About midway through our project, I came down with typhoid fever (at least, that is my best guess of the darkest days of my life). I felt like I was clinging on for dear life, a Typhoid Mary in a hotel bed. It started with a high fever and vomiting. The fever lasted for a week before Azra and James insisted on taking me to the hospital. By then it had progressed to chest congestion.

The swine flu had just entered the scene in Asia, and the hospital was checking everyone for a fever before they were allowed to enter. Ironically, they almost didn't allow me into the hospital when the electric thermometer the doorman used to hold up to my forehead went berserk. "Yes, I know! That's why I'm seeing a doctor!" I pleaded with him.

The hospital was a ghost town. Where were all the patients? Turns out they were in Singapore or London. Health care is free in Brunei, but with limited homegrown talent, the Bruneian government often sends its citizens to Singapore or elsewhere for treatment, and the government picks up the tab. I finally received a brief, squeamish examination by a doctor who didn't know what to do with me other than prescribe antibiotics and send me home.

Days passed and the fever persisted. I felt like someone had poured lead in my bones; even my hair follicles ached. I lost twenty pounds in three weeks. The shrimp-paste smell from the shopping-mall/hotel complex made me vomit, so I wasted away in my hotel room trying to ride out a scary storm I had never met before. I knew I was in trouble when even my chunky thighs turned skinny. For the first time in my life, I was enveloped in a dark vulnerability that comes with persistent illness. *How long will this last? Is my body going to fight this off or not?*

Mama was getting nervous, asking me to think about coming home.

But Mama was also confused about what part of the world I was in: "I just got off the Brunei Tourism website, and I was so confused by all the Asian kids! For some reason, I thought you said Dubai! I had no idea where Brunei even was!"

If I had been in "Doo-By," I might have been off the hook. But sick and in a hard-to-find-and-pronounce country? Those things add up in a mother's mind, and the sum total was: "You need to come home." But the thought of getting on a plane to go anywhere made me collapse with fatigue. At one point over Skype, my sister asked, "Do you think you're going to die?" The question made me cry, but I felt too weak to get out of bed and do anything about it. When you're really sick, having the strength to take even a baby step toward getting better feels like an unbearable task. I needed someone to hold my hand and lead me out of the room.

One day Azra picked me up from my hotel room and insisted on taking me to a different hospital.

Walking through a series of dimly lit empty hallways, feeling so lethargic I could barely walk, I felt like I was handing myself over to the Bruneian national morgue. The attending doctor did little to examine me. He looked at my prescription, massaged his temples with one hand, took a pause for what felt like an entire minute, and said I had been prescribed an incredibly low dosage—it was more suitable for a child. Like the previous doctor, he didn't bother diagnosing me, but decided it was worth cranking up the antibiotic dosage. I was desperate to try something new and shuffled back to the hotel a little more hopeful, downed my new drugs, and put myself back to bed.

Within two days I felt like I had been raised from the dead. The color returned to my face, and my fever went back to normal for the first time in weeks. I had never been more grateful for the Southeast Asian medicine approach of throwing more antibiotics at the problem. I've come to learn over the years that for this region—it usually works.

I got better just in time for Travis to come visit. My chest was still a tad congested, but I was alive in every sense of the word. Travis had never been to Southeast Asia and relished an opportunity for a wild twelve-hour layover in Singapore, followed by the chance to explore this new mysterious sultanate. I warned him that there wasn't a lot for tourists to do in Brunei, but he took it as a challenge to make our own fun.

We drove across the border into Lombok, Malaysia, for cheap beers and seafood. We hunted down underground bars in Bandar Seri Begawan, and found a Chinese restaurant that secretly served red wine out of teapots. We hiked through wild forests and caught pictures of the flighty proboscis monkey with its funny bulbous nose. We took boat rides through quiet water villages and mangrove forests. We sat in the stillness that was Brunei.

In those moments, I saw Brunei with fresh eyes and realized that it takes extra effort to notice the magic of the Far East. All the ceaseless grasping and abrasiveness that seems to plague the rest of the world felt absent. Instead, that noninvasive, low-frequency tone has a receptivity factor that's just as vibrant and interesting as anywhere else. But you'll miss it if you're not paying close attention.

There was nothing wrong with the people or the culture; the problem was with me. I was ignorant of Bruneian and Malay culture, and I needed practice with picking up on the beautiful nuances in cultures that haven't been entirely steamrolled by colonialism or capitalism. Bruneian culture had not caught up with its wealth; it had yet to be corrupted. What could be mistaken as weakness, dullness, or a lack of give-a-damn was actually beauty.

After my close cha-cha with death, it felt good to be by Travis's sunny side again. To hold his hand and walk along the boardwalk. To discover new worlds and new ways of being. I had never felt more alive. My sunshine friend who brightened up dark days had returned, and I wanted him to stay by my side forever.

But as with our time in Jordan, Travis never brought up the future, marriage, or anything long-term. I wondered how long our relationship could survive long-distance without a clearer idea of where we were headed, let alone an end date in sight. He left me again with that bittersweet feeling of *I love him, but what is this?*

***

"Would you like to come to Mass with us?" Azra asked out of the blue one day.

"Mass? Like, as in Catholic Church Mass?" I asked surprised.

"Yes! James and I are going to church," she said.

"Sure, I'd love to go. But I didn't know you were Catholic. I thought you were Muslim," I said.

"Well yes. I am. *Was.* Am. Here's the thing . . ."

I've learned that when someone starts an explanation with "here's the thing," they're about to give you a special peek into something they're trying to work out within the most confused parts of their soul.

"So, I am Muslim, and James is Catholic," she said. "And he gave me a Bible. I read the New Testament, and I cried. I believe in the stories of Jesus. They're so beautiful. But the thing of it is . . ."

"Go on," I nudged her.

"The thing of it is, I'm Muslim. I read the Qur'an and I believe in the Qur'an too. My family is Muslim, and we celebrate Muslim holidays. I saw a priest in France about it, and he says I'm a Christian. So now I'm really confused," she said.

The priest had given too easy an answer, and for her, the construct of being Christian had such an overbearing cultural context that it didn't fit her identity of an independent Turkish Muslim woman. Saying she was a Christian meant the erasure of her Muslim identity, centuries of family heritage, and she understandably wasn't ready to part from that.

Azra, James, and I went to Mass that Sunday night. We joked about being the odd trio in the back of the room: the Turkish Muslim, the American Catholic, and the ex-Southern Baptist in a church service designed for Filipinos. Obviously, we had run out of things to do in our little sultanate.

We put on our Sunday best and proudly took our place in the wooden pews of a crowded sanctuary. We participated in the full service, standing and kneeling at the correct times and awkwardly singing foreign hymns. On the island of Borneo in the South China Sea, nobody knew us from Adam, and we stood in solidarity, insistent on our own dignity in the household of God. It felt good to worship together, right where we were with our mixed bags of faith. It felt like a tiny slice of God's dream for the world—for his children to be one family—hand in hand at the same table, peacefully whole and filled with love and awe.

My Muslim sister Azra was also my sister in Christ, and there was no cute, easy explanation for that—*it just was.* Azra taught me something in Brunei that has stuck with me ever since: Jesus transcends religion. It's possible to love Jesus and still live within the identity of another faith tradition. We love to talk about all of the things God can't do, but what about all the things that God can do? Our human inclination is to package each other up and divide and sort ourselves accordingly, but aren't we all so much more than our firmly held traditions, our slippery soapboxes, and all the ways we have approached God through our foggy cultural lenses? The shtick can only hold up for so long.

I'm pretty sure spiritual anxiety is not what Jesus had in mind when he talked about bringing freedom and abundant life. The essence of the human soul has no right angles or perfect blueprints. It's a dynamic, shapeshifting, pulsating flow of divinity that our very being lives inside of, crying out for a connection with something greater than ourselves. I saw that in Azra the same way that I saw it in myself. We were two young women from traditional faith backgrounds, trying our best to stay afloat in a wild-and-wooly business world. We'd go home each night longing for a connection with a God of love and peace who could touch our hearts and bless our lives.

There was a wise Benedictine monk named Bede Griffiths who is said to have "discovered the other half of his soul" after living in an ashram in India. His attempt to bridge the Hindu and Christian faiths was controversial, as he challenged Western Christians to enlarge their vision of the church to include all of those who are sincerely seeking God.

> God is revealing himself at all times to all men in all circumstances. There is no limit to the grace of God revealed in Christ. Christ died for all from the beginning to the end of time, to bring all people to that state of communion with God, with the eternal Truth and Reality, for which they were created. This gift of eternal life is offered in some way to all without exception. Wherever man encounters God, or Truth, or Reality, or Love, or whatever name we give to the transcendent mystery of existence, even if he is formally an atheist or an agnostic, he encounters the grace of God in Christ.[27]

It changes everything to see every human as a potential member of the household of God.

Then sacraments like baptism and Communion do not belong exclusively to the "saved," but rather, according to Bede Griffiths, they are signs of salvation that "manifest God's saving purpose for all mankind." In other words, they bear witness to a God who is working through all of the earth to make himself known to all of humanity. With this, there's no need to fear dying and being sent to eternal damnation when we figure out that we were accidentally a member of the Almost but Not Quite Good Enough Club. Nobody is going to end up in hell and say, "Rats! I picked the wrong brand of faith in the game of life!"

Is a God that's not full of endless love and mercy worth believing in at all?

Just as we clamor for economic security, we clamor for religious security and comfortable certainty. We're so desperate to stay in the right lane, to be reassured that our chosen path is the correct one. But what if we accidentally wandered outside that lane and accidentally found light and life there too? Would it make our own faith crumble, or would it humble and astonish us? What if we ventured down the wild side streets that crept far from the only orthodoxy we'd ever known and reveled in their beauty and goodness?

My time in Brunei was yet another door that led to a vision of a wider table with a bigger family gathered around. Simply put, loving people of another faith made me want to have them all in the family.

***

The Brunei Ministry of Defense hosts a biennial defense exhibition, and Cambridge Reports was a sponsor that year. We were told the sultan might be coming.

The event was launched with a dramatic theatrical performance of a multi-angled military ambush. Army men rappelled from a helicopter; boats whizzed ashore and dumped off more soldiers. The soldiers cornered off a house and demonstrated a successful attack. I wondered whether there were any veterans present who might be triggered by this very realistic war theater.

After the war show, we filed into the convention center. The crowd began to assemble into a giant semicircle. I got separated from Azra and James, who were on the other side of the room. Unsure of what was happening, I took my place in the circle and waited.

Just then, the sultan walked through the door. Behind him was King Abdullah of Jordan. Having just left part of my heart in Jordan, I was more excited about seeing the king than the sultan, but I was stunned at the coincidence of those two leaders being at the same event. King Abdullah quickly disappeared through the crowd, but the sultan began moving around the semicircle. He did not shake hands like an American politician. Rather, each person took a deep bow when he got directly in front of them.

My heart began racing and my palms started to sweat. I had no muscle memory for this scenario. I was still getting comfortable with air kisses, but this was new territory. A handshake and even air kisses put two on equal terms, but a bow is fundamentally different. My American body had never had to bow before anyone. The thought of bowing to another human being felt wrong, aside from being eight shades of awkward. I watched closely as the goateed, five-foot-nothing Sultan received each bow and then graciously greeted each person. Soon, he came directly in front of me. My body froze up like the shy girl at the prom.

My mind was telling my body to *please bow now so we can end this awkward charade*, but my mind and body were somehow disconnected, as if the nerve bundle that connects the two had been violently severed. My mind struggled to comply with the program, but perhaps my body knew better. My body knew that such an act of worship was blasphemous to give that type of divine allegiance to another human. And my soul knew that bowing to a rich, powerful sultan was a betrayal to how I had come to see all humans on this earth being equal in our sacredness.

His brown eyes locked directly into mine and seared through all rational consciousness. I stood frozen, and he froze, stunned that there was a person in the room who refused to bow. I had disrupted the usual royal mojo, and it felt as if everyone in the room was staring at me. My face burned red hot. *Please can this just be over now*, I thought. After what felt like an eternity, the sultan pivoted and moved onward to the next person without greeting me.

And the world kept on spinning.

Azra, Joseph, and I had a good laugh about it later that day, and thankfully my civil disobedience didn't derail the project. Azra wrapped things up in a nice bow and gave the management team back in Istanbul a green light for me to have my very own project. I'd be in the driver's seat next time, with my own secretary, my own editor, and my own driver.

I survived the sultanate of Brunei, I survived the Sultan, I survived my training, and I would be headed to Ras al Khaimah, one of the seven Emirates of the United Arab Emirates. It was another obscure place on earth to the confused folks back home. I'd go back to Arkansas for a brief visit before heading there. My Arkansas lovies would ask where I was headed next, and I might have been better off saying Timbuktu.

Ras al Khaimah, United Arab Emirates
The wind in the Arabian Gulf feels like a hair dryer to the face. Or the rush of air that comes out of the oven when you're a little too eager to check on the cookies. Cool reprieves are few and far between, but the landscape of the United Arab Emirates is mystically stunning. The UAE is a pristine desert with dunes that stretch like a pure yellow ocean to eternity. Jordan might have been fried chicken, but the UAE is silky banana pudding ready to be topped with cream.

In the hazy distance, a mirage. No, it can't be. Way out here in the sand dunes? As you approach, the wavy image solidifies into a sparkling city of towering skyscrapers. The contrast from primordial desert to flashy modernity is so sudden, you wonder whether you've been out in the sun too long.

Dubai is the Emerald City gloriously made manifest in an Oz-like wilderness. The skyline is otherworldly, with the tallest building in the world, the Burj Khalifa, newly towering over the other tall buildings, which are dwarfed in comparison. Dusk in the desert casts a reddish glow on the cityscape as the warm, colored sands refract the light from a perfect orange ball in the sky.

Ras al Khaimah, known as Julfar by the ancients and known as simply RAK by Western folk abbreviating things, is just north of Dubai, about an hour's drive through the empty desert. It is ruled by a sovereign sheikh and a royal family who control most of the emirate's wealth and assets: a real-estate company with resorts along its beautiful coastline, a port, a small airport, a ceramics company, and a free trade zone.

The company put me up in the Bin Majid Hotel, a rinky-dink budget resort frequented by Russian tourists who craved sunrays like water. "You'll stay there for now. If you want nicer accommodations, you'll have to secure them yourself in the form of a new barter agreement," my new boss, Tiffany Shrill, told me over the phone.

Tiffany was from Massachusetts, but I could tell by her abrasive cadence and pseudo-European-expat dialect that she had been drinking the Cambridge Reports Kool-Aid for so long that her eyes were the deepest shade of money green. She lacked the warmth that Azra maintained in a cold industry. I was a trainee under Azra, and had my own project now, but the autonomy was an illusion. Tiffany was nineteen hundred miles away in Istanbul, but also all up in my chili every time I turned around.

The get-to-know-yous was always a process of sifting out a person for their financial worth. And for me, Tiffany's subordinate, it was no different. How much money would I be making her and the company? That was the question that mattered.

My partner and editorial manager was Miguel, a cheerful, short-and-stocky guy from Miami of Venezuelan descent. He was younger than I was but more seasoned in the industry. I would soon come to learn after having to edit his emails that it wasn't his actual editorial skills that got him the job, but his ability to schmooze with important people. Unlike Stanislaw, Miguel immediately put me at ease with his ability to talk. People with the "gift of gab," as Mama would say, make me feel at home. Much like Mama, he might have been a little scattered and squirrelly at times, but he didn't have a smug bone in his body. The familiarity made me relieved to have him as a partner.

During our first few days on the project, Tiffany flew in to lecture us. She wore a gray power pants-suit, tall clickety heels that were surely torturous in the desert heat, and fiery red hair that had been smoothed to perfection in a French twist.

"The sheikh interview is everything," she said before setting down her green tea and taking a long pause to give us a stern look.

"You can't mess up this part of the project. Do whatever it takes to get the interview," she chomped.

In addition to giving us a four-month timeline, she reiterated the first and main goal, which would also be the most difficult: a face-to-face interview with the ruler of the emirate, Sheikh Saud. If we had his blessing (and photo op), the entire project would fall into place. If not, the project would fail and there would be a tacit understanding that I wasn't cut out to be a Cambridge Reports country director.

Tiffany left town, and our first order of business, Miguel and I determined, was to get better digs. The Bin Majid was dank, dirty, dark, and depressing. The Russian tourists liked to smoke at breakfast, come in loudly at all hours of the night, and sunbathe nude on the beach. I wondered if they just didn't know any better or cared not at all for the local Muslim culture. Miguel and I didn't have a proper office, so we quickly began to wilt in the hotel lobby, breathing stale, smoky air and hearing "Country Roads" sung from the karaoke room for the eighth time that day.

The final straw came on a night that I went on an evening jog at sunset. The Bin Majid beach was narrow. Stretching out directly behind our hotel, hemmed in by rocks on both sides, it formed a small rectangle of beachfront for guests to strip down and sweat out vodka hangovers without being seen by the more conservative public.

I jogged back and forth, back and forth, back and forth before sitting in the sand to catch my breath while staring wistfully at the purple sky. Suddenly a man entered my peripheral vision. He was shuffling through the sand quickly, and I looked around and realized I was alone on the beach. He was too dark-skinned to be Emirati, and he wasn't wearing the traditional dishdasha. I thought maybe he was a construction worker from the neighboring resort—perhaps Sri Lankan or Bangladeshi. Before I had time to blink, he leaned down and grabbed me by the shoulders. A cloud of body odor ambushed my senses as he leaned in to plant his sweaty fish mouth on mine. My adrenaline roared like a dragon on PMS, as I shot up from the sand ready to wage war. I always imagined that I would be more "flight" in a fight-or-flight scenario, but I surprised myself with my instinct to fight back. I pushed him away with all my might until he toppled down into the sand, and then lunged to give him a backhanded pop of the knuckles to the head. His eyes bugged out when he realized I was taller and perhaps stronger than he was. I don't remember what obscenities I yelled at him, but it was clear that

I had come a long way from my demure days. He stumbled up from the sand and ran away, disappearing into the darkness beyond the rock wall.

I reported the incident to the Bin Majid evening staff, who gave me a shrug and an admonition for being alone on the beach in the first place.

The next week, I pitched a barter agreement to the Al Hamra Fort Resort. At that time, it was RAK's main luxury hotel, owned by Sheikh Saud, the guy we were chasing for an interview. I met with the general manager, a stiff French guy of few words. I tried not to sound like Desperate Debbie while stumbling through notes of a pitch and laid out all the reasons he should want the Al Hamra to be seen in our fancy report. Then I held my breath, praying and pleading that he would agree, and thus deliver us from our depressing environment. He said yes the very next day, and Miguel and I gleefully moved uptown.

The Al Hamra Fort Hotel looked like an old Arabian fort with a giant beige gate and stucco villas in the same shade of beige nestled on one and a half kilometers of beaches with the Hajjar Mountain range in the distance. It was the perfect paradise of desert meets beach meets mountains, but mostly it was a relief to be breathing fresher air in a safer work environment.

Everything about our new work environment was dazzling, but the project launch dragged on like a busted garden tiller. Sheikh Saud's office sternly turned down our request for an interview. They didn't give a reason, but we suspected it might have been because of a harrowing story that had just hit the press in America. A housekeeper at a luxury hotel in Minnesota had accused the sheikh of sexually assaulting her after offering to read her palm. No charges were brought, and the sheikh was allowed to return to the UAE after spending a weekend in jail, but the salacious sight of the ruler's black-and-white jail-striped mug shot was being passed around the web. He needed to lie low and avoid the media, and it probably didn't help that we were American.

At the same time, another weird mystery was brewing. It started with a phone call from Mama, who said she had a patient with a friend who wanted to talk with me, "some guy named Randy" who was coming to Ras al Khaimah for business. Mama didn't say why, other than "How coincidental that you're in the saaaame wild place? Maybe that's a sign from the Lord." I was prepared for Mama to eventually figure out what continent I was on, but thought, *Now she's got business leads for me?*

Then my college friend's sister sent a similar message. She worked with Randy at an investment company in Little Rock and said I needed to speak with him. Then another friend who went to high school with Randy sent me a Facebook message saying the exact same thing. Everybody at once was saying, "You need to talk with Randy!" When I asked what for exactly, the answer was always the same vagueness: "I don't know. Something about business where you're at. I think he wants to help you." Was Randy a CIA operative trying to recruit me? My mind ran wild.

We first connected over Facebook, but Randy would not tell me what it was he needed to talk about. He said he'd be coming to the Al Hamra Fort Hotel in the near future and we could talk in person.

I was beginning to pick up on the idea that Ras al Khaimah was some sort of Wild West. Time, law, and energy flowed differently in the Little Emirate That Could. The isolated location and concentrated pockets of wealth made us wonder what was hidden behind all those beige-colored walls.

"What is going on in Ras al Khaimah?" Miguel and I would wonder at the end of a long, frustrating day while smoking watermelon shisha on the beach. Our intuition was pinged just enough to continue aggressively with the project, if only out of wild curiosity.

We were still having no luck meeting with Sheikh Saud, but the sheikh's brother, Sheikh Omar, was warm and welcoming and a grand tour guide. He treated us to a tour of the emirate in his private plane. We soared through the peaks and valleys of the Hajjar Mountains, where we could see Iran just across the Strait of Hormuz. On another excursion, the sheikh took us into the wilderness to see where the Bedouin tribes live a simple shepherd life in the desert. We met an elderly man who bowed respectfully and gifted the sheikh with his ax. Traditional tribes of that region often carry around a tall, slender ax. It's used primarily as a walking stick or a weapon to fight off snakes. The sheikh then gifted it to me.

Giving gifts and outrageous generosity are hallmarks of Arabian culture, especially in the Gulf region. Sometimes the culture felt so wildly foreign, but yet that feeling of nostalgia and déjà vu kept creeping up before it became clear to me: people from the Deep South and people from the Arabian Gulf are really the same. The conservatism, warmth, hospitality, family loyalty, well-meaning earnestness to protect and provide, and the need for drive-thru liquor stores where you want to get your booze but don't want to be seen by your neighbor doing so. Two groups of people who might be suspicious, or at least standoffish with one another, are so much alike.

Tiffany called often—sometimes every night of the week—with the same grinding spiel, berating me for not having secured an interview with Sheikh Saud and thus lagging behind on the budget. "The sheikh needs to lie low and avoid the media" was never a good enough answer.

"I am trying, Tiffany, but he doesn't want to meet with us," I told her each time.

"Do what it takes; MAKE IT HAPPEN," she'd snap.

***

Mama surprised the heck out of me and came for a visit with my sister, Julie. She hadn't really traveled outside of the South, except for my Brazilian wedding, so for her to come all the way to Ras al Khaimah was a very big deal.

I took them on a grand tour of Dubai and showed them all of the glittery things—the flashy shopping places, the superhuman feats of architecture, and bleached-white beaches filled with perfect unbroken seashells, planted for tourists to find. Julie likened it to *The Truman Show*, but Mama was positively dazzled by the ostentatious luster, particularly the artificial archipelago in the shape of a palm tree and the swanky Atlantis Hotel with outlandish blown-glass lighting fixtures made by American sculptor Dale Chihuly.

"I like Dubai! I really like it!" she'd say as if she had surprised herself by her approval.

They returned to the Al Hamra resort in RAK with me to relax while I went back to work.

One night we had dinner at Al Jazeera, the resort's Lebanese restaurant. There was a Filipino band playing, and they opened the floor up to karaoke. I did my usual Norah Jones "Don't Know Why" song and Mama performed her signature Patsy Cline rendition of "Crazy." When we returned to our seats, the Filipina waiter brought us an extra cocktail. "From the table over there," she gestured.

We looked across the room to see two young Emirati men smiling and looking in our direction. Their heads were covered, and they were wearing their traditional white long dishdashas. "Oh! That's so nice!" Mama gushed.

We sipped our cocktails sheepishly wondering who the mystery men were. After about ten minutes, they walked over to join our table. "Hi, mind if we sit down?" the younger of the two asked.

"Sure, thanks so much for the drinks!" Mama responded in her friendly, cheerful Southern-woman tone. Clearly, she had not got the lesson from Celeste.

"Hi, I'm Majid," the older of the two smiled. "And this is my friend Mo."

"Hello. Nice to meet you," Mo said in a stoic and formal tone.

Mo had a baby face with a few patches of stubble. He acted serious but had the face of a child. After getting a good look at him, I realized that his formality was actually shyness. Majid was a bit older and comfortable in his own skin, with a wide grin and slightly disheveled locks peeking out from his keffiyeh. They were mysterious and seemed an unlikely duo—perhaps mentor and mentee? We introduced ourselves, sipped our drinks, and then sat in awkward silence. "Where are you from?" Mo asked finally.

"From the US, all of us," I responded.

"Oh really, whereabouts?" he asked.

We told him about Arkansas, and I was surprised that he had heard of the Toothpick State.

"I just finished college in the States," Mo said. His ability to pull off an impressive American dialect confirmed his high social status. Not too many Emiratis go to American universities.

"Oh yeah, where'd you go?" Julie asked.

"UCLA," he said. "Great school, I love America and miss my life there. I'm so bored to be back home."

"Do you like staying here?" Majid asked us.

"Oh, we most certainly do! This place is so nice!" Mama beamed.

"Oh yeah, good, because his father owns this place." Majid elbowed Mo while flashing a wide smile. Mo blushed. Majid giggled and looked to the side.

"Your father is His Royal Highness Sheikh Saud?" I asked. Of course, he was. Who else in the Little Emirate That Could would have gone to UCLA for college? I had a fresh imprint in my mind of Sheikh Saud's internet mug shot, and Mo was indeed a younger version of his father.

Mo was *Sheikh Mohammed bin Saud al Qasimi, the Crown Prince of Ras al Khaimah.*

My stomach turned and my head whirled, and I soon found myself in the inescapable dependence whirlpool that my industry taught me. The need to seek out people with money and power was the only way to survive. Mo was the person I needed to help me get a meeting with his father. He was my new strategy, my plan.

I turned up the flirt slightly. I hated myself for it, but the child in front of me was my golden ticket to getting the project off the ground. I was caught up in the vortex of human capital. The need to forge a fast connection in order to meet a need. The need to use people for financial gain. *Is this what the Dutch guy who worked in the industry warned me about on Facebook?* I wondered. *Get out before it's too late.*

I held my breath, hoping Mama would—for once in her life—not say whatever thought had just come bubbling to the surface. I felt like the carless teenager whose mother was dropping her off on the first day of school, wanting to scamper away before any embarrassing thing was said. There was too much that could go wrong by an accidentally offensive word salad.

The waitress returned with another round of drinks.

We continued to chat with Majid and Mo. Mama kept it cool, and that made me proud. I was able to relax and actually enjoy getting to know them. They invited us to join them for dinner the following night.

"Pick you up in the limo at six?" Mo asked.

"Yes, of course!" I said, catching a surprised look from Mama and Jules. They still had not caught on.

"Okay great, see you then!" Majid stood, and Mo followed him out. Clearly Majid was a bodyguard and perhaps glorified royal chaperone.

"What was that all about?" Jules asked.

"Mo is the crown prince," I divulged. "I need a meeting with his father for this project to succeed."

"Ooooh, I see," Mama mused. I could see the wheels turning in her head, and it made me sad that I had exposed her to the corrupt side of my job. In her world as a nurse, patients are all equal—one doesn't get better treatment than another—so she'd give just as much attention to her VIP patient as she would her low-income person with no insurance.

I told Miguel about my serendipitous encounter, and he lit up.

"Dude! You have to work this to our advantage. We have to have that meeting if you and I are gonna get paid for this project. Work it girl, work it!"

"What, are you my pimp now?" I asked. Indeed, he was.

Mama, Julie, and I waited in front of the Al Hamra at six sharp. The limo pulled up, and the driver hopped out to open the door for us. The darkness of the interior made Mama gasp. She's chronically claustrophobic and began to panic. "I can't do this. Why don't you girls go without me?" she mumbled under her breath nervously.

"Mama, we're just going down the road. You can do this!" we said. But she had that deer-in-the-headlights, stunned-fear look glazed over her eyes. Her fists were clenched, and we knew there was no walking her back down off the ledge.

The four of us rode away in the dark limo. It felt like a double date already without Mama as a buffer. Maybe I was the one who needed a chaperone.

The limo took us to one of the Lebanese restaurants on the property, a mere quarter of a mile. It felt silly not walking. The restaurant had a special, semi-hidden table for us roped off in the elevated corner of the room behind a row of plants. We ate our mezza in the shadows and watched a belly dancer twirl through the room. Majid and Mo were polite. Mo spoke fondly about college at UCLA, where he reveled in being an ordinary student and was known as "Mo" instead of Mohammed. Now that he was back home, he was the crown prince and everything that came with that: a scrutinized life, on display, a set of expectations, a certain kind of inescapable pressure, and a chosen destiny.

The Arabic music got louder as a belly dancer came twirling closer to our table. She slung her lustrous hair from side to side while orbiting her hips and rippling her belly up and down like waves in the ocean.

"I just love the Middle East!" I overheard an English lady at a neighboring table say. Tourists who spend good money on vacations to the Gulf expect at least one good belly-dancing show to satisfy their imagined stereotypes of erotic, exotic Arabia.

"These girls are all Brazilian," Mo snickered. "The local women don't really do this."

I wondered just what, exactly, the local women did. They were mostly invisible. Absent from business, from government, from the mercantile system. The only women I spoke with were Filipina, in the service industry, or an occasional Emirati secretary. The UAE was a man's world. It seemed the men made all the decisions, got the education, and ran the show.

Given all of this, I imagined Mo and Majid would be pushy guys with a sense of entitlement. But quite the opposite was true. Majid was just along for the ride—Mo's sidekick and chaperone—and Mo was shy, meek, thoughtful, and innocent. He was a kid curious about the world and perhaps bored with his surroundings. But he didn't have a bratty, superiority complex that you'd expect from an entitled royal. Even at his young, wide-eyed age, he wasn't smug. I decided he was nonthreatening enough that we could be friends. He didn't make any kind of romantic moves that night, and Jules and I had a fun time. Julie, usually unimpressed by pomp and circumstance, was slightly giddy about having just dined with a prince.

Mama and Julie went home, and in the days that followed I began subtly dropping hints to Mo via text message that I really needed a meeting with his dad. It felt disingenuous to pursue a friendship on the grounds of what he could provide. But once he got over his shyness, he was an interesting conversationalist and never made any flirtatious moves. He missed speaking American English, and we had what I believed to be a platonic friendship.

Then things started to get weird.

CHAPTER 19

HARK! THE HERALD ANGELS SING

Still in the UAE

RAK might have been a paradise, but what it lacked were the gritty places that make a place fun. Then Miguel and I discovered Klub 88 on the edge of town. It was where all the local service-class Filipinos partied on the weekend.

The bar's sign was a giant yellow smiley face akin to the Wal-Mart rollback logo. Their motto boasted, "A room full of smiles," and they endearingly lived up to it every night. We drank cheap buckets of San Miguel beer and gorged ourselves with Filipino delicacies from their pork menu, absent everywhere else in town. Every night featured a different show with pop songs, earnest choreography, and boy bands and girl bands in DIY matching outfits they had replicated from something they'd seen in a music video. Miguel and I were like kids finding the playground after running around in circles at a big, boring park looking for where the fun was to be had. Klub 88 was the Scene.

But I started noticing the men who would follow me through the desert back to the resort on nights we'd get back late. They'd trail me as I entered the Al Hamra and do little to conceal the fact that they were keeping tabs on my comings and goings. I was too embarrassed to mention it to Mo, for fear he'd think I was flattering myself. After all, he'd never made any romantic gestures, and I didn't want him to know I suspected him of having me followed.

There was also still the mysterious Randy person connected to people from back home. He hadn't yet shown up. Could these guys be connected somehow? I wondered.

Tiffany's frequent phone calls were wearing me down. Some days RAK felt like the twilight zone where I was caught in a web of money, power, and unclear intentions. Klub 88 was the only surefooted place to go—its patrons were service-industry staff and a few off-the-grid tourists having a couple of cold ones at the end of a long day.

One evening Mo called and said he wanted to show me someplace cool. It was a secret part of the Al Hamra Resort. He met me in the lobby and took me down a back corridor, then up a secret staircase that led to another room, and then another secret staircase. A final door opened to the rooftop. For a second I felt like Princess Jasmine on her balcony in Aladdin, seeing a magnificent starry sky through an inky darkness.

"Beautiful from up here, isn't it?" Mo said.

"Yes, amazing," I pondered.

We stood in awkward silence admiring the stars until Mo's voice cracked—"I brought you up here because I wanted to ask if you'd be my girlfriend. I mean, like, my very serious girlfriend."

"Wait, what?" His blatant request made me choke in shock. I hadn't had such a formal request for courtship since grade school check-yes-or-no days. I was mostly surprised by his bold request in light of the fact that there was so much he didn't know about me. My history, my divorce, my plans for the future, or my middle name.

"Mo, I, I . . . " I stammered.

"You don't have to answer right now. But please think about it, will you?" he said sweetly. I was endeared by the preciousness of it all. He never tried kissing me.

"Mo, I have a boyfriend already," I confessed. "I mean, he's not here locally, but I have a boyfriend long distance," I confessed.

"What kind of a relationship is that?" he asked.

The boy suddenly seemed like a mature man. He was right. I loved Travis but knew I could not go on forever long distance, at least, without an end date in sight.

"Think about it," Mo said, before grabbing my hand and leading me back down the secret staircase.

I went to bed that night certain that my late-night stalkers were Mo's minions sent to check up on me. I thought of Queen Noor's memoir in which she writes about the early days of her courtship with King Hussein, when she'd have secret meetups at the royal stables. There were always people around who worked for the royal family.

I tossed and turned that night thinking about the gravity of his request. How would he take it when I officially said no? Even if I wanted to give it a go, it led to a dead-end, some place I didn't want to be: a curated, controlled life behind luxurious walls. I still needed the meeting with Mo's father, but things had already gone too far in the wrong direction.

"Shit shit *shit*!" Miguel said as he poured his French-press coffee at breakfast the next morning. I updated him on the scenario, and he freaked out at how off the rails it had gone.

"I promise you; I did not see that coming!" I told him.

"We need that meeting, but if he feels like his ego is bruised over being rejected by you, we might as well kiss that goodbye. Worse, we could be thrown out of the emirate!" he said.

"Calm down. I don't think it's that bad," I told him. "Mo seems pretty level-headed. I can't imagine him being that vengeful."

But the truth was, I was confused and scared. Everything was uncharted territory, and day to day, it felt as if I were walking in the dark while being pulled in different directions. The company put so much pressure on me to perform in an impossible environment. I was perpetually between a rock and a hard place.

"Now you know why Cambridge Reports only hires females to do this job," Miguel reminded me.

The truth stung. I wondered how Azra and James navigated such situations. It didn't seem that bad in Brunei. I missed Azra and wished she were here to show me how to gracefully navigate choppy, relational waters while still moving the project forward. She was always in control, always airy and unsinkable despite the circumstances. I was surrounded by weirdness and drowning in absurdity.

* * *

One night I was startled out of a sound sleep when my phone rang. The clock said midnight, so I thought it must be an emergency.

"Hello there, is this Natalie? My name is Randy," the voice on the phone said.

Mysterious dude had called me. My heart skipped a beat.

"I'm so glad to finally have you over the phone. I've heard so many good things about you," he said in a warm, Southern tone that was all too familiar.

"Same to you," I lied. I didn't have a clue who he was or what he wanted from me.

He began asking me detailed questions about what I did in Ras al Khaimah exactly. Who I worked for, who I met with, how long I'd be there, and what I knew about the emirate. He quizzed me like a journalist, fast fact-finding and sifting me out for information. "What do you do?" I interjected.

"Well, a lot of things, it's complicated," he said vaguely.

"Okay, so what do you do in RAK?" I asked specifically.

"I'm an investment banker," he said. "And I have some funds of a client I'd like to invest in Ras al Khaimah. This client really wants to help the people of RAK."

"Really? Why RAK? It's mostly affluent. I mean, why not Africa? Who is your client, may I ask?"

"Well not just the people of RAK but also the Filipinos in the service industry. Or projects that help children in the emirate," he said.

"I see," I said but still confused by his illogical request. Of all the children that needed helping.

"If you know of any projects happening, my client has lots of money to invest in this emirate," he pitched me.

I needed to know who his client was to get the full picture, so I continued to rattle on about the emirate, telling him everything I could while playing dumb to his potential criminal activity. It was becoming obvious that he had money to launder—probably a large sum—and was feeling me out for potential places in the Wild West of RAK where his washing would go undetected.

"The gentleman and the missus and the whole entourage will be at the Al Hamra soon," he said.

"Who are they?" I asked.

"They are with the Marcos family of the Philippines. Do you know them?" he asked.

"Uh, not a whole lot, tell me more," I lied again. I was really getting good at playing the ditzy Southern blond.

"It's on behalf of the family of Ferdinand Marcos. He used to rule the Philippines," he said.

"His name rings a bell," I said. Ferdinand Marcos.

Marcos was one of the most detested names among the Filipino people. He had a twenty-year authoritarian regime and was believed to have embezzled billions of dollars from the Filipino government. The infamous kleptocrat is responsible for crippling the country's economy, the effects of poverty and instability still lingering today. He makes Duarte look like Jimmy Carter. And here was a man on the phone, a charming Arkansan with a Southern drawl, working for the Marcos family, asking me to help him bury some of the stolen money from the Filipino people.

Randy was the equivalent of Jason Bateman's character in the Netflix series *Ozark*. Just a downhome guy who somehow got lured into making a deal with the devil for the sake of getting rich quick. "Trust me, you'll be greatly—and I mean greatly—rewarded if you can help us out in RAK," he said.

I wanted to ask him how. How did he get caught up in that web to begin with? Was it worth it? Was the money really worth what it represented: corruption and theft by an evil regime that resulted in millions of people who've lived in poverty? I found it ironic that they wanted to invest in RAK, whose hospitality industry was built on the backs of Filipino women, many of whom had left behind children to work hundreds of miles away just to make ends meet at home.

I thought about all of the unseen forces at work that oppress people around the world. I grew up thinking that the "powers and principalities of the world" mentioned in the New Testament were about personal purity. I would come to know that powers and principalities has more to do with oppressive regimes, beginning with the Roman Empire at the time the New Testament was written. The forces at play that keep people enslaved, poor, and destitute are in opposition to the kingdom that Jesus announced. Powers and principalities are a massive underground entanglement like roots on a grandfather tree. You only see the fruit, or lack thereof, rather than the centuries of growth or starvation that led to the results.

I thought about my own complicity in the powers and principalities. Was it possible that I was chasing dirty money too through my sales in the emirate? Would my success be linked to the past oppression of a generation of Filipinos? I wanted to ask Randy so many things, but I was stunned. I listened to his requests, speechless. By then, it was nearly three o'clock in the morning.

"Okay Randy, I'll look into it and get back with you," I told him vaguely.

I didn't sleep that night.

"I'll help you meet my dad." My BlackBerry lit up with the magic words I needed from Mo.

I was poolside with Miguel and screamed so loudly that kids in the pool stopped splashing to look in my direction.

"Dude, what is it?" Miguel put down his shisha pipe.

"We're getting the interview!" I belted.

The next week, Miguel and I were pulling through the golden gates of the sheik's palace with shined shoes and every hair in place. We parked in the circle drive and walked up to the front door, shocked to find it ajar.

"Should we knock?" I asked Miguel.

It seemed mighty bizarre that there was no security at the palace and the ruler of the emirate had left his door wide open. We knocked and stood awkwardly, waiting for someone to let us in.

"You think they forgot about us? You did say two o'clock, right?" Miguel whispered.

I knocked again, this time louder. We studied the tall Arabian doors. After an awkward five-minute game of knock and wait, I cracked the door slightly. "Hello?" I said, sticking my nose inside.

It was then that I caught a peek of Sheikh Saud sitting in the corner of the room. So I pulled my nose out and knocked again. A Filipina woman came to the door. "Cambridge Reports? Come on in," she said.

Sheikh Saud rose from his corner chair and walked toward us. We introduced ourselves, and despite Miguel's coaching me ahead of time (he had far more of these situations under his belt than I did), I completely forgot to add "Your Royal Highness" when addressing the Sheikh. I tried to make up for it by saying it excessively during lulls in the conversation throughout the interview. At one point, Miguel cut me a side eye as if to say, *we get it; cool your tools!* and I struggled to reel in my laughter like a girl in church.

The sheikh looked just like his furrowed-brow mug shot I had seen on the web. I tried not to imagine him in the black and white jumpsuit, but that was all I could see. Mo came into the living room just then, which seemed surreal out of the context I knew him in.

"This is my son, Mohammed," Sheikh Saud said. "I think Natalie here has already been acquainted with him."

"Yes, correct, Your Royal Highness," I said sheepishly.

The sheikh gestured for us to take a seat on a stiff, shiny couch between a silk Persian rug and various oil paintings. He sat across from us in a wooden Santa Claus chair with crimson upholstery.

Miguel and I stumbled through our list of questions:

"What's the next five years look like for the emirate?"

"Tell us about the importance of the America's Cup being held in RAK this year?"

"What's the fastest sector of growth this year?"

The sheikh didn't have very elaborate answers for any of these. It felt like he was only meeting us because Mo asked him to cooperate. I gave Mo a sly, grateful smile and a nod.

"Thank you," I mouthed as we were being shown out. He smiled back.

The deed was done, and best of all, we had got our much-needed photo of Miguel, the sheikh, and me side by side, smiling like the Cheshire cat while holding up a glossy copy of the previous year's *Cambridge Report: Ras al Khaimah*.

Miguel and I rolled out of the palace and went straight to Klub 88 to celebrate over a bucket-o-beer. The mission was accomplished; the project was saved. We could breathe a little better without Tiffany breathing down our necks every day.

After that day, Mo and I talked. I told him the hard and rocky truth that I was still holding out for a potential future with my long-distance boyfriend. Messy and uncertain as long-distance relationships can be, Travis was the one I could see by my side, always. Mo backed off with dignity. The graciousness behind his big, kind eyes made me imagine he'd be a good partner to someone someday. But that someone would not be me.

Our photograph with Sheikh Saud made all the difference in getting contracts with other businesses and government agencies. We pimped ourselves out with that photo, used it in every sales pitch, and the deals came in one after another. You could feel the momentum. I started asking for more money for the same product as the previous year. If a cement company paid £20,000 the previous year, we might ask for £25,000 the next. Or £50,000 if we knew they could pay it.

My commission checks started rolling in. The sales high is a seductive thing. When your income is directly tied to how many deals you can close, a little success is a strong drug that boosted my self-worth in all the wrong ways. I turned into a moneymaking machine with a bad hair-bleach job. I had no bills, no taxes, and no debt. I was queen of my sales universe, and I wore the hubris like a bejeweled caftan blowing in the sandy, arid breeze.

At the end of each day, I'd come back to the Al Hamra and find a place in the sand, staring at the vast Arabian Sea. I had finally "made it" within Cambridge Reports. I was *good enough*, valuable to the company, successful in a lucrative industry.

But when I allowed myself to be just a little still, I felt the cold loneliness in my bones. I watched the families with small children on vacation and wished I could be one of them, as I imagined— nurtured, loving, connected, and fulfilled. I never spoke with Randy again, but wondered if any of the money I was making was tied to the

Marcos family fund. I suppressed the thought of it and told myself to just enjoy it.

I hated to face the truth of my success: it all came at the mercy of powerful men. Sure, I had worked my hardest. But had I not been a young, attractive blond sitting in the restaurant that day, the project would likely have failed. I knew it, and I stuffed it down with my hummus and pita bread alone at the Lebanese restaurant that night.

The Brazilian belly dancer took center stage again. She was so visually stunning to watch. Her hair whipped from side to side like dancing flames. She was on fire. Perhaps she understood the place I was in. The objectified, fetishized woman playing a part. She danced for me. She danced for the drooling businessmen. She danced for the tourists. She danced for all the women who have ever been hurled to the dance floor unexpectedly. The powerful demand: *Perform!* And whether we like the music or not, we dance the dance for our own survival.

* * *

Christmastime came. The halls of the Al Hamra Resort were decorated in holly, evergreen boughs, and red bows. The dining hall served Christmas pudding and roasted meats. I marched through the lobby on a self-important sales high, scoffing at the fakeness of it all, and strolled up the staircase to my room. The fir trees were the most bizarre for a resort in the middle of the desert. Never mind the fact that Jesus was born in the Middle East, where a decorated palm tree would have been geographically correct, the hotel was catering to its Western clientele who expected the familiarity of European Christmas traditions. Or maybe it was a spectacle for regional travelers who might equate Western décor with seasonal extravagance.

I took the stairs two at a time. A young businesswoman on a roll was hobnobbing with actual royalty, and my status in the sheikhdom was rising faster than I could ascend that grand staircase. No time for pudding. As I rounded the top of the staircase and headed to my room, I could see a choir in red velvet dresses beginning to assemble downstairs.

Wow, they're really reaching far. I rolled my eyes. Ras al Khaimah didn't have a single Christian church in the emirate, but Christmas apparently sells. I was halfway down the hallway when I heard them: "Hark! The herald angels sing, glory to the newborn king!"

They sounded like angels, stopping me in my tracks. I turned back toward the balcony that overlooked the atrium to see the singers, and upon closer view of their faces, I recognized them to be the Filipino service staff transformed into a magnificent choir—singing heavenly Christmas hymns in perfect harmony. Their smiles were radiant.

They shined brighter than anything I'd seen in the UAE. These beautiful souls, the disenfranchised service-class workers of the UAE, were singing about kingdom come. Randy the money launderer said he was trying to "help" the Filipinos of Ras al Khaimah, but ironically, they probably wouldn't have been there if their country hadn't been plagued by the Ferdinand Marcos years of corruption and embezzlement. Perhaps their families wouldn't have sent them to a land far away to make enough income for basic necessities.

Their singing resonated off the tall glass windows and filled the Al Hamra with praise of the coming Messiah. "Oh, holy night, the stars are brightly shining. This is the night of our dear Savior's birth. . . ."

I sat on the floor by the balcony railing where nobody else was around and fought hard to hold back the tears, but without success. There was so much beauty in this act of worship that felt dangerously subversive. In an emirate run by wealthy sheikhs where money launderers were trying to get rich off of money stolen from the poor, there we had the poor singing praises to a Savior who came to shame the powers and principalities that keep people oppressed.

My newfound confidence built on my own flimsy achievements, schmoozing with very important people, dissipated like swirling shisha smoke in the night sky. The Filipino choir shocked me into seeing the gospel in a new light. The Christmas story was less about Jesus being born so he could die to pay the price of our sin and more about Jesus being born to establish his kingdom. His kingdom would always be separate from the kingdoms on earth.

The Gospel of Mark tells us Jesus fasted and prayed in the desert for forty days. There he was tempted by Satan to have all the glittery shiny kingdoms on earth. He resisted. Then after forty days he announced his kingdom. It was upside down from what anyone imagined from the new king of Israel. Mary, mother of Jesus, said it best:

My soul magnifies the Lord,
    and my spirit rejoices in God my Savior,
for he has looked with favor on the lowliness of his servant.
    Surely, from now on all generations will call me blessed;
for the Mighty One has done great things for me,
    and holy is his name.
His mercy is for those who fear him
    from generation to generation.
He has shown strength with his arm;
    he has scattered the proud in the thoughts of their hearts.
He has brought down the powerful from their thrones,
    and lifted up the lowly;
he has filled the hungry with good things,
    and sent the rich away empty.
He has helped his servant Israel,
    in remembrance of his mercy,
according to the promise he made to our ancestors,
    to Abraham and to his descendants forever.[28]

It's no wonder this same passage was banned from being publicly read in parts of India and El Salvador. It's a dangerous thing for the lowly masses to claim that the Almighty God is on their side, independent of the ruling elites.

As the Filipino choir sang loud and proud, tears streamed down my face. My pride was smashed to smithereens, and my hardened, scarred heart had turned to mush. They pulled back the curtain for me to see the glory of God shining brightly and the tender mercy of Christ present at a fancy resort in the Arabian Gulf.

A thrill of hope, the weary world rejoices
For Yonder breaks a new and glorious morn.

Paris, France

It was dark, cold, and drizzly, and I thought I might possibly freeze to death, but I had made it to Paris on Christmas Eve. Notre-Dame cathedral stood, majestic, the twin bell towers disappearing into a foggy darkness as if the low ceiling of heaven had floated down, a snug blanket over a cold city.

Paris was a last-minute plan. Betsy had already planned to meet her mom and boyfriend a week after my arrival. "Why don't you meet us and spend Christmas here?" she asked after I confessed how dreadfully lonely it was in the Gulf over the holidays. Miguel had other plans, and Travis wasn't coming until January. The thought of Christmas alone in the Wild West emirate without friends or family put me in a dark place.

Notre-Dame seemed like the right place for Christmas Eve. Its big, warm presence was a refuge from the cold that enveloped me like a good mother. At the entryway, I lit a small candle and placed it on a large spiral. There were hundreds of little flames, each one a prayer glowing up to heaven from the dim world below.

My prayer didn't have words. I was too tired for words. My prayer was an inner groan for love, unity, and clarity. God already knew the longings of my heart, with or without sentence structure. I watched my little flame dance with the same wild, unpredictable palpitations of my heart. So much of my life had become nebulous like the wintry Parisian air. I was finally succeeding in the country-report industry in which I had trained for the past year, making the kind of money of which I had always dreamed. But my soul was withering under the constant demands to earn more pounds for the company and the pressure to perform in a man's world.

My spirit felt bone dry. My desert days were fun, but they were corrupting. I was repulsed by the fact that I began to sift people out for their financial worth upon first meeting them. Sure, I wanted love and I wanted a family, but mostly I wanted to participate in the kingdom of God—*whatever and wherever that was*—that I wanted to know and understand. But the dark-colored lenses of money and power had obstructed the view.

Paris made me forget my existential troubles, if only for ten days. Betsy and I found a cozy restaurant near Notre-Dame for Christmas Eve dinner. We ordered traditional Christmas mussels with French bread and baby potatoes dipped in cheese fondue. I was hungry, so very hungry. We told old stories and laughed until our ribs hurt.

We stayed in a tiny, elegant Airbnb near the Latin Quarter. Each morning, we'd sleep in late and then dress up in our fanciest scarves and red lipstick to stroll through churches, museums, pastry shops, and whichever direction the chilly wind blew us. "Life's too short to *not* wear red lipstick," we'd say giddily while getting ready for the day.

I bought a gray felt hat with an evergreen ribbon at a vintage shop and received the Compliment of the Year from a Parisian woman on the street who pointed and declared, "C'est magnifique!"

My bones and my blood had a hard time adjusting to the cold winter air, having acclimatized to the desert, but I was a new person—and a little bit warmer—in that magnificent hat.

My business brain had a hard time shifting gears to flourish in a world where time wasn't money. Betsy had always been that friend who forced me to slow down and really taste things. She photographed manholes, savored her croissants at a snail's pace, and could find beauty on the head of a pin. I'd tease her for dillydallying or wanting to idle in a particular place, but she understood better than I did that the magic of Paris is somehow lost when things are rushed. What was time in a city where you could completely lose yourself in a Monet or embody a character from a long-lost novel found in your great aunt's attic? I wanted to stay in Paris for months and explore every corner, perhaps learn to make the perfect macaroon, experiment with watercolors, or live like the wandering Lost Generation of the 1920s, writing my first juicy novel at the famous Café de Flore. With every turn of a side street, there were new steps to take and infinite possibilities.

Betsy and I did all the spectacular touristy stuff—the Eiffel Tower, the Louvre, the Musée d'Orsay, Montmartre, Jardin du Luxembourg, a cruise on the Seine, and a cabaret show—but the best attraction was the food. There is no substitute for basic, fresh ingredients seamed together by centuries of experimentation for the perfect balance of salty, acidic, bitter, and sweet. Every time we felt too chilled, we'd stop at a cozy café for a flaky pastry and a *vin chaud*—hot mulled wine with a hint of spice.

For New Year's Eve, we were invited to a house-party celebration given by Travis's old French roommate, François, and his young and eclectic group of friends. For dinner, the host cooked *poulet au vin jaune et aux morilles*. Translation: slow-cooked chicken in a rich, creamy jaune wine sauce with nutty morel mushrooms and a side of sorcery. In other words, the best meal I've ever eaten and have never been able to re-create. Paired with a 1982 bottle of jaune wine, it felt surreal and serendipitous to be drinking something produced the same year I was born.

Ernest Hemingway has said, "If you are lucky enough to have lived in Paris as a young man, then wherever you go for the rest of your life it stays with you, for Paris is a moveable feast."[29] I was merely a visitor in Paris, but that meal was the movable feast that has stayed with me for life.

That night we sang, we danced, we laughed, we cried. My dehydrated soul was coming back to life again. A spontaneous trip to Paris with a best friend was divine, for pleasure is part of God's kingdom too. In the past, I'd feel guilty for indulging in pleasure for pleasure's sake, but that trip made me see it as holy and necessary. I didn't have to be *doing* anything to be worthy, for merely *being* was enough.

I went straight to the airport from the party early in the morning, mascara smudged and hair wilted. Exhausted but high on life, I had a deep celebration buzz that's a hangover of the heart, and I wasn't ready to return to the sheikhdom.

The project was almost finished, but there were loose ends to tie up and more deals to close before Cambridge Reports would be satisfied and let me off the hook.

I shuddered at the thought that the company owned me. There was no going forward or backward or left or right until they decided it was time. I felt like I had become their indentured servant with a glamorous lifestyle. My life wasn't my own—I belonged to them, as if I were a piece of the organizational machinery and not a person.

* * *

It was almost time to board the plane when an adorable French couple caught my eye. The woman was sitting in the man's lap, and she kept kissing his face whenever she got the urge. They weren't shy about their public displays of affection,, and the sight of it was still a culture shock for me coming from the UAE, where such behavior could land you in jail. I tried not to stare, but I couldn't stop noticing their love and feasting on it with my eyes. It appeared to be both a burning hot fire and a sustained flicker fed by years of mutual kindling.

I noticed their two tots running up and down the gate aisles. The little boy, about four, had a mask over his eyes like Zorro, and he kept pulling it on and off to make his little sister squeal. Then he'd put it on her, and she'd take off running, him following behind giggling. The lovebird parents couldn't be bothered to chase after their unruly children. It was their vacation too, and they were undaunted by capricious childhood on display. I was beguiled by the sheer beauty and goodness of it all. It was a thin moment in an airport with random strangers.

"God, I would like to have this someday," I said in earnest prayer that reflected my deepest longing. It was the first prayer with words I had said in a very long time.

CHAPTER 21

AT LAST

Dubai

Returning to RAK after my Parisian sabbatical felt like going back on a diet after Thanksgiving. Going to the moon might have felt more natural. But I was excited to see Travis again; he was coming to meet me in Dubai for an entire week. He had just completed a deployment to Al Udeid Air Base in Qatar, just a half-day's drive away, but once again, the military made him fly all the way back to Arkansas and in-process before he could return to the Gulf again for vacation.

I wore my very best little black dress to pick him up from the airport.

We checked ourselves in to the Marco Polo Hotel on the scruffier side of town—the old-market district along the water, called Deira. Unlike the glittery, opulent Dubai with gleaming skyscrapers and luxurious real-estate projects popping up on every corner, Deira is the old Dubai along the Dubai Creek with smaller streets, crowded markets, and mosques in need of paint jobs. Wooden dhow boats piled with goods for sale circle in and out of the harbor, gold merchants pedal their wares in shockingly simple storefronts, and the scent of sizzling meat wafts from old shawarma shops that have been there since before Dubai was *Dubai*. Some would say it's the more charming and authentic side of town with traditional Emirati culture.

It's right up Travis's alley, but on his first night, he insisted that we have dinner atop the Burj al Arab—the famed sailboat-shaped hotel that is the iconic image you'd see on postcards and refrigerator magnets. You can't just visit the hotel—you have to either be a guest or have a restaurant reservation. Guests are transported to the hotel in a Rolls Royce pick-up service and stay in a suite for an average price of $24,000 a night.

"What? Why?" I pleaded. It was out of character for him to want something so extravagant.

I tried reasoning with him. "Let's just get a shawarma. I promise it will not be worth it. Way too expensive. You'll be so disappointed at the fakeness of everything."

"Oh, C'mon! It's the most iconic thing here, like the Empire State Building. Might be cheesy, but let's do it anyway," he insisted. "And, I already made a reservation, so you can't say no."

We got all gussied up to go out. His handsomeness took my breath away. After being away from him for a while, I'd forget how striking he was, and then I'd see him in the flesh and my heart would literally skip a beat.

I pulled him in for a kiss, and he smelled different. "What is that on you?" I sniffed his neck up and down. He laughed nervously. It wasn't a bad smell or anything like cologne. I couldn't put my finger on what it was, but he was defusing a vibe that I had never detected before. Something was off.

We went to the Burj and confirmed our reservation in order to get past the red ropes just to get inside the building. You could see all the way up, like entering a giant kaleidoscope with geometric patterns of green, blue, and gold. I couldn't tell whether we were inside a peacock feather or a Jetsons cartoon. We took the long elevator ride to the top and found a seat at the cocktail bar as we waited for our table.

The cocktails were also from another planet. I ordered one with beautiful yellow and red ombre tones and a bobbing piece of rosemary that was on fire. The drinks were expensive, and Travis is cheap, but he slurped down two cocktails like they were water.

What is up with this guy? I thought to myself.

We were escorted to our table in a glass corner overlooking the vast Persian Gulf. The sun was setting, and we ordered another drink. Travis began asking questions about my next assignment: Oman. After RAK, I was headed to another country in the Gulf for a project that was supposed to last eight months.

"What do you want to do *after* Oman?" he asked me. The question caught me off guard. Travis just didn't talk about the future so casually. I sat stunned without an answer.

"Let me rephrase the question: What do you want to do with *the rest of your life?*" he asked me, sweat beading down his face. The shock of it made me answer honestly: "I want to be with you."

"Well, good," he said before letting out a tense exhale. He reached into his pocket and pulled out a small box. He got down on one knee and opened the box to reveal a sparkling diamond ring. With sweat dripping from his brow, he said,

"Natalie, I love you more than life. Will you marry me?"

It was surreal because I didn't see any of it coming. All the signs were there—the fancy location, the scent of nervousness on him, the way he slurped down the liquid courage. Friends who heard this story later have always insisted, "Oh, but you had to have had a clue, right?" The truth is, I didn't see any of it. It was the furthest thing from my imagination. In fact, I wondered if he might be breaking up with me. We had never spoken of "what next." The proposal was the Surprise of My Life.

Proposal stories are usually all romance. But what nobody talks about is the liminal space of the moment that feels a little bit like a death. There's tension in that shift of time. To say yes is to walk through a door into a future that will forever be altered. Even when it's wanted, something in us dies. Everything about my single life would inevitably change. I would say goodbye to my job with Cambridge Reports. I still wanted to work, but I'd be following him in his Air Force career, wherever that would take us around the world.

I didn't quite understand what that would look like, but I loved Travis and couldn't imagine life without him. So, I crossed over that life-altering threshold of time.

"Yes! Of course, yes!" I pulled his face to mine and kissed his nerve-wrought cheeks. He stood up and then slipped the ring on my finger.

"We're going to have a family together!" I said out loud, almost in disbelief. We hadn't even talked about kids.

"Yes. Yes, we are," he said, beaming. "I'm so glad you'll be the mother of my children."

"I can't believe this is happening," I kept saying.

Oh my God, oh my God, oh my God.

I immediately remembered the French family at the airport and cried. I could still see their faces and the clothing they wore. That random encounter was indeed a thin moment when I saw my future in them and knew in my deepest being that that would be us. I stopped believing in my own unworthiness and the curse that Mountaintop church dumped on me when they said I'd *never be blessed again.* That was complete bullshit.

The happiness of that moment has been forever fused into my DNA. I thanked the God of mercy and the God of second chances and the God of love for smiling down on me.

CHAPTER 22

HAKUNA MATATA

Tanzania

Our first test as a future couple came the very next morning. Travis had planned a weekend getaway to India to see the Taj Mahal and other sights in the golden triangle. He had originally planned on proposing at the iconic white marble mausoleum but chickened out over fear that the airport security would find and inspect the ring in his coat pocket.

We found the Emirates Airline check-in counter at the Dubai airport early in the morning. Travis slid our passports across the counter to the impeccably dressed Emirates Airlines attendant with red lipstick and gave me a wink. His wink communicated the relief we felt, having made it to the airport on time, and the check-in line had moved quickly. Soon we'd be relaxing by our gate.

"Sir, where's your visasssss?" hissed the posh Emirates lady with perfect red lipstick.

"Oh, I'm planning on getting it upon arrival," Travis said.

"No sir, you can't do that in India," she said.

"Well, I'm pretty sure I read on the State Department website—or somewhere—that I can just do it when I get there," Travis insisted.

"Well, you read incorrectly," she said. "I'm sorry but you can't go to India without a visa applied for in advance," she said firmly.

"Well, okay then." Travis looked over at me. The look of manly confidence from having a smooth, thoughtfully planned trip quickly gave way to one of shock, followed by dismay. I sensed a low-grade panic setting in.

"Should we go somewhere else?" he asked me.

"Yeah, why not?" I said. "We're here ready to go."

I was traveling with my fiancé with no calls from Tiffany to take for a few days, so it didn't matter if we were headed to Siberia—any place with my new fiancé was a good place.

"Where can we go today? Like, right now?" Travis asked the Emirates lady.

"On Emirates, it looks like Pakistan, Kenya, or Tanzania are your options for this morning.

Roughly an hour later we were on a flight to Dar es Salaam, Tanzania. We didn't have a clue what we'd do there, with no reservations and the wrong sort of clothing. We picked up a copy of *Lonely Planet Tanzania* at the gate bookstore and spent the whole flight reading up on what we could do there.

"I didn't wake up this morning planning on going to Africa," I laughed. But I didn't wake up the day before planning on getting engaged either. It all felt like a bizarre dream.

The Dar es Salaam Airport was hot, muggy, and crowded. It was also dark because they had lost power. We had made it to Tanzania, but soon learned that the visa had to be purchased in local currency. This wasn't part of Emirates lady's travel brief, nor did the Dubai airport ATMs carry Tanzanian shillings. Was this really the only way to get a visa?

"Yeah, mate," confirmed an Australian in line behind us.

Travis moved up the line and approached an official-looking person in a collared shirt. Travis disappeared, telling me to hold our place in the visa line. Turns out you actually can get into Tanzania without a visa if you just need to go to the ATM outside the airport.

We were almost out of the customs line when we were stopped by a man with a white lab coat standing at the customs gate who asked for our yellow-fever vaccination cards.

"Oh great, we won't be able to get into Tanzania either," I said.

"We didn't know we were supposed to get one," Travis answered.

The man looked at us up and down. "Where from?" he asked.

"USA," Travis said.

After a long pause, the man waved us through, "Okay, no problem. Welcome to Tanzania."

Once outside, we were hit by waves of heat and the stench of body odor. A barrage of men, each pandering for our tourist dollars, swarmed us outside the airport.

"Mount Kilimanjaro? Here, here!" a man said.

"Safari! Amazing Safari—elephants, zebras, lions—come, come," another said.

"Downtown! You go downtown!" another said.

"How 'bout Zanzibar. Anyone know how to get to Zanzibar?" Travis asked the crowd. He was still holding the *Lonely Planet* guide to East Africa in one hand, using his finger as a bookmark to the exotic island a few miles off the coast. One driver plugging his "Downtown!" route immediately said "Zanzibar!" and waved to get in front of the other cabbies. Then others joined in "Zanzibar, this way!" It wasn't so much an answer to a question as an echo of whatever Travis had said. Then the first cabbie stepped up his sales pitch, taking our bags from our hands and walking through the driver mob. We had to follow him.

Travis and I looked at each other and decided the man seemed legit enough.

"Yes," Travis said. "You take me there?"

We glanced at each other sheepishly, impressed by our ability to trust total strangers with no credentials other than the quick handling of our bags.

The man escorted us to his beat-up Pinto and drove us to a small plane lot. Our plane had room for six passengers, one pilot, and a single propeller twirling around the nose. I would have been nervous had I not been in a blissfully ignorant stupor with my pilot fiancé.

The pilot, who looked like a boyish Prince Harry, gave the copilot (who happened to be a passenger) a high-five, yelled something out his window, closed it, and the little propeller spun to life.

The toy plane took off like a bird and soared over the Indian Ocean. It was a short joyride. In fewer than twenty minutes we began our descent over pale gray-green waters hugging a jagged green island.

We hailed a taxi from the Zanzibar airport. "Where are we going, exactly?" we asked each other.

"Recommendations, sir? We need a hotel." Travis spoke slowly to our driver.

His eyes squinted on the sides, forming a deep crevice that tracked all the way down to the edges of a wide smile. He spoke in a crisp, Swahili accent. "What? You came all tha way to A-frica with a no reservation?" He chuckled.

"No, that's why I'm asking you," Travis replied coolly. "Where should we go?"

"I take you to Garden Lodge in old Stone Town," he said. "You like it there."

"Great. Thank you!"

"Hakuna Matata!" he grinned and laughed again. He wasn't trying to be cute. *It means no worries*, as the Lion King taught us, and on Zanzibar it seemed to be thrown around like the most important spice in a big cultural cauldron that includes Arab, Persian, Indian, and European influences.

Hakuna Matata was the mantra we needed for our impromptu trip to Africa. It softened all the edges of my fears. It was perfect for two young souls who barely knew each other, lying on a beach discussing their future life together.

We got settled into our simple, clean hotel and set off to explore old Stone Town, the UNESCO World Heritage city where the buildings are made from coral taken from the sea. The stone and shell buildings were badly eroded as if the sea were trying to reclaim its long-lost children.

The wooden doorway and window carvings boasted an elaborate history of trade, art, and luxury. Some looked more Swahili with a filigree of tropical swirls, leaves, and twisty doodles. Others looked more Islamic with geometric and studded patterns and tiered windows. Still others looked more European with Corinthian columns and perfect symmetry. Those doors and windows had seen the collision of cultures over the centuries all in the hot pursuit of commerce. In its biggest heyday, Zanzibar was a trading center for spices and slaves, controlled by Oman in the nineteenth century. As I would later find out with my upcoming project in Oman, many of the traditional fashions in Zanzibar were the same as they are in Oman, the men in dishdashas and small, round hats for a casual look and cashmere turbans for a more formal occasion.

The sun was setting, casting shadows on the dusty streets. Stone Town was stunning, but there was a palpable sadness that hovered in the shadows, maybe an atmospheric hangover from years of the slave trade under Oman's control. It was as if the earth and those old buildings hadn't forgotten the sins of man that took place on its land.

"The landscape has a secret and silent memory, a narrative of presence where nothing is ever lost or forgotten," said poet John O'Donohue of the Irish landscape.[30] The same was true in Zanzibar. If those beaches and those shell walls could talk, they'd recount the horrors they once saw.

Today, Zanzibar is an important historical and tourist spot with a melting pot of cultures.

We learned to say "Jambo," which is the Swahili greeting for "Hello." The locals say it exuberantly with wide, sincere smiles.

"Jambo!" a shopkeeper said catching our eye. She was peddling wooden voodoo masks and bold African prints in bright oranges, fuchsias, yellows, and blues, so we stopped for a wardrobe update since all I had brought were jeans and two sweaters meant for northern India in winter.

We changed and found dinner at a rooftop restaurant overlooking the eastern coast of Zanzibar. It was the time of day when the stunning beauty of sun-meets-moon was nearly over, and the satisfied twilight was melting into darkness. The Indian Ocean was a vast cadet blue mirror, unusually still and smooth. We ordered grilled fish and a couple of Tusker beers and exhaled deeply for the first time that day. The gas flame candle danced between us, and we laughed at our surreal setting. Just one week prior I had been freezing in Paris talking with Betsy about the possibility of her getting engaged when her boyfriend arrived there. Never once did I think it would be me.

How quickly my life was shifting. It was as if my seed of curiosity and imagination had taken root, and a tender bud had formed. Travis held my hand under the table—a habit we started in the Middle East—

and told me what a lucky man he was. I had a hard time believing that; I was the lucky one. Sure, I didn't need a man to sustain me, but the loneliness of my life as a nomadic woman and the longing for a life partner had eaten away at my soul.

I had begun to see God as less of a punitive old man who wanted to smite me and more as a loving mother who sung over me and wanted good for my life. I knew in the deepest part of my heart that God rejoiced in the love and adventure that Travis and I shared with each other. God saw us as *good*.

I began to believe in the God of the backup plan.

If God isn't in the detours of life, where can God be found? The main roads and the perfect plans are not the paths of our biggest growth. What comes after shame or failure is a good mother pouring mercy over everything and whispering, *It's okay, love. It's really all going to be okay.*

***

Turns out there was more to explore on the spice island than we could manage on foot. The next day we saw a sign that read "Scooters for hire." We gave a man our money, and he escorted us to an open field where we could learn how to operate the manual motorinis.

How hard could this be? I thought.

Travis caught on right away, gleefully doing figure eights in the big field like a kid with a new video game. I, on the other hand, had a series of "game overs" in the bushes that made the instructor's eyes widen and his mouth grow taut.

"Sir, I want your money," he told Travis, "but I don't want a disaster. I give you car instead, same price."

We drove away in an old but sturdy Suzuki SUV feeling more confident about our life choices. We headed north and wound our way through red dirt roads and sunny spice groves before ending up on the western coast. The sun was setting over a pale green shallow sea that seemed to go on for miles. We plopped down in the white sand, alone on the beach except for a group of little girls with hair cut close to their scalps and cotton floral dresses. They ran in wild zigzags, making patterns in the sand with wooden wheels on poles.

"Let's stay here tonight," we both agreed. We found a quaint, Italian-run hostel called Paje by Night. But after our frolic in the ocean, we were reminded that time ticks differently in Africa. There was no running water in the hostel, and we had to wait hours for the water to be turned on again for us to have a shower. Energy is scarce in Tanzania.

We passed the time by sitting at the hotel bar in our towels and swimsuits, sipping a "Love Infusion" cocktail, which consisted of cinnamon, ginger, hot paprika, Captain Morgan, Kahlua, and dark chocolate. We made friends with the guy next to us, Johann, a Swedish gospel singer with one blue eye and one brown eye, also waiting on a shower. Zanzibar had a way of making time stand still long enough to make a connection with a total stranger.

Hakuna Matata, Cheers!

The water eventually came back on. We got ourselves cleaned up in time for an African curry dinner and an early bedtime. The sound of the ocean just outside the room was too delicious. The swooshing waves, the breeze coming through the window, and the ceiling fan overhead lulled me to sleep. Around midnight, I awoke to a pitch-black room. The large ceiling fan had stopped spinning, and the generators had ground to a halt. The power was out again. I couldn't see my hand in front of me. The moon outside seemed to have completely disappeared. I wanted to panic. Silence, stillness, and darkness are scary as hell when they are thrust upon you. Or maybe it was one too many Love Infusions. Like being blindfolded against your will, the lack of control is unnerving. The darkness was suffocating and made my heart beat hard and fast.

Hakuna Matata. I took some deep breaths.

Hakuna Matata. I am not afraid of the dark.

Hakuna Matata. I can't see where I'm headed in my new life either, but I know Mother God is there with patience and mercy.

Hakuna Matata

Hakuna Matata

Sleep.

* * *

Hakuna Matata was under our skin. It was a seed planted in our conjoined hearts that set us on a hopeful path for what we wanted our lives to be.

My faith deconstruction and reconstruction would continue. Getting more comfortable with Brother Doubt and learning to appreciate him—that was still happening. Pitching a bigger tent to house my faith in the divine—not going anywhere. But having a partner in my corner to go down that journey together made it a little less scary.

We navigated the things to come for the first time in our lives on the white shores of Zanzibar, where we let go of our fears and all the unknowns of life and embraced grown-up curiosity that, at its deepest roots, was love.

Dear Late Twenties Self,

I'm so proud of you. You're a grown woman now, tall, confident, and comfortable in your own beautiful skin. You've let go of caring about the expectations people thrust on you, the ones that chip away at your soul and leave you empty, and you're learning to listen to your divine inner voice. Stay on the path, you can trust it.

You're in God's beloved family, and I'm sad you ever doubted that for a second. Keep looking for all the places the upside-down kingdom is manifested in the margins and align yourselves with those people. Let them be your teachers.

That man of yours—love him deeply. Revel in the days of fresh minds and toned bodies ablaze. Go on as many wild adventures as you can before the babies come. You've been apart and you're still a little afraid of shifting gears into a new life, but you've found the best partner and soulmate to share your days with, so don't be afraid of big love.

You're going to be wearing new hats in the years to come. It's okay that it feels awkward, and you'll feel like you've lost a part of yourself. But believe me when I say: you're the same soul, just in new skins. It feels scary at first, but you're going to find a new dimension of yourself that's beautiful and generous—lean into it. It's okay to go off-brand for a season and be surprised by the gifts you'll find along the way.

Any lingering shame you have for your past failures, your doubts, or your faith crisis—you need to throw it out with yesterday's doughnuts. Have mercy for yourself. The journey you are on is nonlinear and unpredictable: sometimes smooth, sometimes rocky, sometimes foggy, sometimes murky, and sometimes beautiful. But it's all sacred. Focus less on the agony of the unknowns and more on the delight of curiosity.

Love,
Your Late Thirties Self

THE PART III
River

Part of my ongoing priesthood
is to find the bridges between
my faith and the faiths of other
people, so that those of us
who draw water from wells on
different sides of the river can still
get together from time to time,
making the whole area safer for
our children.

—Barbara Brown Taylor, *Holy Envy*[31]

CHAPTER 23

TURN, TURN, TURN

Tokyo, Japan

TWO YEARS LATER

It's easy to be fooled by the shiny skyscrapers, bullet trains, and high-tech gadgetry, but the deeper truth is that Japan is ruled by seasons. Spring, summer, winter, and fall—all four seasons are distinct and glorious on Japan's main island of Honshu, my new home.

Exactly two years had passed since I left Cambridge Reports and was awkwardly thrust into military life. Mama thought she was getting her daughter back when I married Travis, but right before our wedding he found out he would be reassigned from Little Rock to Yokota Air Force Base in Tokyo. It was an adjustment: the abrupt ending of a fast-paced career, becoming a military spouse, moving in with Travis, moving around the world again, and figuring out what life would look like in those new skins.

In my new season of life, I was learning from the Japanese to embrace seasonal change as deeply sacred. Seasons are the evidence of spirit that is never stagnant: a river that shouldn't be wrangled or co-opted for our selfish endeavors but embraced, enjoyed, and nurtured for the good of everybody. The turning over of the old and welcoming the new—like death, burial, and resurrection—is a cyclical view of the world that goes hand in hand with the way Japanese culture strives for harmony and cherishes renewed beauty.

We pretend to be seasonal in America, but only when it's convenient and cute (pumpkin-spiced lattes! candy-corn M&Ms!). But most of us could have any fruit, vegetable, or flower any time of the year, which leaves us overly indulged and impatient. We often fail to see that there's goodness and divinity in change itself and there's virtue in waiting for the arrival of things in due time.

The most celebrated season, and what Japan is famous for, is the *Hanami* season, or the ten-day window when the cherry blossom, or *sakura* tree, performs her magic and casts a spell on each resting person in the shade of her branches. After a cold and snowy winter, grace bursts forth in the form of tiny white petals in the shape of a star that turns pinkish against a gray sky. The parks and sidewalks are littered with bits of delicate lace that begin falling from the sky like the snowfall of spring, nature's confetti. Known for their long work hours, the Japanese somehow make time to drop everything and embrace the long-awaited arrival of the sakura blossoms. It's a celebration of a sacred beauty that's painfully fleeting. It's a celebration of the regenerative power within the earth. Year after year, light grows, and new things are born.

Hanami is the art of simply sitting under the sakuras for a picnic or a nap, sometimes for hours at a time, with groups of friends or family, or alone. This centuries-old practice dates back to the Heian and Nara periods (710–1185) and is still widely practiced today throughout Japan every March or April, when the sakuras arrive unannounced.

After the strawberry and sakura seasons of the spring, tulip season parades in with its bold, bright colors, followed by azalea season, peaches-and-plums season, and a late summer hydrangea season when the temple gardens come alive with blue and purple puffballs, dewy from the misty rainfall. Finally, autumn marches in boldly, electrifying the air, fresh, vibrant, and positively charged. Waxy orange persimmons pop up in markets and backyard trees. Apple orchards are harvested, baskets sold on the side of the road in the countryside. In October, the orange Osmanthus, or sweet olive blossom, perfumes the air for miles with its sweet, earthy scent. Japanese maples turn into burning bushes dotting the countryside. Tall and mighty ginkgoes burst forth with scores of bright yellow leaves. The humidity from August and September dissipates, and what's left is a dry zing that puts static in your hair and a pep in your step and makes you want to dance through the flashy streets of Tokyo with a new current of energy.

It was during the glorious fall season, my favorite of all, when my belly swelled to the size of a pumpkin waiting on the birth of my son.

It was the auspicious Year of the Dragon, and I was told by Japanese friends that I was especially lucky to be having a baby boy during that year. I was afraid to talk about the pregnancy in terms of luck and fate, as we just wanted to have a healthy baby. Our road to parenthood, still being newlyweds, and adjusting to life together on the same continent—under the same roof—was marked by highs and lows.

The previous December, I had had a surprise pregnancy that ended in a miscarriage. Travis had a surprise deployment two weeks after the miscarriage, and I had found myself on an emotional roller coaster that came to an abrupt stop, leaving me feeling alone and empty at Christmastime, miles from home. The need to lean on community, strangers that had become fast friends, carried me through.

After so many hot, desert days, the Land of the Rising Sun was an oasis of freshness and renewal, but the culture was the most inspiring. The Japanese are among the most mindful in the world. The social responsibility to be considerate of others is unmatched anywhere else. There's a standing side and a passing side on the escalators. Japanese people queue up quietly and wait patiently for one another. Driving is easy because everyone predictably stays in their lanes, uses turn signals, and politely passes when needed. If someone feels that they're coming down with a cold, they'll voluntarily wear a mask to prevent other people from getting it.

Being in Japan is drinking from a deep well of beauty—ancient yet familiar, untouchable yet present. The Japanese are hypervigilant in their care for their neighbors, usually with an earnest smile. I couldn't help but compare them to my fellow Americans who are hell-bent on individualism at all costs. *How can it be that a country that isn't "Christian" is better at neighborly love?* The thought unsettled me.

This is not to say that Japan is flawless and doesn't have its own social problems: a disproportionate suicide rate and an exhausting work culture, for starters. But the essence of the people and the culture was good. I could see the light where the light wasn't supposed to be.

Japanese love to use the word *kawaii* to dote over things that are cute and cuddly. They have an obsession with mascots; not just sports teams: there's a fluffy bird, cat, or whimsical character with big eyes for each prefecture, historical site, and popular local dishes, among others. "Sex sells" seems at first a universal marketing axiom, but in Japan, *cute* sells.

Critical thinking isn't lacking in Japan, but cynicism is. They may be the least cynical culture I've known. Japanese people are quick to show up to the costume parties and cheerfully play along in activities that might elicit eye rolls and sighs from other cultures. It made me notice all the ways I had grown cynical and reluctant to participate in social functions on the base that required commitment.

The first couple of years, I somehow managed to dodge the bullet of getting involved in the Officers' Spouses Club, which was basically the junior league for the military. They were such do-gooders with their fundraisers and theme parties, raising a heck of a lot of money each year for high school kids' scholarships and community needs. I still found ways to justify my lack of desire to participate—namely, being bothered by the fact that there were two clubs: one for officers' spouses and one for enlisted spouses. If you're not familiar with the military, there's a significant rank and pay gap between the two groups. The pecking order trickles down to the spouses (mostly wives) who often wear their husbands' ranks on their sleeves. The club looked like fun, but having just come from working under Tiffany Shrill, I was leery of voluntarily subjecting myself to any catty or passive-aggressive leadership.

Instead, I spent my days wandering the streets of Tokyo (either with friends or alone) and teaching English to a group of toddlers and another class of retirees. I learned pretty quickly that just because you can speak English doesn't mean you can teach it. It gave me a new respect for those who teach for a living. Especially those who teach young children. It's the hardest job in the world, and I wasn't very good at it.

Still, my retirees were gracious and patient with me. They impressed me with their love of *hobbies*. They loved saying the word *hobby*, and they loved talking about their hobbies. Most of them were the same age as my grandparents, but they talked about hiking mountains, dancing, biking, and singing karaoke. One lady had recently taken up blowgun shooting. She loved demonstrating the proper firm stance and how it looks putting the dart gun up to your mouth. They were active and curious and deeply passionate about life and learning new things. I had taken over the class when an actual college professor had to leave. With my lack of experience and curriculum to offer, the class evolved into not much more than sitting and talking over tea, but I felt like they enjoyed me, and I could have listened to them for hours.

Sometimes we'd get into heavy topics like World War II. Many of them were old enough to remember it. It was difficult to imagine that, within their lifetime, our countries were once enemies. They had lived through the horrors of two nuclear bombings and were part of the generation that shared the collective trauma of having to rebuild their lives and their land after unprecedented destruction. And there I was living on a military base that had once belonged to the Japanese but was taken over by the United States when the war ended. By any measure, they could have seen me as their enemy. But those kind and gracious people in their seventies, eighties, and nineties delighted in our weekly conversations, always interesting and meandering, over spiced cake and oolong tea. It perfectly illustrated to me how the worst of enemies could become friends, given the space of a generation and enough conversations over good food and beverage.

I taught until the day my belly was about to explode, and my portable oven could no longer tolerate the overly heated classroom. On my last day, the class presented me with an adorable designer baby towel set. Yoshi, the only man in the group, gave me a special demonstration of how to wash a baby using a paper cardboard cutout he had made himself. He carefully showed me how to cradle the baby's head to make sure you don't get too much water in the baby's eyes. His earnestness and sincerity, like Japanese culture as a whole, was enough to make me cry like a baby when it was time to walk away from that job.

* * *

Henry Wyatt Patton came a week early on November 5, 2012. It was an emergency induction, but the Pitocin kicked in ridiculously fast and he was out a few hours later. Travis had sneaked out to get sandwiches from Subway, and I was worried that Henry would be born while his dad was deciding between Sun Chips or Baked Lays to go with our cold-cut trios.

I've talked about "thin places" in this world; birth itself is a thin moment. Having a front-row seat to the Mystery and becoming a human conduit of divine light and energy is a thin moment of divinity within the pain and mess of life.

Henry was a perfect red wrinkled new potato. His squished face was a miniature version of Daddy. His vocal cords were uncoordinated for the first six months, and he had a squeak that made him sound like a baby piglet when he cried or nursed, which was painfully difficult for what seemed like forever. Our little "Squeaks" was my heart and soul in the form of a tiny boy. I'd cry just looking at him.

I held him close, smelled his fuzzy head, and I knew I was in big trouble.

In Portuguese (and some other Romance languages), the word used for giving birth is *dar à luz*, which literally means to "give the light." As I lay in the hospital bed under the florescent lights of a no-frills military-base hospital, I saw the sacredness of my own body, being a vehicle for passing on the light from its original source—the heart of God, *love itself*, onward from one generation to the next.

As the prologue to the Gospel of John says, the true light through which everything was created and who gives light to everyone came into the world in the form of a human—Jesus. The light that is within us that makes us love and have empathy, care, and mercy for each other is *good*. The love I had for Henry and the love my parents had for me was also the love of Christ.

But I was in trouble. Nothing I had experienced was compatible with the dominant shame-based theology. There were deep stirrings that began during my time in the Middle East that I was never able to articulate, never able to completely flesh out. As I held my perfect son in my arms, a thread began to unravel.

I was still trying earnestly to salvage my evangelical "elevator pitch," to borrow a phrase from author and pastor Danielle Shroyer.[32] Our well-rehearsed understanding of what the gospel means is some version of this: *You're born evil and separated from God by a deep chasm of sin. The only bridge to God is through Jesus.* I had always believed that our true self could not be trusted because our core is evil and despised by God.

As if life itself doesn't beat us up enough, on our day of rest we go to church to get flogged by the man in the pulpit who reminds us how wretched, filthy, and broken we are. Entering confusing and vulnerable adolescence, a time when even more mercy and compassion should be bestowed, we're treated to more shame since we've passed the nebulous "age of accountability," or what some churches have created to soften the notion *you're born evil.* Many Christians have decided this is around age twelve or thirteen, when a child has crossed the threshold from innocent to guilty. In one precarious season of puberty, a child goes from being assured of eternal bliss to dangling over the fire of eternal conscious torment, unless she performs the appropriate ritual of repentance and salvation. We agonize whether we said the prayer correctly so that God would turn his gaze on us and assure our spot in heaven. Then we grow up and pay good money supporting institutions that continue to verbally insult the core of our being, like an abused person who returns to an abuser because they lack self-worth and agency. The fruit of this theology isn't love of neighbor or compassion, but anxiety, self-loathing, and intolerance for others who believe differently.

Where does this take on the Holy Scriptures come from? Our elevator pitch isn't really the gospel; it's the doctrine of original sin, shaped and developed by St. Augustine in the fifth century and taught by most Christians in the West ever since. It tells us that God cannot look at us because of our fallen nature; we are born, some even say, as children of the devil.

Some modern-day denominations, including Catholics and Anglicans, have a more nuanced take on free will and original sin that does not eclipse the original blessing, but the notion of "total depravity" endures in Reformed theology and other evangelical circles.[33] I don't know how many times I've heard it said from the pulpit: *God cannot be in the presence of sin.* In fact, in the creation story in Genesis, it is Adam who hides from God when he sins, not the other way around. But the idea that God detests his sinful creation and cannot look at us has pervaded our consciousness and haunted Christians for centuries. The doctrine of original sin assumes the first sin, committed by Eve, somehow stained human DNA, and these first humans passed this flawed DNA down through all of humanity. So, each new birth is a baby who's flawed, sinful, evil, or in Arkansas parlance, "hell-bent."

Original sin is based on just five biblical texts, and scholars have argued that three of the five came from inadequate Latin translations, most notably Romans 5:12, which says all individuals sinned through Adam. But this passage in the original Greek describes sin as a "cosmic force burdening all humanity in general rather than being born uniquely in each individual."[34] This is why original sin never got off the ground in the Greek world and in Eastern Orthodox theology.

Certainly, not everything can be pinned on Augustine, and there are parts of his writings that Christians continue to find useful, or at the very least—literarily significant. Nonetheless, learning about the doctrine of original sin sent me down a rabbit hole trying to understand the man who set the trajectory for centuries of church history. As I had learned from my own peregrination, I believe the stories of our lives influence the way we see God as much as our cultural and religious heritage do.

Augustine was born into an upper-class family in Roman-ruled Northern Africa. His father was a pagan, and his mother a devout Catholic. From an early age, he was gifted with a brilliant mind, and his parents sent him to school in Carthage. There, he fell in love with a lower-caste woman whom his mother despised. The couple had a son and lived together for thirteen years. Augustine wrote that he "loved her dearly" but ultimately was pressured by the culture of the day and discarded her to fulfil his mother's wishes of wedding his proper match: a Catholic heiress, just ten or eleven years old. The wedding was delayed for a couple of years to give the girl time to mature. As his longtime mistress was sent away, she vowed never to love again.

Frustrated with learning how to suppress his sexual appetite for which his mother ridiculed him during adolescence, Augustine was tortured by shame and haunted by grief. "My heart which was deeply attached was cut and wounded, and left a trail of blood," he wrote. "My wound, inflicted by the earlier parting, was not healed. After inflammation and sharp pain, it festered."[35]

Augustine never married the girl. Instead, he converted to the Catholic faith, was baptized, and made a vow of chastity.

He developed a literal interpretation of the Genesis story of Adam and Eve that had previously been read allegorically by most Christian theologians. The problem of sin, a loss of innocence, and sexual temptation were the fault of Eve. Much ink has been spilled over Augustine's legacy (mostly by wistful, philosophy-loving men who are a bit out of touch, in my opinion), but I don't think the average Christian is aware of the harm that Augustine's contentious views have caused women and people disconnected from power.

"In order to be accorded *imago [Dei]* status, women must pay a price that is never required of men, namely, to become disembodied and degendered as women,"[36] writes Judith Stark in her introduction to *Feminist Interpretations of Augustine*. She makes the case that he had the conceptual tools to extend equality, mutuality, and reciprocity toward women (and other theologians and philosophers at the time did so), but instead he denied the dignity and spirituality of women and opened the gates for misogyny in the church.

I don't know how much I can effectively get inside the head of a man who lived sixteen hundred years ago in a culture far removed from my own, but I imagine it was out of a grieving heart that Augustine concluded that women are the problem, as he sought to forget the love of his youth and declare that even a baby a single day old is a sinner. He wrote in his *Confessions*, "So the feebleness of infant limbs is innocent, not the infant's mind. I have personally watched and studied a jealous baby. He could not yet speak and, pale with jealousy and bitterness, glared at his brother sharing his mother's milk. Who is unaware of this fact of experience?"[37]

Wait, what?

A mother's heart is "unaware of this fact of experience." (And perhaps anyone else with an inkling of common sense.) Who really believes this about their own precious babes? How could I look at my perfect newborn son and not believe that he came from any other place than the very heart of God? And if I believed this about my child, why wouldn't I believe this about everyone else's children?

World travel had influenced my faith deconstruction, but motherhood was the biggest disruptor of all. These confused feelings were compounded by all the light and life I had seen in non-Christian people and cultures in Muslim Middle East and Buddhist Asia. I had found Jesus in all the places he wasn't supposed to be. In all the places that I was told were *dark* and *lacking the sanctification of the Lord*, I had found love and light, blessing and goodness.

This isn't to say that we don't sin, but when the starting place is original blessing rather than original sin, it changes everything. Original blessing hinges on the fact that God called his creation good. And not just mediocre good, but *forcefully good*, in the words of author Lisa Sharon Harper, who tells us about the translation of *tov me'od* in Genesis 1:31. The Hebrew understanding of this goodness was a goodness in the ties between things: humanity and God, our relationship with self, and humanity and the rest of creation.[38]

The divine image of God is written throughout creation and buried like precious treasure in humanity. The power to love, the power to create, the power to care for each other, and restore broken things to wholeness—this is the power of the human soul that is larger and more expansive than the body. The blessings we are looking for are already within us, at home at the "hearth of your soul," as John O'Donohue puts it.

And when we look for this light in our fellow humans, it changes the way we see our children, our neighbor, the entire world, and ourselves.

John Philip Newell, who writes about reconnecting with our "forgotten tune" deep within us, says this about the doctrine of original sin:

> It teaches that what is deepest in us is opposed to God rather than of God. It means that we are essentially ignorant rather than bearers of light, that we are essentially ugly rather than rooted in divine beauty, that we are essentially selfish rather than made in the image of love—the list goes on and on. It is a doctrine that disempowers us. It feeds our forgetfulness of the sacred tune at the heart of our being. And its corollary is the belief that Christ embodies a song that is essentially foreign to us. The consequences, both individually and collectively, have been disastrous.[39]

Why would the fifth-century church need to adopt Augustine's doctrine of original sin? What motivation would they have had for interpreting the Holy Scriptures through a lens that emphasizes the depravity of humankind? Around that time, the calling of the kingdom of God to be separate from the kingdoms of earth fell on deaf ears as the church and the empire became bedfellows. For builders of empire, it was also a convenient means of control to characterize the masses as ignorant rather than light-bearers. The church and government leaders could then become the keepers of the faith, wielding power and authority over a depraved congregation that relied on the church for the disbursement of Truth. It became too dangerous for the people to know they were independent light-bearers who could cry out to the divine anytime they wanted.

Pelagius, a fourth-century English-born monk who spoke Greek and taught in Rome and Palestine, rejected Augustine's doctrine of original sin and taught that "when we look into the face of a newborn child, we are looking into the face of God freshly born among us." He did not teach that we weren't in need of the grace of Christ but rather that Christ came to remind us of the forgotten tune that's deepest within us and restore us to our true depths.[40] Pelagius believed women should be taught to read Scripture independently, a legacy that remained in the Celtic church for centuries.[41] Augustine had Pelagius put on trial in Rome, and with a little bribery Pelagius's writings were destroyed and he was kicked out of the church and exiled to Egypt.[42]

I often wonder how many atrocities would have been avoided, how slavery would have been condemned far sooner, how much less pain and suffering would have been inflicted from one household to the next like a perpetual game of hot potato had Pelagius's teachings become church doctrine rather than Augustine's.

Like everyone else who's ever lived, Augustine was a man wrestling with his own demons and life circumstances as he sought an understanding of the divine presence and sought to be spiritually at home. He and his mother, Monica, have both been named saints, but I can't help but wonder about the spirituality of the lower-caste woman Augustine loved and discarded—the mother of his child, who, like Abraham's Hagar, was used, abused, unnamed, and sent to pasture. How did motherhood change her? How did she cope with a broken heart after losing her partner and son to the merciless demands of Christendom? Did she encounter *El Roi*, the "God who sees"? We'll never know such things because men with power write the history and the church doctrine.

Most importantly, I no longer see the gospel as a story about us being separated by sin from God. *Then what is the gospel*, you ask? The gospel is the Good News, the announcement that God created us good, loves us unconditionally by divine grace, and became flesh to dwell among us and remind us of his true nature. This is the stream of living water that allows us to exhale, restores us to shalom, and transforms us to deeper love and generosity. Shroyer says it best:

> It's the story of a God who is so faithfully *for* us and intent on being *with* us that God became human to help us embody the wholeness and fullness of life we've been made for. It's not a story of separation. It's a story of invitation and participation.[43]

Beginning with my own son, I began to see people differently. If I'm looking for the light in people, the Christ within them, rather than being quick to point out their dark nature or saying they must convert and adopt my brand of faith, it sets me free to love them as they are. I wondered if this is what the apostle Paul meant when he said for women, "Salvation comes through childbirth."[44] The love and mercy of a Mother God is so much easier to understand when the current of love is both received and then passed on from our deepest reserves.

∗ ∗ ∗

Soon, Henry was a rambunctious little toot.

As a new mom in an otherworldly culture, I was a fish out of water. With a husband gone half the time those first few years, my days of being thrust into motherhood alone in Japan were sink or swim. But when the cherry blossoms faded and the muggy Japanese summer rolled around, I caught myself in a full-circle moment.

Rather than going to the swimming pool on the base (which was usually crowded and salty), I found myself preferring instead the banks of the Tama River. Despite my childhood desire to belong to the pool instead of the river, the river forgave me and reclaimed me. It was the perfect space for my mini caveman who came alive in a way that was different from the pool. With wild abandon, he would throw rocks into the water with all his might. He would sit in shallow water for hours if I let him, his pudgy fingers picking up mud, rocks, leaves, and whatever bits of earth he could find. He was still young enough to know that the river was actually better. "As children we were naturally aware of— sometimes even spellbound by—the light that is in all things. But then it was educated out of us. And we began to forget."[45]

One of our most challenging spiritual tasks, then, is to strip away all of the layers of tarnish that have corroded our soul, darkened our true self, and caused us to forget our hidden life in Christ. Fourteenth-century mystic Meister Eckhart said that spirituality has much more to do with subtraction than it does addition.[46] Remembering childhood wonders takes us back to the place of our eternal participation in the divine. "The whole earth lives within us, and in every moment, we are both its creators and discoverers. We only need to reawaken all these early memories."[47]

I wondered if "river culture" is a counterculture that transcends time and place. A place where a moment of joy can be suspended over a moving current. A place where God's love is felt in the smoothness of the rocks, in the sunshine through branches, in cold, moving waters. It's layer upon layer of grace and goodness. It's no surprise that baptisms were traditionally done in rivers, following Christ's own baptism in the Jordan.

My full-circle moment awakened me to all of the goodness and grace around me that I had missed every time I clambered for the *imaginary variable*: that moment in time after I do/achieve/buy/have *fill in the blank*. It's the behavior that looks to the future at the expense of being blind to the present. I'd deceive myself when I'd think everything would just be all right if only I got my hands on it. The imaginary variable was a perpetual dangling carrot, a shapeshifting beast. The imaginary variable was an idol that would keep me from enjoying today.

More often than not, the imaginary variable turned out to be a chlorinated square in concrete, when the river had been in front of me the entire time.

I felt a bit like the older son in Jesus's parable of the prodigal son. When the younger, lost son who has squandered his father's money returns, he thinks his father will be angry, but instead the father sprints out to embrace him, slaughters the fattened calf, and throws a big feast to celebrate. The older brother sulks. He tells the father how faithful, how obedient he's been, and he asks the father why he never gave him the slaughtered calf or a big celebration. The father tells him, "My son, you are always with me, and everything I have is yours."[48]

In the words of Rob Bell, the older son was at the party the entire time and wouldn't embrace it. He created hell for himself by not showing up to the party right in front of him.[49]

How many years had I waited for my day to come, when I was already there to begin with? The country-club pool used to represent all the things I longed for but didn't realize I already had. I was also at the party already and didn't know it. The Spirit of God, who was with me in my early days on the banks of the Saline River, was with me in the driest days of the desert and with me in the trenches of motherhood too. The light that I had just passed on to my son Henry was also deep within me, an eternal well and an eternal friendship with Jesus who calls us friends. Jesus is the "first Other in the universe" and doesn't just enter us when we call on him, he is already the soul friend or "secret *anam cara* of every individual" whether they know it or not.[50]

Motherhood taught me to believe that I am enough—just the way I am. There was nothing my son could do to make me love him more. I love him because he exists. Sure, he'd be naughty and sinful, but his very essence is good and pure. In the same way, there's nothing we can do to earn the love and favor of God. God loves us because God created us. Goodness is our true nature. Blessing is our birthright. Love is our name.

How can the God who created the uni-verse, literally "one song," stop singing over us? The one verse is love.

How can a Mother God suddenly withhold love and mercy? In the words of Richard Rohr, you can't stop the "relentless outpouring force that is the divine dance."

> God is not *a* being among other beings, but rather *Being itself* revealed for any mature seeker. The God whom Jesus talks about, and includes himself in, is presented as unhindered dialogue, a totally positive and inclusive flow in one direction, and a waterwheel of outpouring love that never stops![51]

Just as the universe is ever expanding, I believe with all my heart that there is no end to the love and mercy of the God who created it all. Each day that unfolds in this life is another ride in a current of unceasing generosity.

Because of my rocky childhood and tendency to veer into codependency, at times I would struggle to maintain control of my surroundings. I'd cling to the big rocks in the middle of the river with all my might while the currents were rushing around me, rather than surrendering the things I couldn't control and allowing the current to carry me.

Motherhood was the life-changing force that beckoned me to slow down and try living a contemplative life. To seek silence, simplicity, and solitude whenever I could (even if that meant locking myself in the closet with a candle and a candy bar). I needed to learn this practice because everything else around me wasn't slowing down; it seemed to be speeding up. Living in Tokyo followed by a quick move to Washington, DC, followed by another move to Bangkok, having three kids in three and a half years, keeping the wheels spinning at home, keeping up with my real friends on Facebook and my imaginary friends on Twitter, and hearing from so many amplified voices at once—my attention became increasingly fragmented. Being pulled in a zillion directions, my ADD brain would be overly zinged most of the time. It was easy for the still, small voice of God to get drowned out in all the clamor. As the noisy ambience piled up the imaginary variables, one on top of each other, as the expectations rose, my soul would be left bankrupt.

But the gentle flow of the Tama River stilled my soul every time, calling me back to the heartbeat of God that was with me, inside me, over me, above me, and below me all along. The river took me back to my earliest days when I felt it without even having words yet to express it. From the love of my parents and grandparents at Mommama's round table, to the gushing currents of the Saline River and the pulsating stars on a rural Arkansas night, to the nudging waves at the beach, to the kindness of strangers and the vast sand dunes of Arabia to the drum beats in Asian temples, to the falling cherry blossom petals on my face, and to the steady back-and-forth of my rocking chair during a middle-of-the-night feeding—the heartbeat of God was thrumming along always, wooing me back to a loving God who held all of it.

"What then is the path to holiness?" asks Richard Rohr. "It's the same path to wholeness. And we are never 'there' yet. We are always *just in the river*."[52]

CHAPTER 24

MYSTERIOUS WAYS

Thailand

Nobody ever told me that each of my kids would have a unique scent. Maybe I was the only one in the world who could smell the crowns of their head as they grew and still detect the sweet, earthy scent of their babyhood. Our daughter Magnolia came in like a wrecking ball, born before my doctor could make it to a room that may or may not have been cleaned. She was big, beautiful, and strong like the tree of her namesake, and she smelled like a flower. She was still a baby when we moved to Bangkok, learning how to walk in the dark hallway of our hotel.

Travis got a job as an exchange pilot in the Royal Thai Air Force. We spent a fast and furious year in Washington, DC, where he learned Thai and I survived long hours with two under two. I loved my babies and being a mother, but just as we were getting ready to make an intercontinental move again (and the week of Travis's final Thai exams), I found out I was pregnant again. I had just sold off and given away all the baby gear the previous week. I kept the news a secret until Travis's exams were over, careful not to sabotage the test or give him a heart attack. It was an overwhelming, ill-timed *miracle*. Another move and another pregnancy would take its toll on my mind and body. We were in survival mode.

We arrived in Thailand in November, but it was still hot as blue blazes. It's always a steam chamber in Bangkok, except for two days of the year when the wind gods decide to have mercy. The smells of the street combined with my typical twenty-week "morning sickness" (what a misnomer; for me it was all-day sickness) made for a gnarly adjustment. The stench of fish sauce, spicy curries, chili peppers, piss, garbage, bus exhaust, and the *khlong*, or the polluted water canals, sent me hurling in the streets in front of street vendors, wide-eyed tourists, and my children.

"How's the exotic Far East treating you?" my sister would ask. And I would cry. I wanted to go home. But where was "home" exactly?

I lamented with another American friend in Bangkok that we were cheating our kids out of a "normal" childhood by living in such a gritty, dirty, wild city. Tourists flock from all over the world to seek out Thailand's pristine beaches, monkey forests, waterfalls, and national parks. But in the capital, the lack of green space, fresh air, digging dirt, and the great outdoors, made us ask about our children—*are we damaging them?*

After some thought, consideration, and taking up the lost art of reframing a life in order to retell our stories with grace, I decided that we were actually living in the circus. *And by golly, don't children love the circus?*

"Yes! That's it! Children love the circus." My friend and I sipped Thai tea at a garden café while ruminating on this new metaphor.

In my scruffy little corner of the city, tents sprung up at night selling everything from fidget spinners and Jesus bobbleheads to fake dog poop. Bright pink, yellow, and green lights blinked comically from the *tuk tuks* (three-wheeler rickshaws) that cruised up and down the side *sois* (streets). Fried bananas, sugar doughnuts, roasted peanuts, corn on the cob, and coconut ice cream stands lined the side of my street, always in our faces.

Our neighborhood featured a vibrant cast of characters: The aggressive fruit lady. The smooth Indian Sikh tailor with his curly mustache and magical turban. The tattooed lady who happened to be a man. The friendly toothless woman who slept under the subway escalator and sold her cobalt-blue doodle drawings with funny faces hidden in them. The plant peddler with his goofy grin and floppy hat. The taxi driver with hands full of enormous rings, a magic stone on each finger as if he were soliciting all the powers from the heavens.

Even the Bangkok city logo featured an elephant with a costumed rider holding up a three-pronged baton, as though he were a ringmaster declaring, "Step right up!"

Daring stuntmen on bikes alternated between the road and the sidewalk. This was especially fun walking my newborn baby girl Francina home from the hospital, weaving in and out of these whizzing devils. It was madness!

But I could only distance myself from the absurdity for so long before I caught myself joining the act, taking motorcycle taxis everywhere (without the kids, of course). At first, I'd sit stiffly, white knuckling the back of the seat and hanging on to the driver for dear life. But when stage fright died, I was part of the greatest show on earth, and it was exhilarating. Those same riders whom I once cursed for breaking the law and creating chaos—how soon I became one of them, gleefully whizzing down the sidewalk when I really needed to be somewhere.

Just like the circus, at the end of each night the spell would be broken, and the magic would dissipate to the sky along with the early-morning barbecue smoke and steamy noodle stalls. The side alleys smelled like animals and old dirty popcorn. Somebody was left with a mess to clean up, but the show would go on another day.

* * *

Thailand was exponentially harder for me to understand than I had imagined. There was an energy, *a flow*, that I couldn't put my finger on. I had no muscle memory for navigating this wild corner of the Far East. I had lived in Japan and Brunei, but Asia is not a monolithic culture. Each country and even region within a country are vastly different. Still, Thailand had an energy threaded together with other parts of Asia that made me consider the Far East to be a long-lost relative: a part of myself that I was meeting for the first time.

Time and space were fluid. Things might begin on time or they might not. Things might happen the way they were planned, or they might not. The cab driver might know where I wanted to go, or he might not. It frustrated me, especially that first year, that nothing seemed to be concrete or predictable. When people behaved mysteriously, it might've been over the need to save face, or to avoid the appearance of making a mistake in order to preserve dignity and social standing within a group. Thais value being *jai yen*, literally "cool hearted," more than anything. It takes a lot for them to get spun up about anything. Road rage is almost nonexistent, despite the horrendous traffic.

Maintaining balance and harmony are qualities that are elevated far above all else, which is a beautiful thing when compared with the hotheaded, sometimes violent West. But it becomes frustrating when tranquility is more valued than the need to be transparent, productive, or sometimes have the blazing cojones to get shit done.

As an American, I found the major difference in our cultures to be the indirect way they communicate in order to be polite. *May your yes be yes, and your no be no* is not the case in the Land of Smiles. The phrase *mai pen rai* is the most common filler and seasoning of conversation. It translates to be something like "never mind," "it's okay," or "no worries." It's a delicious phrase, charming in nature. But the subtleties of what it can really mean is usually picked up only by native Thais.[53] For example, if someone was asked if they wanted the last piece of pie, they might want to say yes, but instead they'd say, *Mai pen rai ka.* For a foreigner, they'd take this to mean "No, it's okay. You eat it." But if a Thai person were the one offering the pie, they might pick up on the person's hidden desire to eat the pie and subtle politeness in not wanting to be a bother, and they might continue to offer while also throwing in a *mai pen rai* of their own. It's a circular dance that is understood within the culture and the high value placed on having a *greng jai* attitude, or not wanting to trouble anyone.

The cultural differences were a struggle at first, especially for my military man as an exchange pilot. The phrase "winging it" took on a whole new meaning for him. But the Thais had an impeccable safety record, and somehow his planes took off, did their mission, and landed, and mostly on time. He was rarely late for dinner. Travis found a new family in the Royal Thai Air Force, and they gave him honorary golden wings to signify he'd become one of them.

But the cultural perplexities persisted, and it made me ask the question: Is Thailand living in a different consciousness? The differences were metaphysical—I can't "prove" any of them. But they were as real to me as my hand in front of me. It seemed as though Thais not only saw the world through a different cultural lens but also breathed a different kind of air and embodied an altered state of being.

I write about these differences not to portray them as any more or less human, nor to fetishize them. But I think there's so much to learn from the way they see the world. They do not dominate the world or even their region, so their pieces of humanity's puzzle are often overlooked. But they're valuable pieces of our collective wholeness, and they have something to teach us all.

Just watching them walk down the street and go about the daily grind looked remarkably different than it did in Europe or America. There was little hurry, less frenetic energy spent. It wasn't as though people walked around aimlessly without purpose or direction. But they swanned through town with an elegance and fluidity that seemed less driven by the rational and more by the intuitive. And it seemed to be similar among the different classes. Even learning to drive in Bangkok required a sharpening of the intuition. Nobody seemed to follow the rules, but how do you know which way the motorbikes will go around you; how do you know which way the chaos will flow? After being in the flow long enough for it to get under your skin, somehow you just *know*, and your intuition sharpens for your own good.

In *The Marriage of East and West*, English Benedictine monk Bede Griffiths explains that the difference between the East and West could be understood in terms of masculine and feminine energies, or what analytical psychology founder Carl Jung calls the *anima* as opposed to the *animus*.

I tread carefully here, so as not to feed into any Orientalist stereotypes of Asians being emasculated. But rather, I'm referring to the spiritual and the unconscious. Every human has qualities that are both masculine and feminine. In the masculine, the animus, or conscious reality, is dominant, and in the feminine the anima, or unconscious mind, is dominant. In the same way, the West is ruled more by the conscious or masculine or animus nature of being, while the East is ruled by the unconscious or feminine or anima nature of being.[54]

Again, this isn't to say that men in the East are more feminine and women in the West are more masculine, but rather the collective cultures are influenced by the masculine and feminine unconscious energies that dominate. In the West, the center of gravity is empiricism, rational thought, aggression, grasping, achieving, rigidity, action, and domination. Western clothing is drabber; the colors are more neutral. The architecture has cleaner, simpler lines. In the East, the frequencies are more intuitive, fluid, and receptive. The consciousness is attentive and open, like the image of a blooming lotus flower. The subconscious and unconscious mind is dominant. The colors are more vibrant.

I began paying attention to this vibrancy of color and fluidity in Bangkok. My children went to international schools, but every day on our walking commute, I'd take a shortcut through the Thai secondary school next door to our condo. I tried not to be too conspicuous a voyeur, but watching the flow of life and sense of community was fascinating. While my kids' education was overly structured, with every detail of their day mapped out, in a plush environment that was in some ways *exhaustingly woke*, the Thai kids in their open-air school with no air conditioning and a flooding problem possessed an unbridled joy and deep sense of community that seemed to be stronger and more authentic than what you'd find in the fancy-pants international schools.

The lines were blurred between work duties and play. Boys wheeled each other around in the dolly stolen from the supply closet, falling off and laughing when they'd go too fast. Girls told secrets from the tree house and decorated their own bulletin boards by the front gate. The same teacher that was also the Scouts leader and the PE coach could be seen deboning a chicken in the cafeteria, strumming guitars with boys after school, or giving a lecture to a group of those caught doing something naughty. Kids could randomly be seen mopping the basketball court or busy with sharp knives julienning a young papaya for som tam salad. Though a lot of my observations come from the fact that Thai public schools are underfunded compared with American and international schools, there appeared to be less structure and more *flow*. There was never a short supply of the spontaneous joy that emanates from unconscious, intuitive energy.

Life in the city was still life in the village. Bangkok has thousands of Western tourists and expats, but my little crew still drew attention everywhere like we had two heads on each set of shoulders. It got on my nerves the way so many people wanted to grab our kids' faces and hands without asking, but it sure came in handy when, say, we dropped something without realizing it or my kid was falling down the escalator and suddenly a jumble of arms and hands appeared out of nowhere to break their fall.

There was so much life and light in Thai culture: *the Christ already present*. But the expat church that we were attending never talked about this. Rather, they talked only of the darkness and "satanic hold" that was over the Buddhist culture.

In particular, the leaders of the church were dismayed by the Thai dependence on spirit houses, even for those who had converted to Christianity. Spirit houses were not Buddhist, but rather a tradition passed down from the indigenous animist religion that predated Buddhism. All over Thailand (and in other Southeast Asian cultures), small, ornate wooden houses that look like dollhouses are placed in front of homes and businesses as a blessing for the land that is inhabited and a shelter for the spirits so that they do not share the same space as humans. Remembering my tango with Charlie Bush, the quirky ghost in my Little Rock house, I was a big fan of the concept. Why not just build the ghosts their own houses so they do not share one with you?

Those same church leaders probably wouldn't have a problem with fairy houses (miniature houses we make with our children to leave in the garden for the fairies) and other holdovers from European pagan religion (see: most of our Christmas traditions). The most conservative, God-fearing homeschooling moms I know make fairy-house building a key component of their arts and culture curriculum.

"It's pretend!" you might say, but it's a perpetuated myth that we gleefully tell our little ones—and for good reason! It doesn't feel so "dark" when it comes from our own ancestral spirituality. It made me realize how things *foreign* are often conflated with *dark, evil, or satanic*. But the parallels of animistic beliefs of tiny spirits around the world are uncanny, and if anything, couldn't it be evidence of a universal Christ-consciousness—the divine infused in all the earth?

We had several friends who had come to Thailand as career missionaries, and they expressed their frustration at "making disciples" or converting Buddhists to Christianity. While I don't know the extent of their struggles and I do believe they had the best of intentions, it appeared to me that the starting place was—once again—original sin over original blessing. How confusing it would be when a Thai, who won't even squish a bug out of reverence for its life, is offered the heavy dose of Calvinism that says *we are rotten at our core, and so God killed his Son to pay for our sins.*

Here's the thing: they already knew *the Christ.* They were already deeply enmeshed with the life force that illuminates all things, fills the hearts of the people, makes the orchids bloom and the banyan trees twist and turn and dive back into the earth again. That thing that is the driving force behind the colorful, mosaic temples, the rivers and beaches and monkey forests, the sacred fire and water and the energy felt in the tinkling chimes and the drumbeat processions—*the Christ, through whom and by whom and in whom are all things*—cannot be imported; he is already known well throughout the land. He is always yearning in the hearts and minds of the people for a connection with the divine, with God the Father and God the Mother. "The Christ" is known, even without knowing his name as *the Christ.*

I wonder if the Good News would be more readily received if it were reframed in a way that gave reverence, honor, and credibility for what's already known to be true of a culture and religion. In the same way that St. Patrick spread Christianity in Ireland, not shaming the Celts for their ancient beliefs and practices, but rather adding on to the story that was already present within their hearts.

Nobody corners the market on God; there's never only one household of faith for those who are seeking the divine. As the apostle Paul says, "It is that very spirit bearing witness with our spirit that we are children of God."[55] and so it is that "man was created in this state of communion with God, and all ancient religion bears witness to the memory of this blissful state of consciousness."[56]

I couldn't help but think back to my very first mission trip to Peru as a teenager. I wanted to go back to see that the kingdom of God was already there. Jesus was already among the poorest of the poor in Peru, as he was in Thailand, and I would have been better off learning from them rather than trying to be their White savior. The shame tactics we heaped on those impoverished souls embarrassed me. What arrogance to say to someone who lives in the dirt without plumbing, "Your biggest problem is the dark nature of your soul that needs forgiveness!" The theological impact from the doctrine of original sin blinded us from seeing the image of God already dwelling in those people and in that community.

In the words of Richard Rohr, "From the very beginning, faith, hope, and love are planted deep within our nature—indeed they *are* our very nature (Romans 5:5, 8:14–17). *The Christian life is simply a matter of becoming who we already are.*"[57]

When missionaries come to the Far East to "bring Jesus," more often than not, they are not simply bringing their religion, but they are bringing their culture and their Western mind. The two are inseparable. And so communal worship, where we sit in rows and physically shake hands with one another, sing European hymns and American praise songs, and then hear a sermon that repeatedly highlights the violence of God: *it's lost on the East.*

In the religions of the East—Hinduism, Buddhism (both Theravada and Mahayana), and Taoism—the "powers of nature or the 'gods' are held to be subject to the one supreme Being, by whatever name it may be known,"[58] or the *Ultimate Reality.* The concept of Ultimate Reality may rattle the most studious Christian seminarian, but wasn't it YHWH who, when pressed by Moses to name himself, refused to be named and said, "I AM WHO I AM?"[59] Or, in some translations, "I WILL BE WHAT I WILL BE"? These theological concepts do not compete with one another, but they affirm each other. I've come to see Ultimate Reality and I AM as two beautiful trees side by side whose roots are lovingly holding hands.

In the East, the vehicle for encountering God is often silence, stillness, and yoga. Like the feminine state of consciousness, the mode of spirituality is receptive rather than dominating. The spirituality that is most valued and understood in the East is the *immanence* of God, where the "world does not exist apart from God but 'in' God; he dwells in the heart of every creature." In the West, a higher emphasis is placed on the *transcendence* of God, seeing God as separate from and above nature.[60]

Griffiths urges the Western church to reach out its hands and stretch its divine imagination in order to embrace the spirituality of the East and see where the roots of our trees intertwine, "if it is not to lose its own soul."[61]

The late American Trappist monk Thomas Merton died from a freak accident in Bangkok in the 1960s. The self-proclaimed hippie, poet, and "deliberately irrelevant" spiritual teacher who wore jeans and T-shirts instead of a clerical collar was on a tour of Asia to experience monastic life through a different lens. Coincidentally, I started devouring Merton's dangerous writings during my Bangkok days, and they gave me language for the beauty and Christ-consciousness I felt in Thai culture.

Some of Merton's last writings—found in his journal, published after his death as *The Asian Journal of Thomas Merton*—sought to bridge the religious divide between East and West. Rather than writing off Asia as "heathen" or "non-Christian," Merton had respect for the spirituality they practiced and called on the West to learn the patient and nonhurrying ways of Asia.

"My dear brothers, we are already one. But we imagine that we are not. And what we have to recover is our original unity. What we have to be is what we are,"[62] he said in an informal talk delivered at Calcutta before he died. I often wonder how his work would have played out if he had had more years to write and teach.

* * *

After a full year of struggling to understand Thailand, I let go to the point that I could jump in the river and begin flowing to the rhythm of the intuitive currents. The point at which I stopped resisting and embraced Bangkok for all her wild charms was the point at which I fell in love with the city and the culture. I quit bitching about who she was and who she wasn't, and accepted her for all her wild, mysterious ways. At the very least, life was more fun that way.

Ironically, I learned to be still inside this chaotic city. I took up yoga with a woman named Dodo who was a kind, healing spirit. She taught me to be gentle and caring of myself. I was learning to feel all around me sweet currents of mercy. The Holy Spirit goes where she wants, and though you won't hear it from an evangelical youth group, sometimes the Holy Spirit flows all the way to Far East meditation circles. I learned to say *Namaste*, and mean it, which is, *The divine in me sees the divine in you*. The practice of that taught me to look for the divine all around me.

I learned that when I was looking for the face of God, I'd find him or her. I'd put my earbuds in and listen to music while walking through the streets of the city. There were so many wild, wonderful, and wacky faces that passed me every day. People from all corners of the world, shining as lights, radiant with the fingerprints of God. *My goodness, human beings are so beautiful*, I'd think to myself.

There was a soup lady on my street whose soup was so nourishing it made me cry. Anytime I was sick or in a funk, I'd head straight to her wheeled cart and take my place in line behind shopkeepers and construction workers before ordering a steamy bowl of chicken and rice noodles in a rich bone broth with bean sprouts, cilantro, holy basil, and a hint of clove. I'd add a spoonful of her homemade chili vinegar and a few bumpy slices of bitter gourd. It would go down like nectar of the gods and leave me feeling entirely loved by a total stranger. Her soup told a story of centuries of rising and falling kingdoms, silk and spice trades, tropical breezes and family connection and sustenance. Her soup was divine.

I learned Thai cooking at a school in Bangkok's largest slum district, Khlong Toey. The school was founded by a woman named Poo (her

school and her cookbook were endearingly called *Cooking with Poo*)
who worked her way up from cooking on the street to going on book
tours in the UK and Australia, even cooking with celebrity chef Jamie
Oliver. Her growing school has remained in the slum where she got her
start; she employs its residents and uses a portion of her proceeds to
support other start-ups in the slum.

There was something deeply Christlike in the way Poo connected
people over food and built up her entire community in the process. I
saw it as a peek into the kingdom of God, where the last are first, the
table is wide, all are welcomed, and everybody is flourishing.

It was the subversive truth of the gospel—*kingdom come*. It was the
kingdom where the kingdom wasn't supposed to be. I found myself
wishing I had come to this realization sooner, but in the midst of my
self-loathing, I heard a gentle, almost audible voice whispering back to
me: *mai pen rai.*

CHAPTER 25

BLOWIN' IN THE WIND

Still in Thailand

During our first few months in Bangkok, my morning sickness finally dissipated, and I felt the need for adult conversation and time away from my tots. I hadn't made any friends yet, and with the nature of Travis's job, we were disconnected from the US Embassy. I saw an ad on an expat Facebook page looking for teachers to teach English to a group of Somali refugee women. I knew I was no superstar English teacher, but I reached out anyway and soon found myself in a hot classroom once a week with blank, eager faces staring back at me.

The school was run by the Fatima Centre of the Good Shepherd Sisters of Bangkok. The Fatima Center is the legacy of Sister Louise Hogan, a Catholic nun from Cork, Ireland, who came to Bangkok forty years prior with ten British pounds in her pocket and the mandate to start a mission. The center is known for helping disadvantaged Thai women in numerous ways—providing English education for adults, vocational training, employment making handicrafts, education for young children, a home for pregnant teenagers, and a shelter for victims of sex-trafficking. They meet the needs of Bangkok's poorest of the poor.

With the rising number of urban refugees, they added classes specifically for refugees in transition including English and classes that teach skills for future employment like dressmaking and hairdressing, and a school for refugee children. Bangkok is home to thousands of these refugees, who flock to the city illegally, usually by way of Malaysia, in order to register with the United Nations, apply for asylum, and get in the long pipeline of vetting and waiting in hopes of being resettled elsewhere. The majority of them are denied refugee status by the United Nations, and even for those who get their status, less than one percent of them are ever resettled to another country.

On top of that, Thailand says asylum seekers are illegal.[63] The country was not a consignee to the 1951 Refugee Convention; asylum seekers thus have no protection under the law. Even with UN refugee status, asylum seekers face harsh jail sentences—often with their children in tow—if they are caught without a visa. Bangkok's Immigration Detention Center (IDC) is home to hundreds of refugees living in harsh conditions with no end date in sight. My students were living in a constant state of fear of being caught and detained.

The Good Shepherd Sisters' refugee program was fairly new; I had no curriculum and no direction from the Indonesian nun in charge of the English classes, who barely spoke English herself. Just a scuffed-up dry-erase board and whatever worksheets I had stolen off the web were my tools. The women struggled to retain information week to week. Getting them to be willing to open their mouths and speak English words was an uphill climb.

My saving grace was Lolly, the Somali translator and a refugee herself. Her tall, elegant stature, air of dignity, gorgeous teardrop-shaped face, and bright smile belied the fact that she and her four kids were the only survivors in a family that had been murdered by Al-Shabaab terrorists. Belonging to the minority Ashraf clan, which faced tremendous persecution, she escaped Somalia via the UN and Jesuit Refugee Service and took her place with thousands in the vetting pipeline that included multiple interviews and so much waiting. The hope was that the anguish and the dangers they faced in their home country would end as they'd be reassigned to a new country. It was the promise of a future for her and her kids who had never been to a proper school. Lolly was an educated teacher by trade. She learned English from her father, a Russian-educated shipbuilder.

It was a miracle that Lolly escaped Somalia when she did. Despite her own impossible circumstances, Lolly worked tirelessly without pay to help those she considered less fortunate than herself to learn English in hopes that they would be better off when they were resettled in an English-speaking country.

It's hard to write about Lolly without crying. There isn't a single person who has shaken up my world and made me question everything about faith and God more than Lolly. Originally, I had hoped to be a Christian witness to her. Turns out, she converted me.

* * *

After Francina was born, I had to stop teaching. Having three kids under three and a half felt like treading water most of the time. My days were filled with so much joy and so much exhaustion. Somebody needed a changing, a snack, a time-out, or a hug at all hours of the day.

Lolly and some of my students were the first to visit after the birth with gifts and food in hand.

It's always a race in Somalia to be the first visitor to see a new baby. "We believe the first visitor will have an influence on their personality," Lolly explained, reaching for my newborn. She later came back and gave my house a rug-beating, floor-scrubbing deep clean after seeing how filthy it had become since our first attempt at hiring a housekeeper had ended in failure during the previous weeks. Lolly wouldn't accept any pay and insisted it's just "what you do for your sister."

During my first year in Thailand, my Somali ladies were really my only friends. I'm an insufferable pregnant lady, and I had a hard time connecting with the expat crowd. I was an outsider to the Somali world, but they graciously let me be an insider and a friend. Lolly and her kids started coming over on the weekends. There were few places they could go, as they were always on the run from the authorities. The possibility of being caught and thrown into the IDC was always looming, but so far, they'd gone three years flying under the radar as they waited with the hope of resettlement.

Lolly's kids played well with mine. Omar, her youngest boy, was a bright-eyed snaggle-toothed six-year-old who got along famously with Henry. Both chatty, outgoing boys, they loved being partners in crime and destroying my house. Her youngest girls, eight and nine, were both quick-witted and mature for their age. They loved playing with my baby girls.

Lolly's oldest daughter, Raina, a teen, was biologically her niece. She took Raina in as her own after her parents were also killed. Raina was tough-minded and bright. She'd adapted to Thai culture like it was second nature—spoke the language and got around town independently. Her biggest dream was to get an education and become a pilot. She was one of the top students in her class in Somalia, but she'd been out of school since they'd left when she was fourteen.

I'll never know the full extent of how Lolly made ends meet for her family. She worked odd jobs and received a few weekly food rations from Muslim charities. But usually when she'd contact me with a need, it was for somebody else rather than for herself. She told me about a woman with epilepsy who had been in the IDC for two years and was giving up on resettlement. She told me about a single mother with a little girl who had cerebral palsy and wasn't accepted into any of the schools. And she told me about Istahil, a sick woman on the brink of death with a lung disease who'd been locked up for a year. Istahil's illness was a major blow to the Somali community. They were so used to death, but in the final weeks of the woman's life, the community—many of whom didn't know her personally—sat by her side in prayer day and night, not letting her go a moment alone, until she passed away. Her case was already in the pipeline for resettlement, but having lived in cattle-like conditions at the IDC, without proper health care, she took her last breath before experiencing freedom.

Shortly after arriving in Bangkok, Lolly took on Bishaaro, a Somali teenage girl who had been trafficked to Malaysia by men trying to sell her kidney on the black market. Bishaaro escaped and fled to Bangkok, where she was dumped off at the 7-Eleven alone, scared and penniless. Lolly brought her into her home and cared for her like a daughter.

Lolly struggled way more than she let on, but her spirit seemed to be an unbreakable, never-ending well of hope and generosity.

Apart from motherhood itself, knowing Lolly and her community was the single greatest disruptor to my faith. Part of me still hoped and expected that Christians were the rightful guardians of *the one true faith.* I had still hoped that my real lived experiences would confirm what I was raised to believe: that we were *better.*

"Let them see the love of Christ in you," I could hear the Sunday school teachers of yesteryear say. But I'd get a sinking feeling every time I'd sit still enough to be honest with myself and admit to the very thing of which I was afraid: *We are no better. We are no better than anybody, anywhere.*

It was theologically perplexing and confusing that the most Christlike people I knew weren't Christians at all. They were devout Muslims who were meek and loving and humbled themselves to pray five times a day. I was ashamed that my children had seen them prostrate in prayer perhaps more than they had seen me with my head bowed. I couldn't think of a more righteous person than Lolly. Fruits of the spirit? She was crushing them.

Oh God, do you hear their prayers? I'd ask myself. *They do not pray in the name of Jesus, but do you hear them? Are you near them?*

When I read the Beatitudes, they were the pictures that would come to mind. Mourners who were poor in spirit, meek, merciful, hungering and thirsting for righteousness, pure-hearted, and peacemaking.

Knowing Lolly and her community shattered this platitude for me: *God won't give you more than you can handle.* If every tragedy in my otherwise privileged life is seen as a "test," then why are these people, also made in the image of God and doing their best to see his face, handed a disproportionate number of tests loaded with cruelty and suffering? The implication would be that they somehow *deserve* it or that they brought it upon themselves because they don't follow Jesus. But I wasn't buying that anymore, and there was nothing left in me to believe in a vindictive, transactional God who required merit.

Loving my neighbor as myself took on a new meaning. It caused me to repent of the sins of trying to be the rescuer. Lolly and company didn't need a pitying or condescending kind of love. They didn't need me to try to mold them into my image. They didn't need my brand of Christianity or my wayfaring faith that had become twisted and frayed. They didn't need to be my stepping-stones onto a higher plane of virtuous living. They didn't need me using them to try to heal my own broken bits of my soul.

My Somali friends simply needed me to love them as myself.

I came to understand that loving them as myself meant eating from the same table. Getting to know who they were. Listening to their stories. Finding out what celebrations were important to them. Discovering the happy places of their childhood and traditions. Seeing things of their culture that were truly beautiful. Being open to learning from them. Letting go of the pride that had hardened my heart in the belief that I had nothing to learn from my non-Christian neighbor.

Loving others as ourselves has little to do with being zealous about projecting our own personal evidence of a changed life onto others. It's not trying to make sure they see Christ in us. In the words of writer Beth Watkins, "Instead of asking, 'When they see me, do they see you?' I think a more important question to ask is, 'When I see them, do I see Christ?'"[64]

How different would the world be if we saw the face of Christ in the face of the hungry, the sick, the foreigner, the imprisoned, the lonely, the oppressed, and the forgotten? How would the light of the church shine ever more brightly if perfect love cast out fear as we declare, *Sit at my table. Eat my food. You too are loved and worthy of God's love and peace. You're already in the family. I welcome you, and even if you turn out to be a bad egg and do me harm, I'd rather die loving you than living in fear in my holy huddle.*

I wanted to know what Jesus meant when he said, "Blessed are the poor in spirit, for theirs is the kingdom of heaven."[65] Writer Alia Joy says that the word *poor* in this passage is of the Greek word *ptochos*, describing a destitute state of beggarliness:

It means being completely destitute of any wealth, resources, position, skill, influence, or honor. It is a helpless dependence that knows in itself, it is powerless, weak, naked, and empty. It literally translates to beggarly. It connotes nothing to fall back on. No other route, no short-cuts. No reputation to vouch for you or safety net to catch you because the bottom has already fallen out.[66]

Perhaps Jesus tells us to be close—physically close—with the marginalized because they help us to see a God who suffers with us. They help us to see his kingdom: a kingdom big enough and wide enough to gather up all the lost and forgotten sheep all over this big world.

My mind went back to the story of the dinner party in Luke where Jesus tells the host that he shouldn't just invite the wealthy, powerful, and influential, but also the kinds of people who can't repay him. The great irony is that in the upside-down kingdom of God, these are the kinds of people who often have the most to offer us. The kinds of people we avoid spending time with because they make us uncomfortable, Jesus calls blessed.

I believe the poor see God in ways that we cannot. They teach us what the suave, well-branded megachurch pastors with trendy eyeglasses and ridiculously expensive sneakers do not. Where there is suffering, he is there. Where there are tears, he is there. Where there are forgotten ones, he is there. Jesus told us in Matthew 25 that if we turn our backs on the poor and oppressed, we turn our back on him. But if we lean into the discomfort and sit with the people in the dark places, we see his face.

Thomas Merton says it like this:

The marginal person, the monk, the displaced person, the prisoner, all these people live in the presence of death, which calls into question the meaning of life . . . and the office of the marginal person, the meditative person or the poet is to go beyond death even in this life, to go beyond the dichotomy of life and death and to be, therefore, a witness to life.[67]

The only way I can say it is this: Lolly helped me to see God. My beautiful Muslim friend peeled back some layers and assumptions that had formerly clouded my view, to open up a divine side-curtain that I didn't know existed. Her divine mother love and her tenderness and faithfulness in the face of such impossible circumstances made me see that she was ever close to God's heart—a witness to life. The indisputable truth that I held in my heart was that *my God walked with her too.*

CHAPTER 26

IN A WORLD OF MY OWN

Angry in Thailand

> **Alice:** Would you tell me, please, which way I ought to walk from here?
>
> **The Cheshire Cat:** That depends a good deal on where you want to get to.
>
> **Alice:** I don't much care where.
>
> **The Cheshire Cat:** Then it doesn't much matter which way you walk.
>
> **Alice:** . . . So long as I get somewhere.
>
> **The Cheshire Cat:** Oh, you're sure to do that, if you only walk long enough.

—Lewis Carroll, *Alice's Adventures in Wonderland*[68]

My son Henry has a curious, dark streak like his mom. When he was a tot, we played in the graveyard across from our house for hours at a time. He's obsessed with black holes. He loves Roald Dahl books and Tim Burton movies. So it came as no surprise that he wanted to check out Lewis Carroll's *Alice's Adventures in Wonderland* from the library, complete with the first-edition original drawings by John Tenniel. They were scary as hell. When Alice grows, her neck is stretched like a telescope and her face looks like a doll in a horror movie. The Cheshire Cat does not have the friendly, inviting face of the cat in the Disney version. His grin is a little crooked and maleficent. His round eyes are piercing and hypnotic. The night after we read the first part of it, he woke up with a bad dream.

"What is 'curiouser and curiouser'?" he asked.[69]

I tried to explain the themes in childlike language, but the more we talked about it, the more I realized *Alice in Wonderland* is hardly a children's tale. Lewis Carroll had encoded a story for adults undergoing major life disruptions: a crisis of faith, a crisis of identity, or a crisis of belonging.

The election of Donald Trump was the final straw of my own faith and identity crisis. Knowing that 81 percent of White Evangelicals voted him into office, I felt like Alice spiraling into Wonderland, asking, "Who am I then? Tell me that first, and then, if I like being that person, I'll come up: if not, I'll stay down here till I'm somebody else—but, oh dear! . . . I am so very tired of being all alone here!"[70]

The same tribe that raised me with a strict moral code of conduct had thrown all their principles out the window to give their undying support to a man who had lied, cheated, swindled, and bragged about sexual assault. The same folks who told me to follow Jesus and take up my cross had followed a man who was openly racist, used dehumanizing language against immigrants and refugees, and called for violence at his political rallies.

Sure, many of the voters made their decision based on political party, because of the issue of abortion, but how confusing that the calls for violence, racism, and a campaign built on returning to an age when White people had more power—how was any of that "pro-life"? I realize that these are arguments and points that have been made many times before, by others. Just to say, the last vestiges of my evangelical identity quickly vanished, in late 2016. I loved Jesus, but I was sure as heck not going to unite myself with the coalition of voters who most vocally called themselves Christians. I was angry, but most of all deeply sad and confused.

"I think you might do something better with the time . . . than wasting it in asking riddles that have no answers," Alice said wearily.[71]

Then the pain became personal.

In early 2017, the first travel ban went into effect. It banned people from Somalia from entering the United States. Up until this point, the United States had been a global leader in refugee resettlement in a successful decades-long program. The ban was being touted as "temporary," but it was only the first brick in an unseen wall going up, with the vision of preventing refugees from coming into the United States at all and making asylum seeking on US soil virtually impossible. I wept because I knew exactly what it meant for my Somali refugee friends—prolonged suffering. They would surely have a longer wait time for resettlement without the United States being an option. Canada and Australia were their next options, but the numbers just weren't there. The world refugee crisis was growing, and there simply weren't enough countries willing to take more refugees. Lolly's kids would miss more years of their childhood, without an education, forever in limbo. We cried over the news.

The same friends and family who had regularly asked about our refugee friends simply stopped asking. Was it because they were told Somalis were dangerous? Was it because they were told by the US government not to care about refugees anymore? *Calm down. Don't be hysterical,* I would hear. "It's only temporary," they would say, coldly. Suddenly, our relationships with refugees were seen as *political* and *liberal*. I resented that the work of caring for refugees had been transformed into a partisan, controversial issue.

"DOESN'T THE BIBLE TELL US TO LOVE THE STRANGER?" I wanted to shout from the rooftops.

The caterpillar was back asking, "Who are you?,"[72] only this time his face wasn't as friendly as Wael Karachi's. It was frightening.

"Who in the world am I? Ah, that's the great puzzle," said Alice.[73]

The distance of living in Thailand, disconnected from my tribe, didn't help my estrangement. If I was in the wilderness before, now I was deep in Wonderland. I didn't know who I was, what I believed, or where to turn. The anger was a fire in my belly that made me lose weight and sleep.

"I don't understand why you're so angry," my family would ask. *I don't understand why you're not angry,* I wanted to say.

Prayer and reading my Bible became difficult. Biblical language only triggered bad thoughts of the tribe that had gained the whole world while losing its soul. How they had manipulatively used and abused Scripture for their own political gain. The message was loud and clear: it was never about morality or following Jesus. It was always about power.

CHAPTER 27

WHO'LL STOP THE RAIN

Leaving Church in Thailand

Rainy season. It was that time of year in Thailand when I cranked up the AC and curled up by the window with a book, a cup of tea, and a blanket and pretend it was winter.

It was an art of mental foolery. I'd see the clouds and listen to the rain. I'd invoke images of a roaring fire, flannel PJs, and zippy cool air that carried currents of change. I didn't even like pumpkin-spiced lattes, but I imagined drinking one. My heart and mind longed for a season that was energizing and refreshing. Then I'd step outside into the stagnant steam and I'd be undone. Alas, it was the same hot mess as it always was.

Despite my faith crisis, anger, and disappointment, I was still attending the largest evangelical church in Bangkok. It was a struggle and a stretch theologically, but we needed community. We sang "Great Is Thy Faithfulness" at church, and I was distracted by the need for lyrics alterations. "Summer and winter and springtime and harvest" would be better understood in Bangkok as "summer and hell and steamy rain bath and summer."

The kids liked being able to swim year-round, but for me the summer that never ended was so disorienting.

Why are we so wired for seasons? Our bodies, minds, and spirits are primed for change and continuous renewal. Our spirit needs a time of stillness, reflection, and contemplation, followed by a time of growth, new life, and new beginnings.

I had come to believe that these steady rhythms of life are sacred. I began to find value and blessing in the sacredness of rhythmic, liturgical prayer. Prayers said out loud throughout the day were like mini seasons of the soul. I felt like my own stream-of-consciousness prayers were hemming me into one season. I was suffocating on my own ego. My own dizzying thoughts on repeat had become stagnant and discordant.

I needed voices from the past, the *cloud of witnesses*, to bring rain when I needed rain and shine light when I needed light. Prayers have the power to transcend time and space and speak life into the present.

I was still in Alice's Wonderland, clumsily trying to find my footing in a faith community when my faith was in shambles. I had undergone what St. John of the Cross called the *dark night of the soul*.

Everything I thought I understood had collapsed in front of me. My heart was broken into a million pieces. I had compassion fatigue and hope had been outweighed by despair. I wanted to throw in the towel and render it all meaningless. God felt so distant in all of it. Is there anything more soul crushing than to walk through the dark night of the soul while being warned against backsliding and the temptations of the devil? The final nail in the coffin had been hammered, and I was done with all of it. I was finished with closed systems in which doubt and struggle couldn't be discussed openly. I was forever done with places of worship where you're forced to wear an Everything's Fine mask so that, God forbid, someone doesn't doubt your salvation. I could no longer stomach a culture that had a tense undercurrent of figuring out who's in and who's out.

I was also hurt that, despite my best efforts, there was little to no interest from my congregation in helping Muslim refugees, only the Pakistani asylum seekers who called themselves Christians. Most of the Pakistanis were denied refugee status from the United Nations, not necessarily because their stories weren't horrific or untrue, but because the dedicated people who vet refugees for the UNHCR are forced to triage all the cases, sorting out the most extreme circumstances to be picked for resettlement. With fewer and fewer spots available in host countries willing to resettle refugees, their job becomes harder in deciding who gets refugee status and who is denied.

Nonetheless, these migrant Pakistani families faced tremendous hardship in Bangkok, sorting out where to go next and how to make ends meet. They trudge this path while dodging the immigration police and the never-ending threat of detainment. The leaders of the church we had attended placed a limit on only one Pakistani or family to be allowed in each "Life Group" Bible study that met in peoples' homes. After joining and easily belonging to two different Life Groups, I found out that a Pakistani friend had been on a wait-list for two years to get into a group. It made my blood boil; why would they do that? The income and lifestyle disparity between wealthy expats on government and corporate packages and Pakistani asylum seekers who barely scraped by to feed their families was overwhelming. We all worshiped under the same roof, but our needs and impulses could not have been more different. The Pakistani community was vocal, some would say "pushy," about getting their needs met. Unlike the Somalis, they were not afraid to ask White people in the church for food or money. Instead of actively trying to eradicate all the needs in the church, it appeared as though the church leaders were afraid that too many bugaboos would be a bother to the *right kind* of churchgoers: the ones from wealthy countries who showed up on Sunday with clean hair and deodorant and wrote nice tithing checks.

I would be leaving church again, but this time I would leave on my own accord.

"Why not stick around and try to fix these problems?" it's been asked of me.

But the problem wasn't with any individual at the church, many of whom I maintained close friendships with after leaving. The problem was on an institutional level that was too big for any one person to fix. Travis and I decided that we could longer support a church that is closed to discussing doubt and curiosity, forbids women from holding leadership positions, fails to address White supremacy for fear of losing big givers, and is LGBT nonaffirming. These big institutional things could not be fixed from the inside out; the best thing we could do was to "vote with our feet."

Church is messy, and churches are filled with imperfect people who sometimes hurt each other. But when the institution has big, old chains that do harm and keep some voices silenced, it doesn't matter how sweet the people are or how lovely the "fellowship"—it's just not worth sticking it out to wait for the change to happen when there are plenty of welcoming places of worship that have evolved.

We never walked away from our faith in Jesus, but we needed a break from church. We knew we weren't done with church forever, but we needed to have an actual Sabbath on Sundays. We needed rest. We needed the time to privately work out our theology without judgment.

When I was too heartbroken for words, I needed the words of ancient torchbearers to build me up. I needed words that were formative and restorative. I pulled from the Psalms, the Book of Common Prayer, but mostly *Celtic Daily Prayer*. They saved my faith and brought me peace at a time when I wanted to rage.

They were energizing when I needed to be uplifted, and they were comforting when I needed to mourn.

My Protestant upbringing frowned on liturgical, ritualistic prayers and practices. We were taught that God is a personal God; we have a personal relationship with Christ, and our prayers reflect that as such. Ritualistic religion is empty and dead.

I had heard all these things my entire life, and I had said them.

But the sweetest time of day for my children and me had become our evening prayer time. We'd light our candles, dim the lights, say our personal prayers, and then close with the daily office of Celtic Evening Prayer that ends like this:

Lord, You have always lightened
this darkness of mine;
and though the night is here,
today I believe.

Lord, You have always spoken
when time was ripe;
and though you be silent now,
today I believe.[74]

And the evening blessing:

> See that ye be at peace among yourselves, my children, and love one another. Follow the example of good men of old and God will comfort you and help you, both in this world and in the world which is to come.[75]

The kids would giggle throughout and anticipate the final, "In the name of the Father . . ." so they could fight over who got to blow out the candles. But I hoped with time they would be able to remember and cherish those beautiful prayers and be formed by their strength and encouragement.

I made a vow to always let my children speak openly about their doubts. To let them walk their own faith journey and give them grace to explore. To tell them that it's okay, holy even, to be *curiouser and curiouser*.

CHAPTER 28

BLACKBIRD

Amsterdam, the Netherlands

It was a cold November day in Amsterdam, and I realized eighteen-month-old Francina was unprepared for the biting wind. My "Bangkok baby" had only known hot, humid air, and so I did my best to wrap my scarf around the umbrella stroller, swaddling her arms and icy fingers tightly like an Egyptian mummy on wheels. As mothers do, we use whatever resources are available to care for our children.

We were en route back to our home in Thailand from a visit to our families in America, and we decided to divide up the lengthy journey by staying a couple days in Amsterdam. It was the morning of our departure, and we decided to visit the Anne Frank House Museum before our flight.

It was every bit as sobering as I had imagined it would be. Visitors walk through dimly lit corridors that are part museum and part sacred space, leading to the secret annex where Anne wrote her famous diary while hiding in Nazi-occupied Holland.

I did my best to keep my daughter quiet—she had already got addicted to Dum Dums on the visit home, so I obliged and spent most of my time wrestling her and managing meltdowns. Just as I was blocking her sticky fingers from wiping the walls, I was stopped in my tracks when I saw hash marks on the wall. It looked so much like the penciled lines on bare walls that were in my Henry's bedroom at home. It was a makeshift growth chart, documenting Anne and her older sister Margot's maturity during their twenty-five months of hiding before being found and captured by the Gestapo. It was a relic of their humanity, an insistence on their own dignity, hauntingly preserved for millions to see. In the early 1940s, Anne and her family applied for and were denied entry in the United States as refugees. After their capture, the Gestapo split up the family, sending some to Auschwitz and a quick death in the gas chambers. Anne survived two years before dying of typhus in a Nazi concentration camp in northern Germany. Her body was thrown into a mass grave less than two months before British soldiers liberated the camp. She was fifteen.

We concluded our tour with a video that included famous quotes about the Holocaust from different scholars, theologians, and celebrities. Nobel laureate Elie Wiesel said, "I swore never to be silent whenever and wherever human beings endure suffering and humiliation. We must take sides. Neutrality helps the oppressor, never the victim. Silence encourages the tormentor, never the tormented."[76]

***

Miles away, in Bangkok, something terrible had happened and I still hadn't figured out the details.

I had been texting Lolly to check in on her and the kids, and I hadn't received a response. It was unlike Lolly to ignore me for so long. I texted Bishaaro too but got no response. I reached out to the sisters at the Jesuit Refugee Service to find out if anyone knew of their whereabouts. Everyone seemed to know Lolly, but no one knew where they had gone. We all feared the worst: they had been imprisoned.

The day I got back to Bangkok, Lolly called me on a secret phone under a blanket in her crowded jail cell. She told me about the massive raids, how they went into hiding, how it didn't last long—they were still found and taken to the IDC. As they had no legal protection as UN-registered refugees, she would stay locked up indefinitely along with her children until their case was individually accepted for resettlement to another country. In other words, they would stay in jail until they were hopefully chosen as one of the lucky less-than-one percent to be resettled.

Pope Francis has compared these types of detention centers to concentration camps. No, the prison doesn't kill detainees or perform experimental treatments on them. But human beings are kept like animals, packed more than one hundred to a room that doesn't get enough natural sunlight.[77] There is no door on the bathroom. Lolly tucked her kids into bed on a hard floor in a room where the lights never went off. They received three bowls of rice a day and drank unclean water. Sometimes the water was shut off completely. Some detainees contracted diseases and died before ever finding freedom.

The news sent a shockwave of anger coursing through my veins. The possibility of Lolly and other friends getting detained had always loomed, but I had so many regrets. I regretted not insisting that they stay at my house while I was away. I regretted not taking portrait photographs of Lolly's kids to remember their childhood. Would they even be children by the time they got out? I was angry they were being punished for surviving. My friend who had taught me so much about motherhood, strength, grace, and resilience after surviving hell on earth would have to endure even more torment while raising children to witness it all. I was angry to have to tell my son that he wouldn't be seeing his buddy Omar anymore—how do you tell a five-year-old that his friend is in jail?

The jail allowed visitors to bring food and toiletries. I visited them there. Lolly was like a beautiful bird trapped in a cage. Two metal fences separated us, and it was hard to understand them among the one hundred other visitors who were shouting across the divide, but I could hear Omar asking for a soccer ball, dinosaurs, and bubbles. Her daughters asked for food and puzzles. Lolly was holding a Rohingya refugee baby. Always the nurturer, she introduced me to her "neighbor." She gave me the names and detainee numbers of two Ugandan girls who had been detained for six months and hadn't had a visitor.

"Nobody knows they're in here. Can you please ask your friends to visit them too?" she asked.

It was absurd that they were being criminalized and that the thing that kept me on the right side of the fence was simply my American passport.

I saw Lolly's children as modern-day Anne Franks. Their best hope was for a country to accept their case for resettlement. It was inconceivable that children had to sleep in jail while waiting for a new country. And it was inconceivable that so many Americans were unbothered by our government's travel bans and shutting our borders to refugees. The United States had been a haven for Somali refugees in places like Texas, Michigan, and Washington, DC. But since the annual refugee ceiling had been reduced by more than half, that option would take years longer. The next year, it was reduced even lower, and the following year, it was capped at just eighteen thousand, with scores of resettling agencies shutting their doors. Just like the Frank family, who were turned away from immigrating to the United States, it was unlikely that my friends would ever make it to America.

I asked myself how we got there, why the American church had hardened its hearts to refugees when one of the major themes of the Bible is welcoming the stranger. How did we lose trust in a vetting system that had worked for decades? How did we begin to see refugees as dangerous when there was no statistical evidence to back it up? How did we forget that so many of us are descendants of people who were oppressed and looking for a better life? How did we stop seeing the beauty of American culture as coming from a collision of cultures? How did we lose our way—did it happen overnight, or had it been slowly brewing for a long time?

I wondered how I could begin to dismantle the lie that refugees are dangerous. Despite extensive research, a successful extreme-vetting system, and an extensive faith-based resettlement network, the majority of White American Christians were still in favor of closing our borders to refugees.[78] I wondered how the church swallowed the puff of air that says, "These people are dangerous; we don't want them here; they don't have value; they are not welcome."

The suggestion that refugees are anything other than people created in the image of God who need our shelter and protection is a lie. The rate at which this lie had seeped into our global consciousness was astounding. The lie was told in language that dehumanized refugees during the first travel ban, where our president called refugees from the seven banned countries snakes.[79]

I write about Lolly's virtuous attributes not as a means to justify her worthiness for asylum. Even if she wasn't all of the wonderful things that I describe her to be, she and her children should still be granted safe passage to a country where they'd be welcomed because they're human beings. Seeking asylum is a human right. Refugees shouldn't have to prove their worth, either through virtue or skill.

Anne Frank is famous today because of her diary. But the sad reality is the existence of thousands of Anne Franks who never wrote down their stories. There are thousands of Anne Franks around the world, and *El Roi*, the God who sees, cares for each one of them. Or does he? When we think of Anne Frank and the Holocaust, we feel compelled to quote Wiesel's "never again" and believe we are loving our neighbor as ourselves, since there hasn't been a second Holocaust. But if we are doing nothing about the world refugee crisis and believing the lie that Muslims are our enemy, we are complicit in the suffering of millions.

My friends were in jail, and it was Advent season. I was sad, I was bitter, I was jaded. I felt helpless, watching my friends suffer and being able to do little about it. I was so angry at the attitudes back home, from people I loved dearly, especially those who flippantly declared "It's only temporary" after the first travel ban. How soon they said that and then forgot about it, with no connection to how policy hurts people. *It was never meant to be temporary.* I wanted to have hope for my friends, but there were no words.

My *Celtic Daily Prayer* book gave me words when I had none. When I was too angry to pray. When everything felt reminiscent of the culture that had rejected the very ones who I was praying for.

"God of the watching ones . . ."

Each night before bedtime, my husband and I and our three littles would sit in a circle, light a candle, and pray the evening prayer for blessing during Advent. It was almost as if it was written specifically for my refugee friends, the "slow and suffering ones":

God of the watching ones,
Give us your benediction.
God of the waiting ones,
Give us Your good word for our souls.
God of the watching ones,
The waiting ones,
The slow and suffering ones,
Give us Your benediction,
Your good word for our souls,
That we might rest.
God of the watching ones,
The waiting ones,
The slow and suffering ones,
And of the angels in heaven,
And of the child in the womb,
Give us Your benediction,
Your good word for our souls,
That we might rest and rise
In the kindness of Your company.[80]

Siem Reap, Cambodia

Hildegard of Bingen, a twelfth-century German Benedictine abbess, said that in order to fly like an eagle we need two wings: one embracing God's glories all around us, and the other tending to pain and suffering in our midst. Both involve paying attention.

At different times in my life, it's been easy to do one or the other. Embracing the glories and simply "living my best life" is fun and easy when I'm not thinking about suffering. Or going down a rabbit hole of pain makes me want to marinate in it while ignoring the glories all around me. But Hildegard of Bingen, who I've come to call "Hildy," says that in order to fly high, we need to embrace and embody the paradox.

It was our third Christmas in Bangkok, and Travis and I decided to forgo getting gifts for each other and instead gifted our family a post-Christmas trip to Cambodia. Google Maps estimated the drive to be six hours from our home in Bangkok to Siem Reap. Google Maps is out of touch in that part of the world, but my husband is Clark Griswold when it comes to vacations.

"It's a straight shot due east. The kids will be splashing in the pool before sundown," he told me.

Positive Patty ordered some fancy straps and a tarp to fit all of our baggage on the roof of our small SUV.

"Better than my old man did," he said, recalling that his dad had once strapped everyone's suitcases to the roof of their Volvo but Travis's bag had fallen off at some point and he had had to wear his sister's clothes for a week. "Everything up there is immovable. Solid as a rock," he said.

We left at seven in the morning. Everybody was shiny and caffeinated, especially the guy behind the wheel. About three hours into our trip, we heard the swishing flap of the tarp beating the side of the car and saw its large silhouette waving at the blue sky in the rearview mirror. Travis's bag was gone, then Henry's.

We recovered Henry's bag, but after a three-hour unsuccessful backtrack looking for Travis's, we cut our losses and decided to move all the bags into the car and carry on to the border. It was cramped, but we made do, which left me thinking why we didn't just start off like that.

"Because we had more bags when we started!" barked the driver.

The mood in the car had soured. Our coffee cups were sitting empty in their cup holders, and the only shine left was the sweat on Travis's brow from hitchhiking on the back of a motorcycle against traffic for half a mile to retrieve Henry's bag.

The border crossing was a slow bake in the sun, as our car pulled into a parking spot and Clark Griswold tried to cheer us up as he left us to get the car's documents processed. "At least we have all the right paperwork! We should be in and out."

Meanwhile, the youngest tot had a diaper blowout all over her car seat. We finally walked into the arrivals waiting room when my three-year-old vomited everywhere. She vomited again when it was our turn at the window to stamp passports. We were running out of baby wipes.

The border crossing featured a building where you stamped out of Thailand, after which you walked down a narrow dirt road which brought you to a wooden bridge that spanned a muddy creek marking the border. On the other side, you were technically in Cambodia, but there was another walk of a quarter mile or so until you reached an immigration building.

So, there's this no-man's land between the two countries, where strange things happen. Half-dressed children were playing a bowling game with a flip-flop; men pulled two-wheeled carts packed with goods for export; and a dead body was wheeled by on a stretcher. My three-year-old vomited again. We ran over a snake.

The ETA we pulled from Google Maps didn't account for our lost luggage search, extra paperwork on the Thai side, or the fact that rural Cambodian immigration officials rarely see diplomatic passports at their sleepy border outpost. Travis doesn't speak Cambodian, but he knew the rules when it came to free stuff and he was going to get the visa fees waved, by golly. Eventually one of the officials who looked too young for the job said some things in Khmer to his colleagues, told Travis to have a seat, strapped on his bike helmet, and rode away. Two diapers later, the uniformed man-boy reappeared with a plastic bag full of soup. He emptied it into a Styrofoam bowl. Travis started to ask him for an update, but then sat down, realizing he'd have to wait until the dinner break was over before getting the visas.

It was getting dark as we entered Cambodia, and there were no streetlights. The silhouettes of lone palm trees and water buffalo scattered throughout flat farmlands faded into an inky darkness. A magnificent starry sky is a rare sight for us city dwellers, but the next three hours turned into some of the most stressful hours of our lives. We came close to hitting several trucks carrying livestock moving at tractor speeds in near total darkness. One farmer was using his cell phone as a headlight. Other cars materialized out of nowhere to whiz by us at top speeds.

At hour fourteen of our six-hour journey, we reached our Airbnb and collapsed into bed. Clark got back in the car and went looking for some underwear and socks for the weekend. He may not have outperformed his father's car-packing ability, but he was adamant about not wearing panties this time.

The next morning, I woke up still dizzy from the day before, but pulled myself together so I could go search for some breakfast to bring home. That's when two angels magically appeared. God's mercies had come in the form of the breakfast ladies bearing pots of coffee, fresh croissants, crepes, tropical fruits and juices, and eggs cooked any way we liked. All of God's glory was on display at a beautiful garden table outside by the pool, and I wanted to cry.

Travis was excited and ready to go sightseeing, trying on his odd-sized Angkor Wat souvenir T-shirts and Cambodian underwear from his midnight market run. But rather than be fully present and accept the warm embrace of the most perfect thing ever, I subjected my poor husband to a guilt-fueled sideshow about how undeserving we were.

Remembering our jailed refugee friends in Bangkok, I imagined their heinous travel stories and reminded my husband that "for them, there is no beautiful morning-after with peace and breakfast ladies. Their misery has no end date in sight."

I'm a real treat to be around sometimes.

Travis told me to lighten up and handed me another croissant. Why is it so hard to be fully present and absorb God's good graces?

I find living in the space between a privileged life and the awareness of injustice awkward and confusing. In the midst of my mostly comfortable life, there's an undercurrent of guilt and impending tragedy. It lurks under the surface, threatening to steal joy from whatever feast is before me.

The kingdom of God is often described as a lavish banquet, a party, a feast. As we widen the table to invite more to the party to eat from the bread of life, we can forget to enjoy our participation in the feast. Like the servant in Jesus's parable who is given only one talent, we bury our treasure when we don't relish the moments our cup is brimming with so much grace and goodness that it overflows.

Jen Hatmaker says it like this:

> There is a middle place, holy ground, where we learn to embrace the fasting and the feast, for both are God ordained. There is a time to press onto sacrifice, restraint, self-denial, deferment. There is also a time to open wide our arms to adventure, laughter, fulfillment, neither regards herself as too important or too unworthy to enjoy this life.[81]

The feast is more than just the inner workings of our hearts. It's the beauty in the tangible world; reality itself. It's warm naps and wildflowers on the side of the road. A brand-new box of Crayola 64 (before the kids get hold of them.) The love between a child and a pet. New throw pillows for an old couch. A reunion of friends after years of separation. The ability to laugh at the absurdities in a horrific road trip. And certainly, a private breakfast made by someone else on a morning when I wasn't expecting it. These things are holy, all of them.

My husband has always been the full sun to my partly cloudy skies, and so I took his advice to revel in these moments of glory, adventure, beauty, and absurdity. We explored temples, took ice cream breaks, had cannonball contests in the pool, and left the kids with a babysitter in the evenings so we could enjoy our spicy Khmer food in peace. We celebrated the end of the Christmas season. We celebrated what would be one of our last family trips in Asia before we moved again.

We celebrated without forgetting the injustices around us and understood these things can occupy the same space. Tomorrow would have suffering and tragedy, but it would also have new mysteries to unravel and new wonders to behold.

When I visited my refugee friends in jail upon our return, they asked about my trip. It was during one of their one hour of the week to be in the common space with detainees of both sexes, the closest thing to being out in public. I was reminded that as they spent their days behind bars waiting on a new country, they still took the time to put on lipstick and decorate each other's hands and arms in gorgeous lacy henna patterns. They made colorful vases out of magazine pages folded like origami and beautiful drawings. One teenager was working on a screenplay. They still laughed deeply.

Even in the darkest hellhole on earth, those African beauty queens were taking the time to celebrate womanhood, appreciate beauty, and insist on their own worth, strength, and dignity. They understood better than I did what it meant to be human and alive: that beauty and celebration matter. They continued to teach me far more than I could possibly teach or serve them.

We should pay attention to why Jesus calls the poor and meek "blessed." We have so much to gain by allying ourselves with them. They show us that when all idols are stripped away, all that is left is sacred breath and the glory and enjoyment of the time being. Witnesses to life. And that is where the good stuff really lives. They keep us plugged into the divine circle of self-emptying love. We're filled to the brim with every perfect grace around us, which we can then pour right back out onto others. We love because we are loved.

At the end of this trip, I found myself meditating on Hildy's bird and seeing both the difficulty and the divine genius of it. The two wings of embracing God's glories while having the awareness of suffering was a tricky paradox that felt like tending two tiny flames, one in each hand. It's so easy to let go of one—too easy to *crash and burn*. It's a delicate dance that's become a lifelong pursuit, and I would need more mercy for myself to learn the practice.

CHAPTER 30

SHINE A LIGHT

Bangkok Despair

If irony were a tree, it would be the sacred Bodhi tree that grows out of the visitor waiting area of the Immigration Detention Center, or IDC. The metal awning that shades the open-air lobby has been cut to allow its divine branches plenty of room to stretch majestically into the sunlight. Sashes of pink, yellow, green, and blue are tied around the thickest part of its trunk. It's of the same species of tree that the Buddha fell asleep under before waking up and attaining enlightenment, and it is treated like royalty.

But just on the other side of the gate behind the tree, the people are living like animals. As I would learn from Lolly's endless days in there, the rooms holding the women and children are the most crowded. On a good day, the cell would have around 100 occupants, but usually the number was closer to 150 to 200. Hot bodies in a tight jumble sat on the concrete floor without furniture. There was no privacy and only three bathroom stalls for so many people. The women would get urinary tract infections for holding it for so long. When the water was shut off, the stench and trash piled up. There wasn't enough room on the floor for everyone to sleep at the same time, so they slept in short shifts. Those who had been detained for years often went crazy, beating their heads against the wall. I would continue to hear about deaths and detainees contracting tuberculosis inside that living hellhole.

A palpable tension hung in the waiting area where visitors register. On the really busy days, you could cut the anxiety with a knife—husbands with children visiting their wives, wide-eyed volunteers who didn't quite know what they signed up for, loved ones visiting relatives who got snatched up, sometimes for reasons unknown. The air didn't flow inside this room. There was an oscillating fan on the ceiling and it rotated about, but the blades weren't turning. It was a sad metaphor for that Godforsaken place; outside, it was business as usual in the Land of Smiles, but inside the IDC, the confusion and desperation filled the air like a suffocating gas.

Visitors sat in rows of wobbly chairs and on the floor, double-checking their plastic bags filled with things that might make the lives of the detainees a little more survivable—toothpaste, snacks, Maxi Pads, fresh fruit—everything the jail doesn't provide the inmates.

The scent of Sharpie markers cut through the angsty cloud as folks squiggled the correct detainee number on each bag. We knew the guards would steal some of our goods, but we hoped most of it made it to the person we were visiting.

A loud metal thud signaled that the metal gate was unlocked, and it was time for visitors to go in. We were frisked by an officer and then led to the metal fence where we found our person on the opposite side, clinging to their metal fence. It's impossible to have a decent conversation with everyone shouting loudly, so Lolly and I started passing notes via a guard that paces up and down between the two fences.

Sometimes I'd meet other random volunteers who were there to visit Lolly or Bishaaro as they found their names in an NGO database. Once, a woman complained about Lolly not being very "engaging." This struck me as odd, at first because Lolly was always engaging, present, and sincere, so she must be mistaken. Then I thought, "Wait—even if she wasn't engaging, what kind of remark is that for a visitor to make?" It was the first time the two had met and her comment made it seem like Lolly was being used to entertain her and make her feel satisfied by her good deed. But there was a sort of zoo effect; not only were human beings in cages, but the visitors played the role of tourists who paid for their tickets and now they want to see the big cats do something fierce. Why is the zebra just sitting under that tree over there? It's hot. Are there any refreshments here?

Bishaaro was a popular detainee to visit because of her cute face and big expressions. She learned how to flash her magical smile and deep dimples to show her gratitude, while her big eyes remained scared and exhausted. It made me sad that she had to perform in order to have basic items of survival brought to her.

But for the regular visitors, it was impossible to be in a room with deeply suffering people without absorbing at least some of their pain. We volunteers want to feel wanted and needed—the sugary satisfaction of having "made a difference." It feels good to be the benevolent benefactor. But when you're left sweating in an unresolvable hell, that's when people turn away. It's too much to take in; the injustice and the suffering are hard to sit with. It's easier to hide our faces and write the check or put some pantry items into a collections bin. We like to do good as long as we keep the dark side of suffering at arms' length. Mostly, we're afraid of the questions that come up in our own minds and hearts.

How can God allow this to happen? Do all things really happen for a reason? (Answer: they don't.) What about the dreams deferred that never come true? What about the multitudes of unhappy endings for the marginalized? Could I honestly shout to the woman driven half-insane in this space to stop hitting her head against the wall, because "God never gives us more than we can handle"?

But the answer to the hard question of, Why them and not us? never comes. It's a universe without law and order. Cognitive dissonance with a side of guilt. And for that reason, my days of visiting the IDC were often lonely. I had a hard time recruiting friends willing to go with me. I resented going alone. I resented that Lolly had to suffer longer. I resented that her kids had to endure life behind bars. I resented every time my family would naively ask, "Why don't they just come to America?" when they had just voted for a president who banned Somalis from entering our country while simultaneously dismantling the refugee program entirely. I was up to my eyeballs in bitterness and resentment, and that old feeling of *it didn't have to be this way* was always on my mind.

I worried mostly about Lolly's mental health, being subject to loud noise and no privacy twenty-four hours a day. Watching my friend deteriorate and not be able to do anything about it made me jaded and calloused.

I wanted to forget that awful place; I wanted to pretend as though it didn't exist and carry on with my life. I wondered just what the NGOs in Bangkok actually did to help refugees, as there was nothing they could do to help Lolly and her kids.

The kingdoms of this earth were keeping them oppressed. Keeping them in captivity. Keeping them malnourished and traumatized. Her home country that failed her, the terrorists who invaded and stole everything except her life, the country of Thailand that was not the transitional safe haven she desperately needed, and my own giant, powerful country that decided her nationality was too unsafe to enter for resettlement.

Alia Joy asks, "What does it take to keep the language of hope fluent on your tongue when all you taste is despair and the ash of burnt offerings you never imagine setting on the altar in the first place?"[82]

I didn't know how to speak the language of hope for my refugee friends anymore, but I caught myself praying for kingdom come, usually on the back of a motorbike on my way to the IDC. It was the only spiritual practice I could muster. I had known the words of the Lord's Prayer my entire life, but this would be my first time really *knowing* those words and learning to embody them.

Give us this day our daily bread was always a prayer for Lolly. *Sustain them, O Lord. Comfort them. Get them through today. Give them today's rations.*

I realized that it was also a prayer for me. Even though my expat friends had busy lives, there were strangers I met there, fellow regular volunteers who showed kindness and gave encouragement freely to one another. Just when I'd feel alone in carrying a tiny piece of Lolly's despair, what kept me moving forward was their kindness. A Jesuit priest and a group of French volunteers in particular had a subtle way of carrying on without fanfare, doing hard and holy work that goes unnoticed. Other trailing spouses showed up in minivans full of goods o' plenty to stuff inside the small green basket each visitor was allowed. Once, I showed up late and missed the quota of eighty-five visitors per session when a kind Pakistani man grabbed me by the arm and said, "Give me your food bag. I'll make sure it gets to your girls."

After months of feeling jaded and calloused, I started noticing small miracles. Word of a refugee who had been resettled. A boy whose bail had been canceled who somehow didn't have to go back in. Missing the registration deadline but somehow getting in anyway. There was always a tiny miracle happening.

I overheard a volunteer woman say to a woman whose husband was detained, "Well I wouldn't hold my breath on that to happen, but instead you should breathe with hope."

Breathing with hope became our mantra. Somehow, there was always an enduring flame that glowed in the darkness. Instead of fixating on the utter despair, I tried to pay attention to those glimmers of light. I claimed them for myself too. They were always there in the periphery, pulsating onward. A gentle current of mercy flowed underneath it all.

The odds were stacked against Lolly, her family, and every other unfortunate soul in the IDC. But they were never zero. As long as we had breath, we had hope.

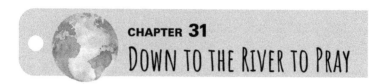

Bangkok Hope

Thailand was under pressure to end the practice of incarcerating minors, so they gave in to a local NGO's longstanding request to open a foster-care program, allowing some children behind bars to be placed with foster families. This was a first for Thailand. To their credit, they let the parents decide whether to separate from their children. The Thai government targeted expat families to take responsibility for the children. Unfortunately, there were more children, mostly unaccompanied minors, who needed families than families willing to host them.

I asked Lolly if she wanted me to take her kids. The question cut so deep. She had to decide what was worse: keeping her kids in a hellhole or separating from them indefinitely. It angered me that she had to make such a decision, but the decision was hers to make, which was a tiny sliver of empowerment.

Lolly was not ready to give up her young three, but her biggest concern was Raina. She would be turning eighteen soon and would be considered an adult, when it would be too late to bail her out under the foster-care program. For weeks Lolly agonized over the idea of releasing Raina, but Raina was tough and ready, she assured Lolly. Lolly and I talked about it for days between the metal fence and over calls from the secret cell phone. If Raina lived with me, she could work on her GED. It would be like going away to college. She'd been out of school since the sixth grade, but she wanted to study more than anything. She had also gained weight from lack of movement behind bars. Raina's two burning goals were to get fit and get her GED.

Travis and I went through the training and prepared our guest room. My teenage niece was coming to stay for the summer, and we thought having another teenager in the house, and a Black girl that looked like her, would bridge the gap to make her feel more a part of our family. If people asked who she was, the two girls would simply be "my nieces."

The day came for Raina to leave the jail and come home with me. We stood by the rainbow-wrapped Bodhi tree as a guard unlocked a wide, sliding metal gate. She paced slowly out, weeping and dazed as if she were unsure how to put one foot in front of the other. It immediately made me wonder if we were making a huge mistake. The trauma of leaving her family with no end date in sight was too much to bear, and it dawned on me we were participating in the added pain.

"Don't worry, I promise, it's going to be okay soon enough," the American director of the foster program whispered in my ear.

Sure, we could give her a nice home with a bed and bath of her own, healthy food to eat, and loving parents, but we weren't her family. It was a frightening transition. Her temporary respite with us was no replacement for the wholeness of staying together in a place where everyone could flourish. We'd all do the best we could, but something was horribly broken, and nobody would rest easy until everyone was out of jail and into safe pastures.

Raina walked around in a fog that entire first week, like a weary soldier who had just come home from a long battle. Her forlorn face and empty stare revealed a girl who had forgotten how to exist in the natural world. Freedom isn't always automatic for someone who has been captive. Especially when they have to leave loved ones behind in an awful place.

Raina came into our home with just a small blue canvas backpack with all of her belongings. It had an American flag on it with a decal that said it was a gift from the International Organization for Migration and US Embassy. All the kids in the IDC had one. The painful irony of getting a gift from a country that banned them.

We went shopping for clothes and a new backpack. Raina was pragmatic and simple, and she didn't think it was necessary to have more than a few pairs of socks or underwear. When I suggested she pick out several pairs of shoes, she insisted, "Enough! I have enough already." I stared at my own overflowing underwear drawer with new eyes: *Nobody really needs twenty-five pairs of panties, how peculiar.* Raina had no interest in acquiring an entire closet full of clothes and shoes. Having her in our home exposed how drunk on stuff we are, our disease of excess. Our material-abundance dependency hadn't yet got under her skin, and I became uncomfortably aware of how there were ways we would harm her and not help.

Raina wasted no time in beginning her studies. She began with science, the first of four GED tests that she'd study for and take one at a time. She spent hours watching YouTube videos, teaching herself everything from photosynthesis to balancing chemistry equations. I marveled at her grit. Nobody was hovering over her asking her to give a damn or teaching her self-discipline. She simply had an opportunity, freedom, and a budding sense of autonomy, and she chased her dream for an education with all her might.

Finding my role in her life was clumsy. I enlisted the help of my beautiful, soft-spoken Algerian friend Gazala who helped her in ways I couldn't: celebrating Muslim holidays and preserving her Muslim identity. She and her daughter were happy to be a friend to Raina and enjoyed her company. Sure, we could easily give up pork and buy halal meat, but I thought about how, if the roles were reversed and my children had to be cared for by Muslims, I would want them to have Christians in their lives to uphold our faith, traditions, and identity. It was important for Lolly, especially.

Raina had been through unimaginable trauma, but she had such a tough, no-nonsense exterior. I hoped she was happy in our home, but I wondered how miserable she was without her loved ones. Knowing when to pry and when to be silent was tough for the socially awkward person I can be.

A trip outside Bangkok was what we all needed, on the neutral ground of God's green earth. My husband, three kids, teenage niece Zoe, and Raina piled into our small SUV and drove four hours through dusty highways and lush forests to Kanchanaburi, home of the River Kwai.

The river recenters and restores our spirit in ways only our subconscious can understand. On the banks of the river, words aren't necessary to feel the spirit of God hovering over moving water and the undercurrent of hope rising out of nothing. Everyone seemed to relax as the tensions of city-living and awkwardness of our new family dynamic were met with merciful breezes, gentle forests, birdsong, and blue skies.

When there are no words, there are elephants. We spent a full day at an elephant rescue center, focused on nothing more than feeding, bathing, and caring for a pack of gentle giants. In the morning, we fed them palm branches and watermelon. We squished up bananas and rice with our hands and rolled them into baseball-sized balls for special treats, "elephant cookies" as we called them. In the afternoon, we went on a languid stroll through the forest and then gave them a decadent mud bath. Rubbing mud over their rough skin was pure pleasure, and it wasn't long before we started giving in to the temptation to rub mud over our skin too. Raina covered the outer parts of her burkini like second skin.

We led the elephants and our group of muddy ragamuffins down to the river for a bath. When we got into the river with the elephants, it was as if some of the chains were loosened in all of us, and Raina gave herself permission to feel joy despite her sadness for her family. I saw the first wide, carefree smiles since she'd been freed.

In the river, we were clumsy, messy, and muddy but tethered together. With our wild hearts beating, afraid yet at peace, we took turns swimming next to the elephants to touch our face to their enormous heads. We were entranced by their big, kind eyes that told a story of how we were all birthed from the same place of love. The elephants were ours, and we belonged to them. Raina belonged to us, and we belonged to her. She didn't belong any less to her incarcerated family, but she was ours now too.

Then one of the elephants pooped in the water and we decided that was enough swimming downstream from giant beasts who can excrete the mass of a small child at any moment.

So we chased waterfalls. At the third station of Erawan National Park, there was a great swimming hole that led to a gorgeous waterfall spilling over to a small cave and a giant rock perfect for standing behind the waterfall.

"Do you want to swim to it?" I asked Raina.

"Yes!" she answered enthusiastically.

"You can swim, right?" was the last thing I remembered saying before her flailing limbs grabbed onto my husband's back as he pulled her safely to the waterfall's edge. We clambered up the slippery rock and passed through, entranced at the watery curtain in front of us.

"This was my dream, you know," Raina shouted over the roar of falling water. "I've always wanted to see a waterfall."

While the others in our group were afraid of the big fish nibbling to get too close to the waterfall, Raina was fearless. This was the start of an unwavering pattern for her. If ever given the choice of "to do or not to do" she was always a wholehearted *yes!* She took no bright, rare moments for granted, and she taught us to bravely jump in feet first, with no guarantees of being able to do it again.

Our time on those tree-lined riverbanks was a piece of kingdom come. That mystical setting was heaven's flamboyant jailbreak seeping over and spilling down onto earth, flooding us with goodness from our heads to our toes. While we didn't forget about Raina's suffering family behind bars, we soaked up the glory of God at the River Kwai. In one hand was the awareness of suffering, and in the other was the wild and wonderful delight of a good and giving God. There it was again: Hildy's bird learning how to fly.

CHAPTER 32

DON'T STOP BELIEVIN'

Celebration in Bangkok

Old memories die hard. Ever since that despairing Christmas with Clyde and his ex-wife, despite having a stable life and a family of my own, holidays for me were still tinged with bellyaches and feelings of estrangement. Holiday cheer comes flooding in like vinegar poured over baking soda, and the suppressed painful residue bubbles up to the surface with the crinkling of wrapping paper or "Jingle Bells." Joni Mitchell's "River" was the Christmas song I could identify with most. Sounds and smells that should tweak the muscle memory of the heart with joy and sense of togetherness instead followed the deep grooves of pathways worn by insecurity and disappointment.

My Somali refugee friends taught me to embrace celebration again. What was moving us forward was the necessity to celebrate every small victory in a big way. Raina told me stories of the wild celebrations they had in the detention center, including a New Year's Eve party they threw for themselves and regular midnight dance parties accompanied by African beats drummed out by water bottles on the floor. Every child's birthday that passed behind bars required the delivery of cake and party hats, thanks to the help of my friend Gazala, who happened to be a talented baker.

Lolly's ten-year-old daughter told me the story of an Eritrean baby girl's first birthday in their room. They had just sung "Happy Birthday" and blown out the candle when they heard a blood-curdling scream resonate off the walls. It had originated in the back corner. A sick Chinese woman was discovered to be dead at the closing of the song. Her relative had realized it was too late. How fast the mood switched from pure sweet joy to utter horror. The guards quickly cleared everyone out of the room so they could remove the body.

"Her smelly clothes were left in the bathroom trash. I couldn't sleep that night," she shuddered recalling the awful story. The IDC was a place of harrowing life and death, and celebration was the antidote to despair.

I'll never forget the day I looked at my phone and had multiple missed calls from Lolly. I knew that could only mean one thing: good news or bad news. It took me a few tries to get through to the secret phone. Her voice on the line was full and resonant and alive.

"We're going to Canada! It's Canada! We got Canada!" she exclaimed.

The day had finally arrived when all of their fears and worries and living moment to moment could finally subside a little with the knowledge that better days were ahead. They were part of the lucky less-than-one percent. The United Nations said it would happen in two months to a year, so they would have to wait it out inside the IDC. But knowing that an end date was in the near future made life bearable again.

Raina heard the news, and we laughed, and we cried, and we celebrated. The separation would not be forever, and the celebration was sweeter than ever.

She took her GED science exam and passed on the first try. She had fallen in love with Bollywood movies and learned Hindi in the IDC by watching Indian soap operas, so we celebrated her victory by taking her to an Indian restaurant.

After a short break and a hard Netflix binge-watch session, she launched into her studies for GED math. Just like the science prep, she spent hours watching YouTube videos teaching herself graphing functions and algebra equations. She wanted to have her hair professionally tinged with gold, and so we agreed that would be how we'd celebrate when she passed math. It struck me as odd that she'd want to change her hair when she kept it completely covered. But after seeing the way the Somalis pierce and paint and doodle on themselves with henna, I was reminded that it was a point of celebration *for her* and nobody else. The need to feel beautiful goes so much deeper than trying to attract a mate or impress people. It's a personal celebration of who we are as humans and as women.

We were getting on with life, one small victory at a time, when suddenly we were hit smack in the head with a ton of bricks. On a routine stamp-in/check-in day at the IDC to show that Raina was still in my custody, the guards, along with Raina's Thai caseworker, told us that her bail had been canceled and she would have to go back to the IDC in two weeks. The office of immigration had new leadership, as they do every October, along with the military and other government workers, following their fiscal-year calendar. The new guy in charge was hard-pressed to show how tough he'd be in cracking down on illegal aliens. It was Thailand's version of "no tolerance." All the foster kids who had turned eighteen had to go back to jail. The previous year, the Thai government had asked expat families (not Thai ones) to take the kids. Now new leadership was asking these same expat families to bring them back. Of all the trauma they had suffered, they'd have to be retraumatized all over again as they waited for their new countries. My heart sank especially for the kids who didn't yet have the promise of a new country.

Raina sat stone cold and emotionless at the immigration office. She was so good at holding her cards. Being invulnerable was an act of survival. The cab ride home was mostly silent. We walked in the front door, and both of us broke down in sobs. It was so unfair. I was sick to my stomach over what was to come.

"I'm just not going to bring her back," I told the caseworker stubbornly. "She'll stay at my house until Canada. I know they won't have the energy to hunt her down."

But when I ran my brilliant idea by her Thai human-rights lawyer, she informed me that if Raina didn't report back, she would be criminally suspect, a fugitive, and it would hurt her chance of going to Canada. I had no choice but to comply.

My anger was justified, but it also shone a light on my own exceptionalism and privilege. "How dare they do this to us?" I asked over and over. It had become personal. I somehow thought that since Raina had become one of us, we'd be immune to extraneous suffering.

Don't they know who we are? said the voice inside my head. *We are American diplomats!*

But they could. We were not given any precious treatment, and our heartstrings that had been intertwined with Raina's had been ripped apart just the same. How would we tell our kids? The difficulty for me was having to explain to kids in preschool and kindergarten how unfair and cruel the world is . . . and appearing powerless to stop it. They had to learn the truth and the cost of building a relationship with someone severely disadvantaged.

With that dark cloud hanging over our heads, we took one last family trip with Raina to the mountains and the beach. We went to an amusement park that had roller coasters, giant Zorb balls that rolled down a green mountain, and ATVs. Raina wanted to do it all, and now it all made sense: Not a day was taken for granted. She never knew when her freedom clock would stop ticking.

One of the unfulfilled goals she had was learning to drive, so we let her try out the ATV track. Once she started the muddy path, the rain started to come down, and I had a heavy feeling. I was stuck between a rock and a hard place in letting her have her fun, freedom, and confidence to try new things, and also seeing that she clearly had no muscle memory for things on wheels.

But the more confidence she gained, the more speed she added to the ATV, throttling the four-wheeler down a straightaway, her pearly white smile shone even brighter against a darkening sky. She was having the time of her life, but a sharp corner was coming up, and Raina needed to slow down. We realized this, but all we could do was look on with horror as Raina twisted the handlebars hard to the right, ejecting herself from the ATV and causing it to roll over on top of her leg.

After several doctor visits, an x-ray, and an MRI, it was revealed that she had a torn thigh muscle and hematoma. She walked with a limp. Thankfully, there were no broken bones, and no surgery was needed. She just needed to rest it for an indefinite period of time until it healed.

"Excellent, now we have to send her back to jail with a gimp leg," I hashed out over and over to Travis in our hotel room each night. We were sick, feeling guilty for ever letting her do it in the first place. Our brave girl complained little, popped ibuprofen, and got on with it. All of it.

With days remaining before she had to return to the IDC, she wanted to take the GED math exam, despite not feeling quite ready. She passed with flying colors, and we had reason to celebrate again. On the night before she went back, we went to the salon for a massive color job and styling of her long hair. Her gorgeous curls suited her personality, but she wanted to return to jail with silky, gilded hair. The sight of her in the mirror took our breath away. She was a goddess. We took pictures from every angle, misty eyed at the bittersweetness. She might be going back to jail, but she would do so feeling beautiful and dignified.

The next day, we hugged her long and tight and watched her walk to the other side of the metal gate in front of the Bodhi tree. She had four months of freedom and personal growth on the outside, only to find herself back in a cage again, a butterfly with broken wings.

In a most unlucky twist of fate, the same day Raina went back Lolly and her other kids were taken out of the IDC and bussed miles away to another facility. They had thought they would be reuniting that day behind bars, but without any notice, they passed each other like ships in the night. With no warning, all of the mothers and children under age eighteen had been relocated. It would be days before I'd hear from Lolly. She didn't have access to a phone, and I didn't know where the new facility was.

The switcheroo set off a panic both inside the IDC and for loved ones on the outside. Even resolute Raina was losing her mind over not knowing where her mom and younger siblings had been sent and how they were being cared for. Rumors were trickling in from people in the new facility who had been taken to the doctor and got word out that they were hungry in there; they didn't have enough food or access to a phone. The new facility was supposed to be a "shelter" rather than jail. This was Thailand's hastily executed attempt at ending child incarceration.

"Please don't worry about visiting me until we can get my mom and siblings out," Raina said.

Eventually Lolly was able to make a phone call. I was able to visit her, and shortly after Lolly and her younger children were eligible for bail. The Thai law opened a door to allow bail for single mothers with children. We quickly filed the paperwork, but Lolly miraculously raised her own bail money, making phone calls from jail. A Somali boy showed up at our doorstep with hundreds of dollars in cash that in just a few days he had collected from churches, mosques, and neighbors in the poor East African community of Bangkok. He was like the boy who had some bread and a few fish that Jesus used to feed the five thousand. It was a subversive reminder that we were not alone; the village had all of our backs. After weeks of waiting, we got the call from the jail telling us that Lolly's bail had been accepted. She and her younger kids (but not Raina) would be released that evening.

Standing over six feet tall with flawless makeup and wearing the same red hooded capelet that she had been wearing the day she was incarcerated a year prior, Lolly sauntered out of the metal gate, past the Bodhi tree, and into the streets of Bangkok with the grace and dignity of Cleopatra. She carried the trauma deep inside, but in that moment she was free and shining like the sun.

One of the jail guards asked to have his picture taken with her, as if she had gone from slave to celebrity on the other side of the fence. It felt a little strange, but it was also a reminder that there was still kindness and humanity underneath the cruelty of the system.

She and her kids stayed at my house for two weeks while we sorted out her living arrangement. We launched a GoFundMe campaign, and in less than two weeks, enough dear friends and family near and far had helped raise money to support Lolly's medical care and living expenses for her time left in Thailand as she waited for Canada.

Reintegration into normal life was a foggy, uphill climb. Lolly walked around with that same glazed look that Raina had when she was released. Like a soldier with PTSD, her memory was in shambles, she'd forget she had a phone, and she easily got lost. "The UN asked me if I needed a mental therapist. I told them no, but now I wonder if I'm all right," she confessed.

She and her kids had thick black callouses on their ankles from sitting on the floor for so long. The first few weeks, the kids couldn't eat much at a time; their stomachs had undoubtedly shrunk. Her nine-year-old needed glasses, and they had cavities that needed filling. Thanks to the generous donors, she was able to take care of all of their health needs.

* * *

That November, we had three holidays to celebrate: American Thanksgiving, the Prophet Muhammad's birthday (Mawlid), and the Thai holiday Loy Krathong. Thanksgiving was at my house with all of our friends and neighbors, along with Lolly and kids and my Algerian friend Gazala and her daughter. All that was missing was Raina.

I assembled three long tables to create one massive banquet table that stretched from my dining room to my living room. The tables were decorated with Thai warty pumpkins painted gold and bright purple orchids. I tried to plan carefully, configuring who would sit where in order to blend expat friends and refugees to make everyone feel comfortable. I decided to separate men from women and put all the kids at one end. Lolly helped doodle gold leaves and name cards on butcher-block paper covering the tables. I marveled at our Pinterest-worthy dining room with glowing pride.

"We have so much to be thankful for," I gushed to my husband.

But when the guests arrived and began to be seated, I was surprised that Gazala had seated herself all the way at the end of the table in some of the kids' seats, and Lolly had followed suit, despite helping me with the table arrangements just hours prior. The kids were confused about where to sit, and before long, musical chairs ensued.

"Gazala and Lolly, your seats are down here," I casually pointed out.

"Oh yes we saw them, but we can't sit by you. You're drinking alcohol!" Gazala replied.

I knew Muslims didn't drink, but keeping a distance at the table was a first for me. I wanted to ask what the threshold of distance was required: Two feet? Five feet? *How far away do you have to sit from your infidel hostess?* I had drunk with Muslims many times during my time in the Middle East, and my occasional glass of wine had never been a problem for Lolly or Raina. They didn't drink, but they never had a problem with sharing a meal with us while we did. Was it just Gazala who had a problem with it, or had Lolly secretly had a problem the entire time and just never told me? My pride was wounded, and I felt shamed in my own house at my own holiday.

The hot buttered truth is that diversity is messy. We love to idealize and romanticize diversity, so long as we feel comfortable. We jump on photo ops that show how accepting and diverse we are, but then retreat to our friend groups who look and think like us. But intentionally choosing to integrate our lives into the lives of those from different countries, religions, and socioeconomic backgrounds doesn't roll up nicely like a cinnamon roll. It squishes out the sides, gets scrunched in unexpected ways, and sometimes gets a little burned. I learned a lot that day about letting go of expectations and simply letting things be. Seeking out true diversity is a gift worth pursuing, but also an exercise in checking our egos at the door.

Our week of celebration continued with Gazala's Mawlid party to celebrate the Prophet Muhammad's birthday. She had a grand feast prepared of Lebanese food and Algerian sweets. All the neighborhood children were there, the majority non-Muslim. They took turns participating in a candle-lit henna hand ceremony in which each child was stamped with a ball of henna before getting a lollypop. Gazala had loaned us all gorgeous Algerian dresses for the occasion. My girls looked like Arabian princesses trimmed in silk and gold, and by the end of the party they had eaten so much honey tamina that they became sugar drunk, twirling around and around to the Arabic music like a pair of tiny dervishes.

Our holiday week continued with Loy Krathong, Thailand's most beautiful holiday. On the night of the full moon, everyone takes to the rivers and water sources to float tiny rafts made out of banana leaves, flowers, and incense sticks. Some float lanterns into the night sky.

The origins of Loy Krathong are ancient. Like the spirit houses, it's rooted in animist beliefs that predate Buddhism. It is believed to be a payment of respect to Mother River, to release the old and welcome the new. Not unlike Thanksgiving, it is a time of reflection and gratitude.

My first year in Thailand, I didn't participate in Loy Krathong. I had thought it might compromise my Christian beliefs. But as the day came around every fall, I began to see such beauty in it. Honoring the divine feminine that sustains all life is written into the hearts of humanity throughout the world. It is the manifestation of a deep awareness of a Mother God. We are most afraid of what we do not understand.

The idea that we can't copyright the experience of God scares the pants off most of us. But if we dig deep enough in our own Bible, we'll find references to other gods and goddesses as the ancient Near Eastern people sought to understand the divine. El and YHWH were not the same Gods. Proverbs 3 has a poem about wisdom that, according to Princeton Theological Seminary Professor of Old Testament Literature Mark Smith is an allusion to the mother goddess Asherah—"she is a tree of life to those who lay hold of her; those who hold her fast are called happy."[83]

The tree of life plays a critical role in the Bible's opening poem, and its final saga as a centerpiece of the new Jerusalem (Revelation 22). The tree-of-life motif is seen around the world, weaving itself into many religions throughout history. If anything, isn't it evidence of an abiding intuition in the hearts of humankind of a good, life-giving, regenerative God?

I've come to see holidays around the world as the best way to see the Christ in a particular culture. That magical spark and deep joy that seeps into our minds over a marked moment in time is divine. We are hardwired for celebration; our deepest impulse is to participate in a welcoming feast. The rallying together over the sake of pure fun, joy, tradition, and unity is something supernaturally felt in the air, even if the culture is foreign and the thing being celebrated is of another religion. It unites the classes and brings people together, and I believe the Spirit of God delights in this. Christ lives in it.

Thomas Merton writes, "The fact remains that our task is to seek and find Christ in our world as it is and not as it *might be*."[84]

Learning to celebrate deeply with someone of another faith is like opening a door that you've only seen one side of your entire life. The other side of the door is a different color, maybe a different texture, but it is warm and welcoming and an invitation to the pursuit of truth. Celebrating holidays with friends of another religion wasn't an abandonment of my Christian faith, but an invitation to let our roots intertwine.

Bede Griffiths writes, "The truth is one, but it has many faces, and each religion is, as it were, a face of the one Truth, which manifests itself under different signs and symbols in the different historical traditions."[85]

I had seen those other faces of truth reflected in my Buddhist and Muslim neighbors. And once I saw them, they couldn't be unseen. The nameless, faceless God, *the Great I AM*, was alive in the heart of humanity everywhere. From the most warm and familiar traditions to the most foreign and unusual—Christ is present. I can no longer decide *who's in* and *who's out*, for the inescapable love and mercy of an unnamable, untamable God covers our heads to the heavens and flows on the ground beneath our feet.

* * *

Lolly and her kids made it to Canada at last, just a few months before we left Thailand. With her UN-purchased airfare in hand, Thai authorities drove Raina directly from the jail to the airport where she was met by Lolly and the kids. After long hugs and tears and rejoicing from their Somali community in Bangkok, it was time to cross the threshold into freedom. With fresh henna hands and new oversized coats and neck pillows, they waved and blew kisses and walked arm in arm past the security gates into a new life. Thanks to UN funding and local volunteers, they moved into a nice apartment near Toronto. The kids thrived in their new schools, Raina began finishing her high school curriculum, and she and Lolly went to work at a bakery. They sent me pictures of themselves throwing up peace signs, decked out in red and white apparel and maple leaves. They sent videos of themselves chasing Canada geese in the park and shivering at the first chill of winter. They were Canadian, and proud of it. In another miracle, Bishaaro was released from the IDC two years later to be resettled by the United Nations in Canada, where she reunited with Lolly and her kids, the first real family she ever had.

Their safe passage and new life was a piece of kingdom come, and I'm lucky to have been a witness to it. I'll always remember them as the ones who expanded my notion of the family of God. They too were accepted exactly as they were in the eyes of God, deserving of a flourishing life in peace, wholeness, and security.

CHAPTER 33

I Come to the Garden Alone

County Carlow, Ireland

The rain beats down harder, the sky seems to be darkening, and the light softens inside the quiet country Irish church. Travis and the kids are waiting for me in the car, as I give in to an impulsive, curious fit to check out this random single-storey Gothic church on the side of the road. We're on a stopover trip on our way back to the United States from Bangkok. What is it about this church that called out to me to pull over? If stones could talk . . .

I catch a chill in the air and tighten the scarf around my neck.

Once my eyes adjust to the dim light, in the shadows on the side wall of the sanctuary there's a large inscription that takes my breath away. *Surely these words are not here by accident,* I wonder. What a random, bizarre piece of Scripture to be so prominently displayed.

It says:

And that rock was Christ.
1 Corinthians 10:4

The apostle Paul is referring to the rock that Jewish tradition says accompanied the Israelites in the desert for forty years, providing them water whenever it was struck by Moses. He tells the Corinthians that this rock was literally *Christ*. Perhaps it's just coincidental that the church nearest the heaviest dolmen in Europe bears such an inscription on its wall.

But for St. Patrick's Ireland, I think it makes perfect sense. Author Thomas Cahill tells us that St. Patrick's approach to spreading the gospel in Ireland was unique among early missionaries in that he didn't try to erase the culture and religion of the people in the land. He took what they already intuitively knew, of the divine being present in all living things, and added to their story.

St. Patrick told the Irish about a good God that wasn't shapeshifting, nor at odds with their deeply held beliefs. With his own "earthiness and warmth," he won the Irish's affection and trust, as well as rejecting the way of the empire surrounding them. While the rest of Europe was bloody and chaotic after the fall of Rome, he led Ireland in the way of unprecedented peace.[86]

Monastic communities that followed in Patrick's footsteps grew into large population centers. It was a time of great scholarly and artistic flourishing—fruit that is still enjoyed today and felt in the warmth and hospitality of the Irish people. Weathering centuries of invasions by Vikings, Normans, and English, the Emerald Isle managed to preserve ancient knowledge lost to the rest of Europe. Irish monks and scholars spent the better years of their life copying ancient literature and history, while illuminating beautifully detailed Gospel manuscripts with brightly colored swirls and knots and animals.

While the Irish were Christianized, they unashamedly kept their pagan culture and legends, continuing to tell their children stories of fairies, spirits of the forests, and Druid folklore. Their indigenous beliefs, along with local legends, were celebrated and passed down with new converts. Sometimes they joined forces with the gospel.

For example, one of Ireland's most noteworthy female saints from the fifth century, St. Brigid (whose mother was said to be a Christian and whose father a Druid priest), was mythically woven into the story of the Nativity. Brigid was believed to be a goddess before transforming into a saint. Legend has it in Celtic lore that she was the barmaid at the inn in Bethlehem where Mary and Joseph sought shelter and were sent to the stable. When the Christ child was born, Brigid turned from barmaid to midwife and wet nurse, delivering the Christ child and nursing him.

These Celtic legends were not forgotten with the revelation of Christ, but rather were whimsically folded into the story—an old testament to the new. The Celts weren't slaves to legalism or bothered by historical inaccuracies. Those things didn't matter, but the meaning behind the story was the guiding light: a good and loving God born among us. The divine came to participate in our commonplace life, sanctifying the ordinary as holy and intimately dwelling in our lives. One minute dear Brigid is on the job serving beer, and the next minute she's delivering the Son of God and nursing him at her breast.

What might seem as irreverent or sacrilegious, I've come to see as kind and merciful. The stories didn't compete or cancel each other out. They became enmeshed. In the words of philosopher Ken Wilber, the evolution of consciousness is a path defined as "transcend and include."[87] Such is the way when the story of Jesus becomes intertwined with culture and tradition.

For the Celts, says Alexander Shaia, "Nature tells the story that the gospels amplify."[88] After a period of darkness in winter, the light begins to grow again. Their understanding of the Gospels was a marriage of two great incarnations—Christ in all of nature, that divine spark or energy that animates the universe and lights up humanity (or what the Gospel of John calls the Word or *logos* of God), and Christ as human dwelling on the earth.

And that rock was Christ is a shocking, provocative declaration for modern-day Christians who have divorced God's self in the cosmos with God's self in Jesus Christ. This isn't some romanticized idea from yesteryear that I'm trying to usher into the present.[89] As a mother grappling with what theology to teach my children so the next generation will be more loving, it has huge implications for how we treat our fellow humans and the earth.

Tragically, the separation of spirit from matter has tainted the way we see all of humanity. It's much harder to love our neighbor if we don't see the divine, *the Christ*, within them. It makes it much easier to characterize entire swaths of people groups who don't have "Jesus in their hearts" as the enemy. In the past, it was used to justify violence against indigenous people, and in the more recent past we've dismissed thousands of casualties from wars in the Middle East as collateral damage. US Senator Lindsay Graham, when asked about the cost of going to war with North Korea, justified the damage by saying, "If thousands die, they're going to die over there."[90] The lawmaker and the constituents he represents are proud of our country as a "Christian nation." But this type of thinking is a direct result of a theology that cares more about souls than it does bodies. Moreover, it continues to pervade modern-day missions that typify non-Christian cultures around the world as savages living in darkness, rather than seeking to learn from the wisdom already present within a community.

* * *

The rain clears the next day and we make it to the Glendalough monastic site. *Glendalough* literally means "the valley of the two lakes." The lakes are perfect glass, reflecting the surrounding Wicklow Mountains. County Wicklow is known as Ireland's "Garden County." The gloriously green valley between the lakes cradles a jumble of ancient silvery stone ruins, churches, a tall, pointed minaret, and a scattering of centuries-old tombstones with Celtic crosses. The site was originally founded by St. Kevin, a sixth-century hermit and miracle worker who lived in a cave.

I am fascinated by the legends surrounding St. Kevin. The kooky stories are a fusion of myth and tradition, but the more I learn about them, the more I can feel that curious itch creeping up again and leading me to an imaginary door called Alluring Expressions of Faith. These doors used to scare me, but now I only see them as exhilarating.

Over the centuries, Glendalough was built up as a monastery in the Middle Ages and later a pilgrimage site. For generations upon generations, pilgrims have journeyed to Glendalough to rest in the sacred energy of the landscape and perhaps lean into the quiet and nurturing way of St. Kevin by visiting his dwellings.

One of the pilgrimage markers is a magical healing stone called the Deer Stone. It's a big, flat rock with a hollowed-out, round indentation. These types of *bullaun* stones are prehistoric, believed to have been originally used as mortar-grinding stones. But when the land was Christianized, early priests brought them into monasteries, believing they retained special powers. Legend has it that St. Kevin cared for one or two orphaned twin babies, and when he needed milk for them, a doe shed milk into the basin of the stone. To this day, pilgrims still come to the stone to pray and drink water from the basin, believed to have healing properties.

In another legend, Kevin was so connected with nature that a blackbird laid eggs in his hands, and he held still for days until the chicks took flight. His statue marker has a bird next to his serene face, and his face bears an uncanny resemblance to the Buddhas I see in Thailand: seated upright, spine flat as a board, face relaxed, eyes open but not wide-eyed, and just a hint of a grin. It's the same expression of divine grace that humans have been seeking out since the beginning of time. It's the pursuit of the divine that touches all matter and burns brightly within—from rocks to humans.

John Philip Newell threads together a long chain of mystics throughout the ages who have preserved the Celtic theological tradition, usually in opposition to the dominant empire and religious elites. It's been passed down from the misunderstood Pelagius to Ninian, whose church formed St. Patrick. Then onward to the ninth-century philosopher John Scotus Eriugena, to Julian of Norwich, Teilhard de Chardin, George MacLeod, and in the imagination of George MacDonald. In the tradition of John who heard the heartbeat of Christ when he leaned against Jesus at the Last Supper, the mystics in the Celtic tradition tuned their ears to the heartbeat of God in the whole universe. The forgotten tune of the presence of God in all things is both a symphony all around us and a stirring deep within.[91]

The "Garden of our Origins," says Newell, is the forgotten tune, a yearning for love, unity, and wholeness buried deep inside humankind. Sin and evil have corrupted and altered our natural state, but *deeper still* is something holy and beautiful. Salvation is less of a sudden, abrupt transformation after saying the perfect combination of magical words

and more of a waking up to the reminder of who we are in Christ—
made in his very image and born in unending love:

> The gospel of Christ reveals the dearest and most hidden
> of truths, that we are what Christ is, born of God, and that
> at the heart of every human being and every creature is
> the Light that was in the beginning and through whom all
> things have come into being.[92]

I think about the light that illuminates all things as being
inescapable. We are all just basking in the light whether we know it or
not. Whatever metaphor we use to approach the unnamable I AM, the
source of it all, matters less than the wild pursuit of a good God who
stalks us all our days. Whatever structures we're handed, systems we
overturn, or alchemy we stumble on to feel more sanctified matters less
than the experience of divine Love that's poured over our heads, floods
our feet, and spills onto others. How arrogant to think our little thread
is the only lane that the Almighty travels.

"That rock" can apply to a number of things, from a utilitarian
household object and grinding stone to a tool of magical healing. It can
be a portal tomb to the afterlife, or our grandmother's kitchen table.
It can be the inanimate objects that become holy things in a sacred
space—the sewing table, the potter's wheel, or the tattoo parlor. It is
possible that Christ is present in all of it.

It can be all of our earnest efforts to be touched by our Creator, and
all of the mundane places of our lives where the Spirit gives us a wink
unexpectedly. It can be the unlikely miracles in the darkest nights that
catch us by surprise and take our breath away. It can be the friendships
that remain after all of our failed attempts at making a transaction with
a God who doesn't need one. It can be the misfits, the outcasts, and the
least-likely influencers becoming our biggest teachers. Or the return to
a house of worship after being harmed by it. It's all of the calloused
parts of our lives where it's hard to see any signs of new life. The old

habits that we can't shake. The stories we carry from our ancestors' past—the things we can't erase even if we tried. The new mercy that we find growing under our deepest shame. The heavy things we carry that are no longer of use that suddenly die and produce new life. This is the rock; this is the Christ. This is his life hidden within it all and our life hidden in his.

In Ireland, I found a piece of my own resurrection with this scandalous truth: If even the rocks are saturated with the love and energy of Christ, then how much more are you and I?

Dear Mid-Thirties Self,

Pretty soon, you're going to have to go through another hairy journey called "repatriation," and it's gonna be a lot. On top of that, a global pandemic is gonna sweep over the planet and things will get really weird and sad.

You'll sit at Mommama's round kitchen table one last time before her house sells and she moves into an assisted-living facility. Returning to your first altar of mercy will be bittersweet, but it's a portal of peace. You've spent the last decade chasing all of the big things like exotic adventures and mountaintop experiences. But returning to Mommama's table one last time will show you that the deepest joy is in the small, ordinary, childlike experiences of our lives.

When you can temporarily suspend the pain of your childhood and meditate on the moments where you remember a time when you unflinchingly gave and received love—the days long ago before your heart was tarnished with pain and your ego began to grow—you can dwell in a little divine space (if only for a moment) where you know without a shadow of a doubt that the mercy of God will never be withheld from you and it was with you the entire time.

It's an odd place: returning to your old world that seems to be mostly the same way you left it, and then realizing you are a different person. It's like looking at two identical pictures—the kind we looked at as children—and being asked, "Can you spot the difference?" The difference is me! You don't know how to fit in, and maybe you never will again.

At first it feels like the hard-earned wings that you've grown have been forcibly removed so you can inch around and munch on stale leaves again. It's not that the stale leaves aren't delicious or valuable or even nurturing. It's just that when you've tasted other forbidden fruits that you've found to be delicious and life-giving, it's hard to go back to just a one-note flavor that's been sanctioned as the only way.

For those who have walked the path of faith deconstruction or spent years abroad, there's a tendency to get frustrated at the perception that other people haven't changed at all or "don't get it." But the perception that things have stayed exactly the same is mostly an illusion. Nothing is static; things might move slowly at times, but the Spirit of God stalks the whole earth, wooing us back to Love, and inviting us into a more expansive light where we can love better and welcome more to the table. There's mercy at the beginning of our journey, and there's mercy at the end of it. The same is true for everyone, even the ones who break our hearts and confound us with their closed-mindedness. We might think we're morally superior, but this is also an illusion. We're really all on the same path.

You're going to get frustrated with people whose beliefs baffle you. You'll learn how to have constructive conversations, and you might lose your temper a few times. Breathe, and work on your fragility. Remember that you've had the privilege of having proximity to many kinds of people, and for that your vantage point comes with luck as much as it has work. You'll need to tap into your deepest reserves of empathy and generosity for the years ahead.

Resist the temptation to shame people. Just like you've learned with your own children—shame doesn't produce more love or change a heart. We should hold each other accountable, but we can do that while also calling out each other's goodness and looking for the light within. Don't stop believing in original goodness, hard as it will seem in a divided America. The servant example of Christ fulfilling Isaiah's prophecy that "he will not break a bruised reed or quench a smoldering wick"[93] shows a better way to react to those whose lights seem to be burning so dimly that they're almost imperceptible. They're producing smoke, but there's no real flame. We've all been there—by way of either pain, shame, or being improperly loved—our very fragile lamps can fade. Remember when that was you? When we see people's lamps fading, instead of stomping them out, maybe try tenderly trimming their wicks and pouring more oil into their lamps. This is the way of mercy. Love calls out love and reminds us of our true nature.

Sincerely,
Your Pushing-Forty Self

ACKNOWLEDGMENTS

My first thank-you goes to Travis, who is washing the bedsheets and cooking spaghetti and meatballs as I type this. He didn't flinch when I casually mentioned several years ago that I wanted to write a book, and he's cheered me on every step of the way. He was the first to read an early draft and correct all of my mixed metaphors, and he pushed me to the finish line in the trenches of pandemic living by helping me homeschool the kids and keeping an endless rotation of meals and snacks going. He is still the full sun to my partly cloudy skies, and this book has had more light and love infused into its pages through his unwavering support. I love you!

I'd like to thank my intelligent tribe of sisters who set aside their busy lives during a crazy year to slog through a long manuscript and offer up their honest feedback, brilliant suggestions, and validation for my work. Jane Monnier, Kallie Culver, Joy Felix, Rachel Bierman, Emily Parks, Valerie Kurlansky, Aimee Hubmann, Natalie Svendsen, Breanna Randall, and Constance Dykhuizen: I love y'all to pieces, and I'm so lucky to call you friends.

I owe a tremendous amount of gratitude to my Somali sisters for shaking up everything I knew about God, life, suffering, and resilience: Lolly, Raina, and Bishaaro—I'm forever changed and blessed by knowing you, and I love you all.

This book might not have happened if it weren't for the help of Mimi Khinphang, who helped keep the wheels spinning at my home in Bangkok so I could sit down and write a decent sentence. You are a bright light, and the world is better off with your presence. We love you so!

I'd like to acknowledge the following friends, teachers, and elders who have encouraged my writing or inspired the content of this memoir in some way: Natasha Naragon-Holmes, Lauren Byers, Jessica Hope, Megan Montgomery, Arva Tatman, Judy Goss, Debbie Harrison, Jennifer Rock, Rob Bell, and the Something to Say Class of 2020, Ryan Kuja, Charlie McScallywag, Duangduan Phuengphan, Nada

Hamrouche, Nicole Wood, Andy Page, and the dedicated servants of Christ at the Good Shepherd Sisters in Bangkok, including Sister Louise Horgan and Sister Immaculate Seku.

I'm grateful to my editor at Paraclete Press, Jon Sweeney, for giving me the opportunity to tell my story and for making it better, along with Jeffrey Reimer, Michelle Rich, Rachel McKendree, and the entire team at Paraclete Press.

I'm thankful for our American church family for giving us a soft place to land during our repatriation and welcoming us with open arms. Rev. Dr. Paul Johnson and the good saints at Hughes Memorial United Methodist Church in Washington, DC—worshiping with you makes us feel as though we've merely scratched the surface of the mercy of Christ.

The love of my family has given me the courage to heal from past trauma and use my voice. Cheryl Schilb, Rusty Schilb, the late Mark Toon, Julie Toon, Jesse Toon, Charles and Ann Greene, the late Mildred and Tom Toon, and so many aunts, uncles, cousins, and nieces: you have loved me well and carried me through it all. Thank you!

And finally, my children, Henry, Magnolia, and Francina, have opened my deepest well of love and expanded my heart, as they inspired the themes of original blessing for this book. They were and still are some of my biggest teachers in life. I don't know what it's like to be a writer who crafts in complete silence, but the sound of laughter, singing, feet trudging up and down stairs, slamming doors, and occasional cries is the beautiful soundtrack to my life, and I wouldn't trade it for the world. I hope you kids know just how deeply you are loved and cherished. May you be courageous in your love and *curiouser and curiouser*. Mommy loves you forever and always!

NOTES

1 Silas House, *A Parchment of Leaves* (Durham: Blair/Carolina Wren Press, 2020), 70.
2 Julian of Norwich, *Revelations of Divine Love* (n.p.: Digireads Publishing, 2013), 60.
3 William Faulkner, *Requiem for a Nun* (New York: Vintage International, 2011), 73.
4 Ant Grimley, quoted in John T. Skinner, "Prayer, Pilgrimage, Peregrinate," The Yoke, http://theyoke.org/prayer-pilgrimage-peregrinate.html.
5 Nora Chadwick, *The Celts* (London: Penguin, 1997), 210.
6 Genesis 12:1.
7 Terry Tempest Williams, *Refuge* (New York: Vintage, 1992), 148.
8 James 1:5.
9 Luke 14:12–14.
10 Richard Rohr, "Transforming Our Pain," Center for Action and Contemplation, February 26, 2016, https://cac.org/transforming-our-pain-2016-02-26/.
11 John Philip Newell, *The Rebirthing of God* (Woodstock, VT: SkyLight Paths, 2014), 13.
12 Acts 9:1–19.
13 Richard Rohr and Mike Morrell, *The Divine Dance* (London: SPCK, 2016), 43.
14 John 9:1–12.
15 Rohr and Morrell, *The Divine Dance*, 49.
16 Barbara Brown Taylor, *An Altar in the World: A Geography of Faith* (San Francisco: HarperOne, 2009), 203.
17 Galatians 4:5.
18 John Philip Newell, *Christ of the Celts: The Healing of Creation* (San Francisco: Jossey-Bass, 2008), 28.
19 Newell, *Christ of the Celts*, 29.
20 Psalm 145:9.
21 Hadith Qudsi, *Radical Love*, trans. and ed. Omid Safi (New Haven: Yale University Press, 2018), 20.
22 Genesis 3:19.
23 Jewish Virtual Library, "U.S. Foreign Aid to Israel: Total Aid (1949-present)," https://www.jewishvirtuallibrary.org/total-u-s-foreign-aid-to-israel-1949-present.
24 John 4.
25 Luke 10.
26 Rachel Held Evans, *Inspired: Slaying Giants, Walking on Water, and Loving the Bible Again* (Nashville: Nelson Books, 2018), 33.
27 Bede Griffiths, *The Marriage of East and West* (Tucson: Medio Media Publishing, 1976), 33–34.
28 Luke 1:46–55.
29 A. E. Hotchner, *Papa Hemingway* (Cambridge, MA: Da Capo, 2005), 57.
30 John O'Donohue, *Anam Ċara: A Book of Celtic Wisdom* (New York: HarperCollins, 1997), 93.
31 Barbara Brown Taylor, *Holy Envy* (San Francisco: HarperOne, 2019), 25.
32 Danielle Shroyer, *Original Blessing: Putting Sin in Its Rightful Place* (Minneapolis: Fortress, 2016), ix–x.
33 Ronald Rolheiser, *Sacred Fire* (New York: Penguin Random House, 2017), 333.

34 Charles Freeman, *The Closing of the Western Mind* (New York: Vintage, 2005), 288, 290–91.

35 Saint Augustine, *Confessions*, trans. Henry Chadwick (New York: Oxford University Press, 2008), 109.

36 Judith Chelius Stark, introduction to *Feminist Interpretations of Augustine*, ed. Judith Chelius Stark (University Park, PA: Pennsylvania State University Press, 2007), 36.

37 Saint Augustine, *Confessions*, 9.

38 Lisa Sharon Harper, *The Very Good Gospel* (Colorado Springs: WaterBrook Press, 2016), 30–31.

39 Newell, *Christ of the Celts*, 19.

40 Newell, *Christ of the Celts*, 21.

41 John Philip Newell, *Listening for the Heartbeat of God: A Celtic Spirituality* (Mahwah, NJ: Paulist Press, 1997), 13.

42 Freeman, *Closing of the Western Mind*, 292.

43 Shroyer, *Original Blessing*, x.

44 1 Timothy 2:15.

45 Newell, *Rebirthing of God*, 39–40.

46 Richard Rohr, "A Spirituality of Subtraction," Center for Action and Contemplation, May 18, 2015, https://cac.org/a-spirituality-of-subtraction-2015-05-18/.

47 Valerie Andrews, *A Passion for This Earth* (New York: HarperCollins, 1990), 15.

48 Luke 15:11–32.

49 Rob Bell, *Love Wins* (San Francisco: HarperOne, 2011), 169–70.

50 O'Donohue, *Anam Ċara*, 15.

51 Rohr and Morrell, *Divine Dance*, 43.

52 Rohr and Morrell, *Divine Dance*, 58.

53 Nanticha Ocharoenchai, "It's Not Okay: What They Really Mean by 'Mai Pen Rai,'" Coconuts Bangkok, February 18, 2016, https://coconuts.co/bangkok/features/its-not-okay-what-thais-really-mean-mai-pen-rai/.

54 Griffiths, *Marriage of East and West*, 5.

55 Romans 8:16.

56 Griffiths, *Marriage of East and West*, 55.

57 Richard Rohr, *The Universal Christ: How a Forgotten Reality Can Change Everything We See, Hope For, and Believe* (New York: Convergent, 2019), 65.

58 Griffiths, *Marriage of East and West*, 12.

59 Exodus 3:14.

60 Griffiths, *Marriage of East and West*, 12.

61 Griffiths, *Marriage of East and West*, 23.

62 Thomas Merton, *The Asian Journal of Thomas Merton*, ed. Naomi Burton, Brother Patrick Hart, James Laughlin, and Consulting Editor Amiya Chakravarty (New York: New Directions, 1975), 308.

63 Human Rights Watch, "Ad Hoc and Inadequate: Thailand's Treatment of Refugees and Asylum Seekers," December 12, 2012, https://www.hrw.org/report/2012/09/12/ad-hoc-and-inadequate/thailands-treatment-refugees-and-asylum-seekers.

64 Beth Watkins, "When We See Them Do We See You?," January 29, 2018, http://www.iambethwatkins.com/2018/01/29/when-we-see-them-do-we-see-you/.

65 Matthew 5:3.

66 Alia Joy, *Glorious Weakness: Discovering God in All We Lack* (Grand Rapids, MI: Baker Books, 2019), 41.

67 Merton, *Asian Journal*, 306.

68 Lewis Carroll, *Alice's Adventures in Wonderland* (Greenwood, WI: Suzeteo Enterprises, 2017), 52 (dialogue arrangement by author).

69 Carroll, *Alice's Adventures in Wonderland*, 7.

70 Carroll, *Alice's Adventures in Wonderland*, 11.

71 Carroll, *Alice's Adventures in Wonderland*, 59.

72 Carroll, *Alice's Adventures in Wonderland*, 33.

73 Carroll, *Alice's Adventures in Wonderland*, 9.

74 *Celtic Daily Prayer: Prayers and Readings From the Northumbria Community* (San Francisco: HarperSanFrancisco, 2002), 22–23.

75 *Celtic Daily Prayer*, 25.

76 Elie Wiesel, the Nobel Acceptance Speech delivered in Oslo on December 10, 1986, Elie Wiesel Foundation for Humanity, https://eliewieselfoundation.org/elie -wiesel/nobelprizespeech/.

77 Chris Rogers, "The Christians Held in Thailand After fleeing Pakistan," BBC News, February 26, 2016, https://www.bbc.com/news/magazine-35654804.

78 Gregory A. Smith, "Most White Evangelicals Approve of Trump Travel Prohibition and Express Concerns About Extremism," Pew Research Center, February 27, 2017,http://www.pewresearch.org/fact-tank/2017/02/27/most -white -evangelicals-approve-of-trump-travel-prohibition-and-express-concerns -about -extremism/.

79 Kylie Atwood, "Donald Trump Compares Syrian Refugees to Snakes," CBS News, last updated January 13, 2016, https://www.cbsnews.com/news/donald-trump -compares-syrian-refugees-to-biting-snakes/.

80 *Celtic Daily Prayer*, Evening Prayer for Blessing during Advent, 230–31.

81 Jen Hatmaker, *Of Mess and Moxie: Wrangling Delight Out of This Wild and Glorious Life* (Nashville: Nelson, 2017), 24.

82 Joy, *Glorious Weakness*, 199.

83 Mark Smith, Interview by Jared Byas and Peter Enns, *The Bible for Normal People*, podcast audio, September 23, 2018, https://www.podbean.com/ew/pb-2z3tp -9a92d9

84 Thomas Merton, *Seasons of Celebration: Meditations on the Cycle of Liturgical Feasts* (New York: Farrar, Straus and Giroux, 1965), 90.

85 Griffiths, *Marriage of East and West*, 20.

86 Thomas Cahill, *How the Irish Saved Civilization* (New York: Doubleday, 1995), 124, 137, 148.

87 Ken Wilber, *A Brief History of Everything* (Boulder, CO: Shambhala, 2017), 27.

88 Alexander Shaia, interview by Rob Bell, *The RobCast*, podcast audio, December 10, 2017, https://robbell.podbean.com/e/alexander-shaia-on-the-mythic-power-of -christmas/.

89 For more reading on this, see the works of John Phillip Newell and Alexander Shaia.

90 Erik Ortiz and Arata Yamamoto, "Sen. Lindsey Graham: Trump Says War with North Korea an Option," NBC News, last updated August 2, 2017, https://www.nbcnews.com/news/north-korea/sen-lindsey-graham-trump-says-war-north-korea -option-n788396.

91 Newell, *Listening for the Heartbeat of God*, 1–7, 24.

92 Newell, *Christ of the Celts*, 56.

93 Matthew 12:20.

ABOUT PARACLETE PRESS

PARACLETE PRESS is the publishing arm of the Cape Cod Benedictine community, the Community of Jesus. Presenting a full expression of Christian belief and practice, we reflect the ecumenical charism of the Community and its dedication to sacred music, the fine arts, and the written word.

Learn more about us at our website:
www.paracletepress.com
or phone us toll-free at 1.800.451.5006

SCAN
TO
READ
MORE